My Youth

(As I Remember It)

Bryan De Vouge

iUniverse, Inc.
New York   Bloomington

My Youth
(As I Remember It)

The views expressed in this work are solely those of the author and do not necessarily reflect the views of the publisher, and the publisher hereby disclaims any responsibility for them.

iUniverse books may be ordered through booksellers or by contacting:

iUniverse
1663 Liberty Drive
Bloomington, IN 47403
www.iuniverse.com
1-800-Authors (1-800-288-4677)

Because of the dynamic nature of the Internet, any Web addresses or links contained in this book may have changed since publication and may no longer be valid.

ISBN: 978-1-4502-0591-7 (sc)
ISBN: 978-1-4502-0592-4 (ebk)

Printed in the United States of America

iUniverse rev. date: 12/30/2009

Foreword

My name is Bryan De Vouge and I've decided to write a book, a memoir of my childhood growing up in the beautiful Gaspe Peninsula of Quebec. At sixty years of age I felt the time was right to do so. I retired from my job as a Stationary Engineer at INCO Metals Ltd. ten years ago and have been doing a whole lot of nothing since. Well, I've travelled quite a bit spending most of my winters in Florida and part of the summers travelling in Canada. I have also read hundreds of books.

I believe I have a unique story to tell, you see I grew up in the 1950's with my sister, mom, dad, grandmother, grandfather, great-grandmother and great-grandfather on a farm and all of us lived in the same very large farmhouse. Many people that I've met over the years are fascinated by this and wish to hear more. I have told several of my stories to friends and relatives over the years especially at family gathering I have attended over the past ten years. Many of my cousins had not known their great-grandparents and wish to know more about them.

When I moved to St Catharines, Ontario in 1967 and attended grade thirteen at Lakeport Secondary School Mr. Dunn was the head of the English Department and also my English teacher. He was different than most English teachers in that he was always asking his students to write essays and short stories. Most teachers that I had previously had wanted us to read books and then do book reports on them. So I wrote essays and short stories. Every week Mr. Dunn picked his favorite from our class and got that student to read his or her essay or short story at the front of the class. He picked my story to be read almost every week and at the end of the school year Mr. Dunn approached me and told me that he thought that I had a future as a writer. I was flattered but I told him that I was more interested in reading books than writing them.

In 2005 I attended this three-hour seminar given by Ms. Vicki Gilhula who was at that time the editor of "Northern Life" which is a Sudbury community newspaper. She lectured us on memoir writing and then gave us forty-five minutes to write a short story about our youth in Sudbury. Since I had moved here at the age of twenty I wrote about the experiences of the first few days when I moved to Sudbury in October of 1968. At the end of the forty-five minutes my story was only half finished but she asked me to read what I had written. I went up to the podium, adjusted the microphone and read my story to the twenty-five or so writers and wannabe writers assembled there. When I finished reading my half a story I then announced " I'll have to tell you the rest." When I finished everyone seemed to like my story because there was enthusiastic applause and smiles all around. Because I like telling stories so much I decided to tell another one and it also went over very well and later some of the writers there told me that they had really enjoyed my stories.

I knew that Ms. Gilhula taught a longer writing course and I asked her if she thought that I should take a creative writing course.

She replied, "Get a pen and some paper and write your stories. Don't worry. Someone is going to read them"

A few years later when I turned sixty I started putting my childhood memories down on paper and I informed my sister Donna that I was writing a book. She quickly agreed to also write a few chapters about mom, dad and me.

So here we go.

1. In The Beginning

I was born on September the fourth, 1948 in the beautiful city of Montreal, Quebec. My parents Frances and Herzil De Vouge had met and later got married there in 1947. You can see that they didn't waste much time.

My father worked for a construction firm as a foreman and my mother worked in a bank as an assistant manager.

Ten months after I was born we moved to the Gaspe Peninsula, back to the farm where my father was born way back in 1917. I think that dad missed living by the ocean and he had been offered a job at the Sandy Beach Boatyard building long liners, which are fishing boats.

Mom, dad and I left Montreal in July of 1949 on the long six hundred plus mile drive to Brilliant Cove (now known as L'Anse-a-Brilliant) in the Gaspe Peninsula, the maritime part of the province of Quebec.

Many years later my father told me how they heated up my milk bottle while they were on the road. Back in 1949 there weren't any bottle warmers to plug into the car's cigarette lighter like I had for my children in the seventies and eighties. When it appeared I was hungry and wanted the bottle dad simply stopped the car, opened the hood and wired a baby bottle to the exhaust manifold. Then after driving for fifteen or twenty minutes he stopped the car once again and retrieved the warmed milk. Hey, it worked.

When we reached the farm in L'Anse-a-Brilliant I met my grandmother Ruby, My grandfather Leslie, my great-grandmother Angelina and my great-grandfather Elias for the first time. I've been told that they were very happy to see me.

My great-grandfather Elias De Vouge moved from his father's farm in Barachois to L'Anse-a-Brilliant in 1889 where he acquired farmland and married my great-grandmother Angelina Leggo. They built a farmhouse and started a family having a daughter Olive who died when she was only one year old. My grandfather Leslie De Vouge was born in 1892 and was the only surviving child.

When Leslie grew up he married Ruby Dell Leggo and they decided to stay on the farm with Elias and Angelina. However my grandfather decided to build his own house on the farm but he attached it to his father's house thus making one rather large duplex. It actually had eight bedrooms in total, seven upstairs and one on the main floor.

My grandparents Ruby and Leslie had five children Cyril, Herzil, Glen, Denzil and Leona. When they came of age all of them except for uncle Denzil moved away to places such as Nova Scotia, Ontario and Montreal.

In 1949 when mom, dad and I moved to the farm we moved into the old part of the house that was built in the 1880's. This part of the house was called "the old end". My great-grandparents, grandparents and uncle Denzil lived in the newer part of the house called "the new end".

Although we lived in the old end of the house which was more than sixty years old I liked it better simply because we had a view of the neighbouring farms and the Atlantic Ocean when we looked out our kitchen window. When my grandparents looked out their kitchen and dining room windows they saw the highway, fields and woods. I preferred looking at the Atlantic Ocean.

This beautiful place that we called Brilliant Cove or L'Anse-a-Brilliant was where I spent most of my childhood. It was an ideal place to grow up. I am so thankful for the opportunity I had growing up on a farm.

2. The Fabulous Fifties

I was born in 1948 and grew up in the 1950's, the most fabulous decade of the 20th century. I may be prejudiced in making that statement because I think that most people would pick the decade of their childhood as being the best. However there are countless millions of people who strongly agree with me. There have been many surveys that attest to that fact.

The 20th century started off with events leading up to the First World War in 1914. After the war ended the roaring twenties resulted in the stock market crash of 1929. The great depression of the 1930's ended with the starting of the Second World War in 1939. The warring forties was certainly not a pleasant decade. But then the fifties came and people were happy once again.

I consider the fifties to be the transitional decade; the out with the old and in with the new decade. Things were changing and changing fast. In the music industry out went the dreary big band sound accompanied by gray haired vocalists and in came the modern country sound of honky-tonkers like Hank Williams and young exciting rock and rollers like Elvis Presley.

The auto industry boomed and the big three automakers General Motors, Ford and Chrysler competed with each other to see who could come up with the best work of art car every year. Cars were built big and beautiful with big powerful motors and big stylish fins. More people than ever before bought cars and everyone went on Sunday drives because gas was cheap and plentiful.

The fifties was a rebuilding decade after the Second World War and the Korean War. The economy was on the upswing and jobs were plentiful. Men worked and women stayed home to raise the kids and run the household. For the good life only one salary in the family was required. Life was good.

The only negative thing that I can think of was the start of the cold war. People were afraid of Communists and people in North America were afraid of a possible nuclear attack by the Soviet Union. I must say however that paranoia existed in the USA more so than in Canada. In L'Anse-a-Brilliant we weren't too worried about the Russians coming to bomb us.

When I moved to the farm with my parents in 1949 we didn't have electricity, running water or an indoor bathroom. We had manual water pumps and an outhouse. My parents and I had to adjust from the modern city of Montreal where all the comforts of modern life were taken for granted to the farm where the old ways of life lingered. My grandparents and great-grandparents who had lived on the farm all their lives had yet to experience the convenience of modern utilities. In fact they had done quite well without them. In those days unlike today you didn't really need electricity to function normally. Today, however, if the power goes off for a few hours we are lost without it. How are we going to make dinner? Is the food in the fridge going to spoil? We look at our watch and worry how long is it going to be until they get the power back on. How will we make a coffee? In the 1950's we didn't have these problems. There was always a kettle of hot water on the wood or oil stove.

The first modern convenience to come to the farm in L'Anse-a-Brilliant was electricity and it came in the early fifties. I remember the hydro poles being installed and the house being wired. When the electricity was turned on my mother turned on an electric light that night and did not light the old coal-oil lamp. When I visited my grandparents and great-grandparents at their end of the house however the coal-oil lamps were burning brightly. They had not turned on the new electric lights, as they still liked the old ways.

Next to come to our house was running water when my grandfather installed a new electric water pump and tank reservoir. I didn't have to go outside anymore to get a drink of cold water from the pump.

The last modern convenience to come to our house was our new bathroom, which my grandfather installed in 1958. I loved it but if it was occupied and I needed to go I still went to the old outhouse behind the house rather than wait.

Another great thing that came to Canada in the 1950's was television but it did not make it to L'Anse-a-Brilliant until the early sixties. Someone must have forgotten that country people in out of the way places needed television service as much as the good folk who lived in the towns and cities of the nation.

We never had a telephone until 1962 when we moved to Murdochville the copper mining town, which was eighty miles away from our farm. In those days phone numbers were only four digits and ours was 2306.

Growing up in the 1950's we didn't have any computers, televisions or video games. We didn't need them because we had the wondrous outdoors and other things to entertain us. The 1950's were the best decade ever. I know this because I was there.

3. Grandpa Buys Me A New Tricycle

Now that I'm a senior citizen I've forgotten many of my childhood birthdays and what gifts I received on those joyful fourth days of September that rolled around once every year. I do remember that on my twelfth birthday my dad gave me a brand new 22 caliber repeating rifle which was not that unusual a gift for a boy growing up in the country. Of course that would be a different story if I had lived in the city.

The birthday gift that I consider to be my all-time favorite was given to me by my grandfather on my third birthday. While I do not have any memories of that actual day the gift I received is forever etched in my memory because I used it for many years. It was a brand new shiny red tricycle and I can only imagine the joy I felt when my grandfather presented it to me.

For the next several years I made good use of that tricycle. I rode around and around the path that encircled our rather large farmhouse. When I got too big to ride my tricycle I took pleasure in teaching my sister Donna to ride it. She was five years younger than me and she made good use of my tricycle as well.

But even if I was too old and too big to ride the tricycle some days I felt like going for a ride around the house so I stood on the footrest behind the seat, grabbed the handlebars and pushed along with my right foot. It reminds me of the way the youngsters ride a skateboard today.

When any family member mentioned "Bryan, don't you think that your a little big to be riding that tricycle that way?"

I would reply, "Yes I could use a new bicycle." Hint. Hint.

4. Mother Baugh Can't See Me

In 1952 when I was four years old I was too afraid to go outside by myself. You see, I was afraid of Mother Baugh who was a witch who if she saw me outside of my house alone would swoop down on her broom and spirit me away. I would never see my family again.

In those years before I started school I didn't have any friends or playmates my age. The children who lived on the three adjacent farms were all several years older than me and it was from them that I had learned of the existence of Mother Baugh. I must inform you that it wasn't the older boys that had told me this. It was those innocent young ladies Geraldine Hodgins and Orion Baird. They had explained to me that Mother Baugh did not kidnap girls and would only grab young boys who were playing outside alone. Mother Baugh would not go inside a house so I would be safe there.

In the spring and summer the weather was beautiful and my mother would say to me

"Bryan, Go outside and play" but I would just tell her that I wanted to stay inside. She did take me to the beach to swim and lay on the sand but when we got back home I would immediately go inside with her.

My mother finally figured out that I was afraid to go outside and asked me why. I told her that Mother Baugh would get me if I went outside the house alone. She said that was nonsense and there was no such thing as a witch on a broom named Mother Baugh. She said that those girls were just trying to scare me and not to believe them.

Should I believe the girls or should I believe my mother? At that time I chose to believe the girls and I continued to stay indoors during the daytime and would only venture outside if someone were with me. Now, at the age of sixty I can still remember how terrified I was of Mother Baugh, the witch.

There weren't any streetlights in L'Anse- A-Brilliant in those days so when nighttime came it got really, really dark outside. So I went outside and played. I was all by myself. I would run around in the tall grass and roll down the hill that was close to our house. I couldn't see very much, only the light shining through our kitchen window. I had come to the conclusion that

6

Mother Baugh could not see me in the dark and thus could not come on her broom and kidnap me. Mom would come outside in the dark and call me to come inside the house. She would say that it was too dark to be out at this time of the night and that I had to get ready for bed. I would resist of course and try to stay out in the dark as long as possible. When my mother started to exhibit anger I would reluctantly reenter the house for the evening. Mom would look at me and say "Bryan, why are you so afraid of going outside to play in the daytime and why are you not afraid at night?"

"Mother Baugh cannot see me in the dark" I replied.

A year later when I was five I lost my fear of Mother Baugh. I would go outside by myself and play day or night.

5. Uncle Denzil

In 1949 at the age of ten months I along with my parents made the move from the big city of Montreal to a country farm in the Gaspe Peninsula. In the big duplex farmhouse in L'Anse-a-Brilliant I met my grandparents Ruby and Leslie, my great grandparents Angelina and Elias and one other individual who was to be my first playmate on the farm. He was my uncle Denzil and he was twenty-eight years old and a bachelor.

Uncle Denzil and I took to each other right away and we became fast friends. The first thing he did was teach me to walk at ten months of age. He had a lot of time to spend with me because he was unemployed at that time. When I became a toddler uncle Denzil would bounce me on his knee while he hummed fiddle tunes to me. At times he would get out his fiddle and play my favorite tunes such as "St. Ann's Reel" and "Maple Sugar".

My dad and uncle's Glen and Cyril were all fiddle players but my uncle Denzil was the best and I never got tired of listening to him play.

This friendship with my uncle Denzil continued on when I was three and four years old. I remember one day I ran into my grandmother's end of the house and I asked Nanny "Where's uncle Denzil?"

"He's upstairs in his bedroom sleeping his life away and it's after twelve o'clock in the afternoon" she said. "It's about time he got up."

Another time I was playing with my uncle Denzil and my grandmother said "Denzil, you spend so much time playing with Bryan, why don't you get married and have some children of your own?"

And that's what he did. In 1952 when he was thirty-one years old he married Ina Leggo who was only eighteen. As you may have guessed there's a story there.

When he was thirteen, uncle Denzil's best friend was Embert Leggo who lived across the river on the other side of L'Anse-a-Brilliant. Embert already had three brothers and in 1933 his mother gave birth to a baby girl, which she named Ina. Embert invited Denzil over to his house to see his baby sister Ina and he suggested that when she grew up that Denzil marry her. Baby Ina's father Elvin informed Denzil that he would have to wait until Ina was eighteen before he could marry her. So it appears that on the day she was born Ina was betrothed to my uncle Denzil by her brother and her father.

Fast forward eighteen years to 1952 and my uncle Denzil De Vouge and Ina Leggo got married in our local Anglican church in L'Anse-a-Brilliant. They moved to Murdochville and their first daughter Daphen was born in October of 1953. Later another daughter Laurel (1955) and a son Dana (1961) were born.

Throughout my youth I had occasion to hear my uncle Denzil play his fiddle at parties and family gatherings. I was so proud of him; of how he was a master fiddle player and everyone that heard him play felt the same way I did. They all wanted to hear him play more.

As the years went by and I became a teenager my mother would inform me of an upcoming party or family event. Because there would often be nobody there my own age I would usually say, "I don't think I'll go" but after thinking for a minute I would ask, "Will uncle Denzil be there?"

My mother would reply "Yes and he's bringing his fiddle. "

"Then I'm going I would reply."

Most of the time I would be the only teenager there but I was there for basically one thing, to hear my uncle Denzil play his fiddle.

When my mom, dad and sister Donna moved to St Catharines, Ontario in 1966 my uncle Denzil and aunt Ina moved their family there as well.

After I moved to Sudbury, Ontario to work I saw aunt Ina and uncle Denzil less and less, maybe once every two years or so. I have fond memories of a special anniversary party at my parent's house in St. Catharines in 1977. Expatriate Gaspesiens from there and other cities in Southern Ontario came to celebrate my parent's thirty years of marriage and my aunt Ina and uncle Denzil's twenty-fifth wedding anniversary. Aunt Dot and uncle Glen came up from Nova Scotia as well. A good time was had by all as there was square dancing downstairs in my parent's rec room and of course uncle Denzil played his fiddle.

In 1984 my parents now having been retired for a few years moved to Port Mouton, Nova Scotia and my aunt Ina and uncle Denzil moved to Nova Scotia as well but to Tatamagouche to be near my cousin Laurel who lived in Truro. It was about a two-hour drive from my parent's place.

I made many trips to Nova Scotia thereafter either with my family or my sister Donna to visit our now elderly parents. I remember mentioning to Donna when we passed by Truro that some year we should stop and visit our relatives there but we continued on as we were extremely anxious to see our parents two more hours down the road. Donna and I did stop in Truro in 2004 and again in 2006 and had the pleasure of reuniting with several other relatives that live there as well. My uncle Denzil, a widower and now in his mid eighties would give me a hug, embrace me, put his hands on my shoulders and say "Bryan, you're a big strong man." I knew that was the best of compliments coming from him. He had great respect for a big strong man.

When I saw uncle Denzil in 2006 he was eighty-six years old and he looked good. I asked him if he still played the fiddle and he replied, "Yes, Bryan and I'm better than ever. They want me to play all over Nova Scotia and I was up to Pembroke, Ontario to play in the Canadian Fiddling Championships. Fiddlers from all over come here to learn my tunes and several bands here and in the USA are now playing my tunes.

The last time I saw my uncle Denzil was at my mother's funeral in August of 2007. He had a massive stroke and passed away on September 4th. 2008 at the age of eighty-eight. I have a picture of him on my computer that was e-mailed to me by my cousin Laurel. It was taken just a few days before he passed away and in the picture he was sitting in a chair in his apartment playing his fiddle.

On our yearly trips to Nova Scotia to visit our late parents my sister Donna and I would always listen to a recording of our uncle Denzil's fiddle music on my truck's stereo. When I want to listen to his music at home I just pop the cassette into my stereo and listen to that beautiful music. I close my eyes and I can still see him there playing his fiddle. Uncle Denzil will always be my favorite musician.

6. My Cat Timmy

One of the most special days of my life was September the fourth 1952. It was my fourth birthday. I do not remember anything about the actual day, whether it was sunny or raining but I do remember that I did receive a birthday present from my parents which I still consider to the best present I have ever received. It was a very small yellow and white striped kitten and I named it Timmy. I don't remember to having asked for a kitten but nevertheless that was what I received.

My mother taught me how to care for Timmy and I would often give him a saucer of milk when he was hungry.

In those days many farmers had a pet, usually a cat or a dog. The dog, which was usually, a big one would be a watchdog and serve as a protector for the other farm animals. The main predators in our area were foxes and they sometimes played havoc with a farmer's chickens. A good watchdog would protect the hens and keep the foxes at bay.

Cats did a good job of keeping the farm free of mice. I don't remember anyone having a more exotic pet although Irma, Wayne and Verna Leggo had a pet rabbit: I think its name was Bunny.

As the years and Timmy and I got older and bigger a bond developed between us. We played together and I used to dangle some wound up yarn or paper attached to a string if front of him and he would chase the yarn and try to pounce on it. At other times I would sit on my favorite chair listening to the radio and Timmy would sit in my lap dozing and purring away.

One thing I did not like was when Timmy brought me special gifts. Timmy would approach me with a dead mouse in his mouth and drop it at my feet. I would tell him "No, I don't want any dead mice." I don't think that he understood me because the next day he would present me with another dead mouse.

Timmy was a very smart and clean cat. He was always licking his paws and cleaning behind his ears. When he wanted to go and do his business he would always go to the door and meow to go outside.

When Terry reached full adulthood he had grown to be a very large tomcat, quite larger than most. I remember when people visited us and saw Timmy they would say "Wow that is one huge tomcat. Does he scratch?"

I would reply, "No, go ahead and pet him. He won't scratch you."

As Timmy got older he started to do something that was very worrisome to me. He would take off for two to three days at a time. I would look for him especially along the highway where I thought that he might have been hit by a car while crossing the road. But he always returned albeit sometimes a little worse for wear. One day I saw him coming home walking very slowly. He was limping and he had tuffs of hair missing from his coat. One of his ears was ripped and there was dried blood on it.

Timmy had been going into the woods where there were many wild animals who could do him harm. There are bobcats and lynx in the Gaspe Peninsula as well as bear, moose, deer and other smaller animals. I don't believe there were any wolves or coyotes at that time. What I was really worried about was that he was fighting with a much bigger animal. I knew that was a battle that Timmy could not win. I was also hoping and praying that he had the good sense to stay away from any porcupine he encountered in the woods. I remembered hearing of dogs that had come home from a sojourn in the woods with their snout full of porcupine quills and their owners had to put them down. I did not want that to happen to my cat Timmy. Each time that Timmy came home from the woods hurt my mother and I would nurse him back to health. My mother being a former nurse always knew what to do.

One day when I was twelve years old and Timmy was eight he came home from one of his trips into the woods. I did not see him but my dad did observe him staggering home very slowly. My dad knew that something was terribly wrong because Timmy did not come to the door but instead crawled under our house, which had no basement. My father tried but was unable to coax Timmy out from underneath the house. Eventually my father saw Timmy walking up in the field behind our house. When dad approached him Timmy hissed and snarled at him and dad observed that he was frothing at the mouth. Instantly my dad knew that Timmy must have had a run-in with a rabid fox and that now Timmy had rabies, a deadly disease which could be passed on to humans. He went and got his 22 rifle and shot Timmy to put him out of his misery. Dad buried Timmy so that we or any other animals would not be exposed to his deadly rabies.

Fortunately I wasn't at home when this all happened and didn't find out about it until days later when my mom explained to me what had happened and why. I was very much saddened by this bad news but because I had grown up on a farm I understood why Timmy had to be put down. As strange as it may seem almost fifty years later I had completely forgotten about how Timmy died. When I was planning to write this book I called my sister Donna who was only seven years old when this happened. Donna informed me what had happened and slowly my memory of this incident returned. I suppose that unpleasant memories of one's childhood get sent to the furthest recesses of one's brain never to be retrieved again. I do remember that my parents asked me if I would like another cat to replace Timmy and I said, "No, no other cat can ever replace Timmy."

7. A Spoonful Of Gin, A Juice Glass OF Beer

In 1952 when I was four years old I used to watch my mother make my father a gin drink when he requested it. In those days in Gaspe gin was the favored alcoholic drink of the majority of the men. My mom would pour a shot glass measure of gin into a glass and then add a mixer such as Collins Mixer or soda water to it. My dad preferred the Collins Mixer making a drink commonly known as a "Tom Collins".

I would continually ask my dad for a taste of his gin drink and he would always say "no you're too young to drink alcohol."

"Just a small sip " I would say.

One day when I was pestering my father for a taste he replied "If you want to taste my gin you'll have to taste it straight from the bottle. I'll give you one spoonful."

"No, Herzil" said my mother. "Don't give it to him straight."
Dad replied "One spoonful won't hurt him" and he filled the spoon I was holding with pure gin. Being very careful and making sure not to spill a drop I put the spoonful of gin in my mouth and swallowed it. I let out one hell of a large shriek when the gin burned my mouth and throat. I tried to spit it put but it was too late for that.

"It tastes terrible," I said. "It's awful"

"Would you like some more? asked my father.

"No!" I replied. "I don't want a sip of that gin ever again."

The next time I asked my dad for a drink of gin was about twelve years later when I was sixteen years old.

Although my dad only drank gin once in a while he loved to have a beer on a hot day when he came home from work. When I asked him for a sip of his beer he would go to the kitchen cupboard and get a small four-ounce juice glass. He poured a few ounces of his O'Keefe beer into it and handed it to me. I took a little sip and was surprised to find that it tasted good. I liked it a lot and from that day forward when my dad opened a beer he always gave me a few ounces in a juice glass when I asked for it.

A few years later when I started school I was skinny and sickly. I didn't have any energy and couldn't keep up with the other kids when I ran or played sports. My parents took me to the doctor and it was decided that I needed a tonic to perk me up a bit. It didn't seem to work as I was still as skinny as ever and I didn't have an appetite.

My father remarked that I was just skin and bone and I needed a real tonic, one that would give me an appetite. He prescribed beer and he said that I was to drink half a bottle in the morning before I went to school and the other half when I got home from school. I don't really know what my mother thought of this but dad was the boss.

My grandmother however was angry with my father and told him that he was going to make his children into alcoholics. He listened to his mother's advice but he did not change his mind in any way.

The end result was that at the age of eight or nine I was drinking one beer per day and keeping it a secret from my teacher and classmates at school. I was actually drinking more beer than my dad because he didn't drink a beer every day. Also my younger sister Donna was drinking a small juice glass of beer when dad had one.

Believe it or not my dad's prescription of a beer every day cured me. I became energetic and finally got an appetite. I ate better and became healthy. I became an athlete and I was good in the sports that I was involved in. I finally put some meat on my bones and my dad judged his project a complete success. He then stopped the practice of giving me a beer every day. He did however give my sister and I a small glass of beer each when he had one. In fact my sister Donna watched our father like a hawk and when he ventured to the fridge to get himself a beer she would run to find me and say "Bryan, come quick. Dad is opening up a beer."

Donna would then run to the cupboard and get us juice glasses and approach dad for her share as she called it. Because my mother didn't drink beer dad would finish off what little was left in the bottle and then open a new one for himself.

My grandmother's prediction that my sister and I would become alcoholics did not come true. As we grew older we lost interest in pestering our father for a glass of beer. Perhaps because it was available to us at such a young age we simply lost interest in it later. Throughout my adulthood I have consumed very little hard liquor or beer. The only time I drink beer is when I spend the winter in Florida. Sometimes after a long walk on the beach and I'm feeling parched I find a small seven ounce mini bottle of "Bud Light" very refreshing. This past winter I drank five or six of them.

8. He Drinks Out Of A Sugar Bowl

In the summer of 1952 or was it the summer of 1953: I really don't remember which summer it was. I was only four or five but I do remember the day my father came home from work and told my mother that the next day he would be stopping by in the early afternoon for a coffee. He would be bringing one of his co-workers Captain Bill along with him on their way back from inspecting a fishing vessel that needed repairs. Dad worked at the Sandy Beach Boatyard building long liners, which are actually big fishing boats. They were also called trawlers.

I looked at my father and said "Dad, are you bringing a real captain here tomorrow?"

"Well that's what they call him" dad replied. "Captain Bill."

I was very exited because I had never met or seen a real captain before. But I wondered why this captain was building boats instead of sailing them.

The next afternoon I was eagerly awaiting my dad and Captain Bill's arrival at our farm. When they pulled up in my dad's car a tall man who must be Captain Bill got out of the car and they came into our house. Captain Bill was wearing an authentic captains hat with a white top and a shinny black bill. It had a crown and anchor crest on the front of it. I was impressed, wow a real live captain.

My father introduced Captain Bill to my mother and I, and then my mother announced that the coffee was perked and ready. Captain Bill and dad sat down at the kitchen table and mom served them each a mug of coffee along with a plate of biscuits.

All of a sudden my mother noticed something amiss and said "Captain Bill. I must apologize because I've given you a chipped coffee mug. Here, let me get you a new one."

Captain Bill looked at his chipped coffee mug, and then looked at my mother and said, "That's nothing Pat. At home I drink out of the sugar bowl."

Then he finished drinking his coffee out of the chipped coffee mug.

I was wondering why Captain Bill called my mother Pat when her name is Francis and later that evening I asked my dad why.

My dad replied, "Oh, he calls everyone Pat. It's a saying like how's it going Bryan or how's it going John? I've heard other people say it as well."

"But he says that at home he drinks out of a sugar bowl." I stated.

Dad replied, "He probably does Bryan. He probably does."

9. Hank Williams Died

I was born in Montreal in 1948, moved to the farm in the Gaspe Peninsula in 1949 and the radio was a big part of my life in the 1950's as far as entertainment was concerned.

As long as I can remember the radio was on when I awoke in the morning and was on until I went to bed in the evening. Except for my uncle Denzil playing his fiddle the few years he lived with us the radio was our sole entertainment on the farm. We didn't have any television on or computers to entertain us and no record player to play mom's old 78 rpm records; just the radio. We had an abundant number or radio stations we listened to but I considered the best ones to be the country stations coming to us from Boston, Massachusetts.

Hank Williams was the first superstar I remember whose songs I loved to listen to on the radio. Hank was born on September 17, 1923 in Alabama and was a pioneer of the honky-tonk style of country music. He became a country music star in 1948, the year I was born and by the time he made his Grand Old Opry debut in June of 1949 he had become the first country music superstar. Along with his band, The Drifting Cowboys he cranked out hit after hit and had eleven number one records such as "Hey Good Looking", "Kaw-Liga" and "Your Cheating Heart". I remember when I listened to the radio I didn't have to wait very long until they played a Hank Williams song. Although there were lots of good singers on the radio they played a Hank Williams tune once ever fifteen or twenty minutes or so. I knew the words to all his songs and I would sing along with the radio. Although there were several singers I liked both male and female Hank was my absolute favorite and he still is to this day.

After midnight on January the 1st. 1953 Hank Williams was sleeping in the back seat of his Cadillac enroute to do a show in Canton, Ohio when his driver stopped at a gas station. When the driver checked on Hank in the back seat he found that Hank had passed away.

When I woke up that morning I went downstairs to the kitchen to have my breakfast and there was a Hank Williams song playing on the radio.

While I ate my breakfast they played another Hank Williams song and then another and another. I was only four years old and I knew New Years Day was a special day but I wondered why there were playing Hank Williams songs back to back to back.

I asked my mother "Mom, why are they playing only Hank Williams songs this morning?"

"Hank Williams passes away during the night Bryan. He died."

"Why did he die mom?" I asked. "He is still young." In fact he was just twenty-nine years old.

"His poor old heart just gave out" was my mother's reply. She was obviously saddened as tears were running down her cheeks. I was very sad as well. My favorite singer had died and died young but even after his death new Hank Williams songs that had been recorded but not released were played on the radio and I knew that his music would never die. It would carry on forever.

My other favorite singers that I heard every day on the radio were Johnny Horton and Johnny Cash. But once again we lost another great talent when Johnny Horton died in a car crash in 1960. Fortunately Johnny Cash lived to a ripe old age and provided us with great music for many, many years. In fact Johnny Cash was voted the number one performer in country music by CMT. Hank Williams was rated number two even though his career was very short.

In the early fifties a new type of music started to be played on the radio and it became known as rock and roll. There were several new stars but the first real rock and roll superstar was Elvis Presley. I loved his songs just as I had loved Hank Williams's music.

Everything was going fine and Elvis was pumping out the hits when in December 1957 we learned that he had received his draft notice. We were very dismayed when on March the 24th. 1960 Elvis joined the US Army and was sent to Germany to serve. On that day the radio stations played Elvis and nothing but Elvis all day.

I was overjoyed however when new hit songs were being played on the radio for the next two years while Elvis served in the army. Elvis had previously recorded several songs to keep us entertained while he was away.

Elvis was discharged from the army in March 1960 after serving two years. We were all happy to have him back to keep making more hit records. On the day he was discharged Elvis songs were played on the radio all day as well. Unfortunately like many other stars Elvis died too young.

When my mother passed away a few years ago I inherited the big family bible. In the front there's a section where all births, deaths and marriages are recorded. Of course all the deaths of my mother and father's ancestors are recorded there along with one non-family member. In the family bible my mother wrote

Elvis Presley (King of Rock)
Born 1935 Died Aug 16, 1977
Aged 42 years

When television came to the Gaspe in the early sixties it became my entertainment of choice but I still listened to the radio from time to time. These days when you turn on the radio you can listen for a month of Sunday's before you will hear a Hank Williams song. Right now I'm going to put a Hank Williams CD into my computer and listen to his hits that were recorded sixty years ago and listen to that beautiful music while I check my e-mail and then play FreeCell and Hearts.

10. Buy Gap Some Cough Medicine

In the early fifties my great grandmother Angelina (Granny) and my great grandfather Elias (Gap) were still living. They stayed in the newer part of our big farmhouse with my grandparents.

Gappy, as I called him had developed a bad cough and since he was eighty-five years old Granny was worried about him. That evening she came out to our end of the house to see my dad.

Granny handed my dad some money and said "Herzil, tomorrow after work I want you to go into Gaspe to the drugstore and buy Gap some cough medicine. He's got a terrible cough and it's keeping both of us awake all night. He wants a bottle of that De Kuyper gin and says that will cure him but I want the proper cough medicine for him.

Dad took the money and said that he would be sure and do that the next day.

An hour or so later my great grandfather Gappy came to my dad and told him that he needed a bottle of De Kuyper gin and he didn't need any cough medicine.

In those days in Gaspe and throughout the province of Quebec De Kuyper gin was the preferred drink of the older men. They didn't drink rye whisky like Ontario men did, or vodka or wine. They loved their De Kuyper gin, which was imported from Holland. They claimed that it could cure a cold. They used to say that " it was good for what ails you and if nothing ails you it's good for that to. Years later some young men described it to me as harsh and rotgut gin.

The next day dad who worked at the boatyard at Sandy Beach drove the few miles into Gaspe after he finished work for the day. He bought the cough medicine for Granny and the De Kuyper gin for Gappy

When my dad got home he delivered the cough medicine to his grandmother and snuck the De Kuyper gin to his grandfather.

Gappy told Granny that he would take a spoonful of the cough medicine before he went to bed that night but he didn't. Instead he had a few swallows of the De Kuyper gin.

The next day when my dad got home from work he visited his parents and grandparents to see how Gappy was doing.

Granny said "Herzil, that was good cough medicine you bought Gap yesterday. He took one spoonful and he slept all night and didn't even cough once.

Gappy winked at my dad and said, "Yes, that was good cough medicine that you bought me."

11. Gappy (Elias De Vouge)

Gappy was my great grandfather Elias De Vouge who was better known by his nickname than his real name. Some people also called him Gap but he will always be Gappy to me.

Gappy was born down in Barachois in 1867 the year of Canada's Confederation. He moved to L'Anse-a-Brilliant when he married Angelina Leggo (Granny) in 1889 and started farming there. He was also a fisherman as most men were in those days combining fishing and farming as their occupation. He was not a tall man like my grandfather Leslie and my father Herzil. He was of average height but he was a tremendously strong man and he used to perform feats of strength. I have been told that he used to lift those kegs of nails weighing up to four hundred and fifty pounds up off the floor and onto the counter at the general store. When he was young he was known as the strongest man on the Gaspe coast. I only wish that I had inherited more of his strength than I did.

In 1948 Gappy was walking along the road to go to the store when a logging truck lost it's load and unfortunately several logs fell on him and broke one of his legs in eight places. He was eighty-one years of age at the time and was lucky to have survived this horrible accident. His leg had to be amputated and he spent the rest of his life in a wheelchair.

As a child I would go and visit him in his end of the house and immediately hop on the footrest of his wheelchair.

Gappy would say, "Bryan, I guess you want to go for a ride" and then he would take me for ride in his wheelchair singing songs to me as he wheeled me around the house. The songs were in English and in French and were the songs that fishermen sang as they rowed their flats out to the net moorings. Gappy chewed tobacco and there was a spittoon attached to the side of his wheelchair. He sometimes would stop momentarily and spit into the spittoon. I don't remember him ever missing his mark. He was always available to take me for a wheelchair ride. I don't think there ever was a time when Gappy said that he was too tired to wheel me around. He always enthusiastically wheeled me around anytime I wanted a ride.

One day my mother said "Bryan, go tell Gappy that I'm going to give your baby sister Donna her bath now."

I did so and when Gappy and I returned my mother placed Donna in a washbasin in the kitchen sink and bathed her. As Gappy watched tears began to flow down his cheeks. Later I asked my mother "Why did Gappy want to watch you give Donna her bath and why did he cry?"

Mom replied "He lost his only daughter Olive when she was a baby and he's remembering her. He loves having a baby great granddaughter living here in this house with him. He loves all his great grandchildren."

And we all loved him as well.

In the late 1940's before Gappy lost his leg he would walk down to the harbour and sit on a large flat rock the size of a couch that became known as Gap's Chesterfield. It was located right close to his old stage, which is a building like a barn where fishermen store their equipment and bait etc. I have a photograph of him sitting there posing for the camera. This photo turned out to be a famous one because it is displayed at one of Canada's National Museum's in Ottawa. It is black and white and is entitled "An old fisherman in Gaspe, Quebec" or something to that effect.

Gappy passed away in 1954 at the age of eighty-seven when I was around six years old. It is strange but I have absolutely no memory of his passing or his funeral although I was right there at the time. I guess unpleasant memories are suppressed and tucked away. However I do remember the good times we had going for many rides on his wheelchair while he sang fisherman songs to me.

12. A Dog Bites Me

In the mid fifties when I was about seven years old I used to go over to the farm next door and play with Orion Baird. She was much older than me: in fact she was a teenager but I was very grateful she took the time to play with me as there were very few children of my own age around.

One summer day I took my new red, white, and blue rubber ball and went over to Orion's house to see if she would play with me. We decided that one of us would stand on each side of the house and throw the ball over the roof to each other. It was very difficult to catch the ball when you didn't see the ball till the last second and you had to run and position yourself to catch it.

At the corner of our property and Orion's parents property there was a small lot with a small house on it. It had once been the local schoolhouse many years before and had been converted. This lot was fenced in on three sides and open to the old road on the fourth. There was a family there with a daughter who was about a year younger than me. They had a small dog that I think was some kind of terrier as it had a very hairy face. It used to bark a lot especially at people who walked by on the road.

This day the dog was loose and came over on Orion's property. This time when Orion threw the ball over the house I failed to catch it and it rolled away. I ran to get the ball and the dog ran towards it as well. I got to the ball before the dog did and picked it up. The dog was barking at me and looked angry. It bit me on the leg. I tried to get away but it kept on biting me. Orion heard me screaming and came running around the house. She made the dog stop biting me and chased it away. My leg hurt a lot where the dog bit me and Orion took me home to my parents. I was crying and in terrible pain as Orion explained that the neighbour's dog had bitten me.

While my mother washed the blood off my leg and cleaned the bites with iodine I told my dad that he should go and shoot the dog. My dad was a big strong man but I could see that he didn't want to do something like shoot the neighbour's dog.

My dad had brothers and uncle Cyril who was my dad's oldest brother was visiting the farm that day. When he found out what had happened to me he came out to our end of the house and asked my dad if he was going to do anything about it. My dad must have said no as I thought my uncle was a little angry when he left.

My uncle Cyril was a tough son of a gun and I figured that he would do something about the dog. And right I was because he went into my grandparents' end of the house and got one of my grandfather's rifles. He then went down to the corner of our property where the dog was still loose. The dog started to bark at my uncle Cyril and came towards my uncle on our property. Uncle Cyril shot the dog with one shot and killed it.

Hearing the shot we went outside to see what had happened. We saw the dog's owner come out of his house, observe his dead dog there and angrily shout at my uncle Cyril. My uncle must have informed the neighbour why he had to shoot the dog but we could not hear what was being said. I found out later that my uncle had informed the neighbour that he had more bullets for the gun.

This result would not happen today because it would not be politically correct and it would cause so many legal problems. But in 1955 in our community it was considered Gaspe' justice.

I had always been a little scared of my uncle Cyril but that day I was very thankful and proud of him.

13. Dad Built A Boat

When we moved from Montreal to my grandparent's farm in 1949 my grandfather was a fisherman/farmer who captained his own fishing boat. My father noticed that his dad's fishing boat was looking old and worn and he asked grandpa "How long are you going to fish with that old boat?"

My grandfather replied "My boat is only going to last a few more years but if I had a new one I would fish until I can collect my old pension in 1957."

My father replied, "In that case I'll build you a new boat. I'll work on it in my spare time and it'll be ready when you decide to scrap your old boat in a few years.

Dad worked up at the boatyards in Sandy Beach building long liners and for the next few years most if not all of his spare time was spent on his new project. Instead of working from a set plan dad came up with his own design of what he thought a fishing boat should look like. Then dad built this weird contraption out behind the house. I was only three years old but I knew what a boat was and this thing didn't look like a boat to me. When I asked my father what that thing was he explained to me that it was a cradle to hold the boat that he was going to build.

For the next year I watched as my dad did the many different things required to build a fishing boat. I watched as he steamed wooden planks so that they would bend without breaking to form the pointed end of the bow. Finally I thought the boat was finished but my dad informed me that there was still a lot more work to be done before the boat could be launched into the water. Two masts had to be put up and sails installed. An engine, transmission, a propeller and other accessories had to be installed as well as navigation lights etc. The cabin or cuddy had to be finished below the deck and bunk's installed where the fishermen would sleep when they were out on the Atlantic Ocean for three or four days at a time fishing until they filled the hold up with cod. A stove had to be installed in the cuddy for cooking and to provide heat on cool nights out on the water.

In the spring of 1953 the boat that my dad had built for my grandfather was ready to go. It was painted white and now it had to be named. It was a tradition in the Gaspe to give a fishing boat a feminine name and usually a fisherman would name his boat after his mother, his wife or his daughter. That was not the case this time however as my grandfather named his new fishing boat the "Herzil" after my father. When he asked why he did this my grandfather replied "How could you name this beautiful boat for anyone other than the man who built it'"

The "Herzil was indeed a beautiful boat. It was not shaped like the traditional Gaspe fishing boat, which had both a pointed bow and a pointed stern. The "Herzil" was built long and sleek like a schooner and it had a rounded, inclined and squared stern like a yacht. It was fifty-two feet long with two masts and two sails. Instead of the traditional put-put-put small horsepower marine engine it had a larger and much more powerful Cadillac engine with a manual transmission and a stick shift. Instead of a rudder controlled by a hand held tiller it had a multi-spoked steering wheel like a big ship. Its name "Herzil" was written in big black letters on the stern along with "Gaspe" its homeport. L'Anse-a-Brilliant harbour was actually it' homeport but it's in Gaspe Bay so I guess that's why Gaspe was written on the stern. It's name "Herzil" was also written on both its sides up close to the bow.

Now it had to be transported from our farm where it was built down to the harbour where it would be docked. That was to become quite a task because the tractor that towed it could not use our driveway and make a ninety-degree turn onto the road. The "Herzil" had to be hauled to the old road and down to the harbour and this meant basically in a straight line through our farm and the next farm over. This meant that fences had to be taken down to let the boat pass and then put back up again. It was a slow process but eventually grandpa's new boat was launched into the water and tied up at the wharf. But it still wasn't ready to go fishing. Big beach rocks had to be collected and installed in the hold on the bottom and sides to act as ballast to make the "Herzil" sit lower in the water making it more stable when it was operated by the engine or by the sails.

The "Herzil" was the nicest and fastest fishing boat in the harbour and many people came and took pictures of it. Many years later I acquired two paintings that were made of it, one a small painting and the other a much larger one. Both paintings depict the "Herzil" out on Gaspe Bay coming in to port returning from a fishing trip.

After my grandfather's new fishing boat was launched in the spring of 1953 Grandpa and his crew fished for five seasons in it. My grandfather retired from cod fishing in the fall of 1957 and sold the "Herzil" in the summer of 1958 but not before our extended family and some friends went for one last sail on a beautiful July day.

14. My Sister Is Born

On October 19, 1953 my father drove my mother the twenty miles to the Hotel Dieu hospital in Gaspe'. Much later he returned home alone and told me that I now had a baby sister named Donna. He told my grandparents and great-grandparents that mother and daughter were doing well.

The next day dad told us that he was going to Gaspe' to visit my mom and my new baby sister Donna at the hospital maternity ward. I got my coat and got ready to go as well.

"Hold on" my dad said. " You're too young to visit the hospital. You have to be at least ten years old to get in to visit your mom and sister."

I had just turned five the previous month and I was real disappointed that I was not allowed to visit. I decided to take matters into my own hands and quickly went outside and got in the back seat of my dad's old 1936 Buick. I made sure to close the door without slamming it and lay down on the floor so my dad wouldn't see me.

My dad exited the house, got in the car, started it and we were on our way. I was as quiet as a church mouse as I knew that my dad would take me back home if he discovered me in the car with him.

Thirty minutes later dad parked his Buick in the hospital parking lot and exited the car. I got up off the floor and got out of the car as well.

"What are you doing here?" dad asked. "You hid in the car. You shouldn't have done that"

"I want to see my mom and my baby sister" I replied.

"Well we'll have to go see the sister" dad said.

I found out that the sister that dad had mentioned was a nun who was all dressed in a black robe from head to toe. At the time I didn't know about nuns, as we were Anglican and not Catholic. My dad explained to her what had happened and how I wanted to see my mom and baby sister so bad that that I had hidden on the floor in the back seat.

I was afraid of the nun and that she was going to be angry with me. However she looked down at me and she was smiling.

"You know a child has to be ten years of age to visit a patient" she said, "How old are you?"

"I'm five years old " I replied.

The nun was still smiling and looked down at me and said, " You really were determined to see your baby sister today weren't you? Well I think we will make a rule change for today only. Today you have to be five years old to visit a patient."

My dad said "Thank You sister" and then turned to me. "Bryan what do you have to say to the sister?"

I looked up at the sister and said, "Thank You very much."

"You're quite welcome young man" she replied.

My dad and I rode the elevator up to the maternity floor and went to my mom's room. It was not a private room but a ward and there were other ladies there as well.

My mom told us that we had to go down the hall to see Donna. We came to a big room with a really big window. Looking in I saw several babies in little cribs, some in blue blankets and some in pink blankets. All of them seemed to be sleeping.

A nurse came and asked which baby we wanted to see and my dad said " the De Vouge baby."

The nurse didn't bring my baby sister out to see us but brought her up to the window and we looked at her through the window. She weighed over seven pounds but she looked small to me. She had these tiny hands with even tinier fingers. I could see that my dad was happy and that he liked her and I liked her as well. My mom told us that she and Donna would be back home in a few days.

When dad arrived home with my mom and baby sister Donna, I along with my grandparents and my great-grandparents were eagerly awaiting. We were all very happy that we had a new addition to our four generational family on the farm.

15. First Day Of School

In the 1950's in the Gaspe there wasn't any kindergarten or junior kindergarten. You started school in grade one when you were six years old or five years old and turning six before the end of December. Since I was turning six in September of 1954 I was eagerly looking forward to starting grade one at Belle Anse Consolidated School. However it was not to be. When the first day of school rolled around my mother told me that I couldn't go because I was too sick. I had a minor illness, which made me sickly and weak, and my mom told me that I needed a while to recover before I could attend school, which was fourteen miles away by bus.

I was disappointed of course but I had no say in the matter. My mom had reminded me that I could already read a bit and that she and my father would home school me until I was healthy enough to go to school.

A few months later I was feeling much better and wanted to start school but my mom said that it would be better to wait until the new school term started in January to start school. She wanted to be sure that I was really over my sickness before sending me off to school.

Christmas came and went. I was feeling good and healthy and my mom sent me off to school on the first day of school in January. It was my first ever school bus ride and I sat in the second last row of seats at the back of the bus. It was exciting because when we drove over a bump the kids at the back of the bus would all be thrown about a foot in the air and would all let out a cheer.

When we arrived at the school one of the older girls took me to the grade one classroom to introduce me to my teacher. It was either Geraldine Hodgins or Verna Leggo: I don't remember which but they were the only two girls a few years older than me in L'Anse-a-Brilliant.

My new teacher did not looked pleased when she was told the circumstances of why I was starting school so late in the school year; four months late in fact. She told me that she was taking me to the principal's office to talk to the principal.

The principal was a man and my new teacher introduced me to him and explained that I was a new student. She also stated that she did not think that I should be starting school so late in the school year. I had already missed four months of schooling and I would be so far behind the class it would be almost impossible for me to catch up. She said that this would be disruptive to her and the class. It wasn't fair to her class.

The principal turned to me and said "Young man, do you understand what your teacher is saying?"

"Yes" I replied "But I can already read, write, add and subtract."

"Really" the principal exclaimed and then he asked me if I knew my ABC's.

I said "Do you want to hear them frontward or backwards?"

"I've never heard them backwards before" he replied. "Go ahead and recite them backwards."

I very quickly recited them backwards in a musical rhyme without missing a beat like my father had taught me. I could see that the principal was impressed and I said to him "Do you want me to say them frontward?"

"No Bryan, that won't be necessary" was his reply.

He turned to my teacher and said, "Could you bring me a grade one reader?"

The teacher returned with the same reader that my dad had used to teach me to read at home. It was the traditional grade one book about Dick and Jane and their dog Spot. I opened the reader and started reading out loud about Dick, Jane and Spot. The principal stopped me and asked me to read the last chapter in the book. I did without any problem whatsoever. The principle then asked my teacher to get a grade two reader and she left the office. He asked me "Who taught you to read?"

"My dad taught me to read about a year ago and since I was too sick to come to school my mother has been teaching me mathematics at home."

My teacher returned and handed me a grade two reader which I opened and started reading to both of them.

"Oh my God" the teacher said. "He's reading better than my grade two class."

I asked the principal "Would you like me to do some addition and subtraction?"

"No thank you" was the reply. "Mr. Bryan De Vouge welcome to Belle Anse Consolidated School."

I couldn't wait to get into that classroom to begin my education.

16. Learning The Facts Of Life

In the previous chapter I talked about the beginning of my first day of school in January of 1955 and the reason I started four months late because of sickness.

The first big disappointment of my first day at school happened at our break for lunch. My mom had bought me a brand new Roy Rogers lunch pail with a picture of Roy Rogers sitting on his horse Trigger on it. It also had a thermos inside with the same picture on it. I was very proud of this lunch pail and thermos set, as I was a real Roy Rogers fan. My mother had met Roy Rogers and his famous horse Trigger at an appearance in Montreal and had actually talked to him and his wife Dale Evans. I was very proud that my mom had met these famous celebrities. At lunchtime we all went down to the cloakroom to retrieve our lunch pails and take them to the gymnasium where tables were set up for us to eat our lunch. I grabbed my lunch pail and in my hurry to keep up with the other kids I dropped my lunch pail on the floor and broke my thermos inside it. In the fifties thermos bottles were very fragile as they had a silver coloured glass inside that could not survive a fall. The milk that was my drink of choice for lunch was all over the place. This was a major disappointment breaking my new Roy Rogers thermos on my first day of school.

That day I learned things from the teacher that you would learn in a normal classroom setting. However it was not in the classroom that I learned things that I considered to be more important than reading and writing.

You see these fascinating lessons were given to me by some older boys who were around ten or eleven years old and who delighted in teaching a new six year old student the facts of life and other things. These so called lessons were taught at both morning and afternoon recess and at lunch break.

The first thing that these older boys informed me was that there was no such thing as Santa Claus. No one lived at the North Pole and flew down on a sleigh pulled by Rudolph the red nosed reindeer. Santa Claus did not land on my roof and climb down the chimney to leave presents under the tree if I was a good boy. This was certainly a shock to me as less than two weeks previous Santa had left me several nice presents under the tree. I had received presents from my grandparents, aunts and uncles, mom and dad but Santa had left the really good ones. I did not know if I should believe what these older boys were telling me but when you're six years old you usually believe everything someone tells you. The boys explained that adults tell us about Santa so that we'll make sure to be well behaved all year long so that Santa will bring us presents. They told me that my father was the one who ate the milk and cookies I had left for Santa, not Santa Claus. My father and mother had bought these presents for me and not an imaginary Santa Claus.

The next thing I learned was that there was no tooth fairy. I found this hard to believe because I had recently pulled one of my loose baby teeth out and had placed it under my pillow. The next morning when I awoke there was a twenty-five cent piece under my pillow as there had been every time I had lost a tooth. The older boys informed me that my mom was the real tooth fairy who had done this. Another Surprise.

The third thing that I learned was that there was no Easter Bunny. Again I found this hard to believe because on Easter Sunday morning I had found Easter eggs hidden all over our house and my mother had explained that that the Easter Bunny had hidden the eggs well so I would have to look in every nook and cranny for them. Maybe this explained why after I thought I had found all the eggs that the Easter Bunny had left me my mother would suggest that there might be one behind the bread basket or in the cupboard behind the cereal box and she was always right.

The next lesson that the older boys gave me was the most important and by far the most confusing. I already knew that babies came out of your mother's belly because I had a sister Donna who was a year old and when my mother was pregnant I remember her putting my hand on her belly to feel the baby kicking. So I already knew that a stork did not deliver a new baby to my mother that she had ordered.

The older boys then explained to me how a lady gets pregnant. I was both shocked and horrified at their explanation. I could not envision that something like this was possible but the older boys assured me that what they were telling me was correct. The lecture ended there because I didn't want to discuss it any further.

When I got home from school that first day in January of 1955 I ran up the driveway and was greeted by my mother at the door. When she asked me if I liked school and had I learned anything today I told her that I loved school and yes, I had certainly learned a lot on my first day of school.

17. Churning The Butter For Granny

On the farm in the early fifties Nanny, my grandmother milked the cows and pasteurized the milk. She worked the machine that separated the cream from the milk.

Granny, my great-grandmother who was in her late eighties was the butter maker. When it was time to make up a supply of butter for our extended family she would get out her old churn and churn away. The churn was an old-fashioned one made of wood and it looked exactly like a wooden barrel only it was much smaller. It had a wooden lid with a hole in the middle where the plunger was inserted.

Granny didn't need a recipe to make the best butter I ever slapped on a slice of fresh baked homemade bread. She had made the butter so many times she knew exactly how many handfuls of salt she had to throw into the mix.

I started helping Granny churn the butter when I was about five or six years old. If I visited my grandparents and great-grandparents in their end of the house Granny would always ask me if I wanted to help. She would say "Come here young fellow and churn this butter for a while. Bryan, you have lots of energy and give your granny a little rest."

I would then takeover for her and push and pull the plunger up and down, up and down and kept doing it until I thought my arms were going to fall off. When Granny saw that I was getting really tired she would say, "Ok Bryan, I'll take over now. You've done a good job thickening up the butter. I'll churn for a little while longer and then I think the butter will be ready."

When the butter was ready Granny would put it into a mould and make one pound bricks like you buy in the supermarket. She would wrap the bricks of butter in the proper waxed paper and store it away. It was certainly delicious butter and I judged it to be much better than the store bought variety.

As I got older, bigger and stronger I got more vigorous and better at churning the butter. As Granny lived into her nineties and got too elderly to work the churn any more my grandmother took over the butter making and I helped her as well.

A few years later the cows were gone. I don't remember if my grandparents sold them or ate them. In any case we had to find another source for our butter. My mother would send me over to Rupert Leggo's, which was three farms over from ours. Nora Leggo still made butter the old fashioned way and I was surprised and delighted to discover that her homemade butter was just as good as Granny's was.

My great-grandmother Angelina Leggo De Vouge passed away in 1957 at the age of ninety-two. I treasure my memories of churning butter with her so many years ago.

18. The First De Vouge

My great, great, great-grandfather was Pierre Andre Marie De Vouges and he was the first De Vouge to emigrate to North America and all the people in Canada and the USA bearing the surname De Vouge or De Vouges are descended from him. Pierre was born in La Haye D'Ectot, France on January 1st. 1806 and lived there with his parents close to the English Channel in Lower Normandy. When he grew up he moved to the island of Jersey in the Channel Islands to work for the Charles Robin Company, which was a global company with Channel Islands, UK heritage. It was there in Jersey where he married Jeanne Francoise Boulier on August the 12th 1836 in St Peter's Parish, Jersey, Channel Islands.

In the 1800's the Charles Robin Company had become the largest fishing company in Canada and had many fish processing facilities along the Gaspe coast and in other parts of the maritime provinces. They exported their preserved salted and dried cod to many countries in Europe such as England, France, Spain and Portugal. The Robin Company also exported to many of the tropical islands in the Caribbean. Their product, salted cod, was dried and cured in the sun was unique in that it was good for up to eighteen months without refrigeration.

Point St. Peter was the main schooner port for the cod fishery in the Gaspe area in the mid 1800's. The area was totally controlled by the Robin's Company and Pierre De Vouges was sent from their main office in Jersey to be the new Harbour Master at Pointe St. Peter.

Pierre arrived with his wife Jeanne in 1838 and took up residence in Pointe St. Peter. Because this was an English community Pierre now became known as Peter De Vouges. Jeanne got pregnant and later received word that her father had passed away back in France. She had to go back to France to settle her father's estate so she took passage on a ship and sailed back to France as soon as she was able to. While she was in France she gave birth to Peter Jr. her first son and after spending some time in France she returned to her husband in Point St. Peter.

Their second son and the first De Vouges to be born in Canada was Thomas Phillip De Vouges. He was born in the middle of the winter on February 16th. 1842 and he is my great, great-grandfather.

Peter was a religious man and wanted his newborn baby boy baptized as soon as possible. He was Roman Catholic and the church that he attended was several miles away in Barachois. Nevertheless he hitched up horse and sleigh and proceeded to his church to have his baby boy Thomas baptized by his priest. However the priest said that he was too busy to baptize the child and that Peter would have to come back on another occasion. Disappointed with his priest Peter began the long winter sleigh ride back home to Point St. Peter. On the way Peter decided to stop at the local Protestant church, which was St Peter's Episcopalian Church in Mal Bay and ask the minister there to baptize his son. The minister readily agreed and baptized Thomas Phillip De Vouges right then and there. Peter and his family changed their religion to Episcopalian, which later became known as the Anglican Religion. Besides his new church was much closer, only about a mile away.

When the church burned down and had to be rebuilt Peter was the largest contributor to the cause donating ten pounds, which was a lot of money back in those days. Peter was one of the founders of St Peter's Church when the Episcopalian Church became the Anglican Church.

Peter lived the rest of his life in Point St. Peter and passed away in 1879 at the age of seventy-three. His wife Jeanne lived another eleven years and passed away in 1890. They are buried in the St Peter's Anglican church cemetery.

I don't know much about my great, great-grandfather Thomas Phillip De Vouge. He was born in Point St Peter on February 16th. 1842. He married Elizabeth Jane Amy whose ancestors were from the island of Jersey. They had nine children, six daughters and three sons. Their second child and first son Elias De Vouge was my great-grandfather.

Elizabeth De Vouge passed away in 1901 at the relatively young age of sixty-one years. Thomas was widowed and he passed away in 1914. They had lived in Barachois and the 1881 Canada census listed Thomas as being a farmer and an Episcopalian. There are still some of his descendants and my distant cousins living in the Barachois area.

In August of 2008 I visited my great, great-grandfather's grave site at the local Anglican Church cemetery in Barachois. I was with my son Zac and it was the first time that I had visited Thomas's resting place.

19. Fast On The Draw

Cowboys and Indians was perhaps the favorite game my friends and I played in the early and mid-fifties. We didn't have television as of yet but in those days if you had the opportunity to go to a movie theatre chances were that it was a western on the screen. Therefore playing Cowboys and Indians was a preferred pastime. We would get a gang together and go into the woods, which were very close. We would pick two teams, the Cowboys and the Indians and then go off in slightly different directions. We would then try to locate and ambush each other. Once everyone on one team was captured or killed the game was over. Sometimes the Cowboys won and sometimes the Indians won. It didn't matter to me if I was an Indian or a Cowboy because I was very good at capturing members of the opposing team.

For a bit of variety sometimes we were the sheriff and his deputies on a posse hunting the bad outlaws who had robbed the bank in our dusty little western town. In this case I always wanted to be the sheriff or one of the deputies and hoped and prayed to be on the good team. If I was picked to be an outlaw my heart wasn't really into it and I will admit that sometimes I surrendered to the posse a little too easily.

To be a good Indian or Cowboy one must dress the part with the proper clothing and accessories. I had an Indian headdress with several multicolored feathers located at the front just above my forehead. I also had a rawhide cord with one single gray feather located at the back of my head. I had a rubber tomahawk and a bow and arrow set with rubber suction cups on the tips of the arrows. I was therefore well equipped to be an Indian.

When I was seven years old my mother bought me a cowboy outfit. In addition to the cowboy hat I had a bolo tie, a western vest with fringes and chaps for riding a horse. I also had a gun belt with a pair of shiny six shooters. They had white imitation pearl handles and I loaded then with those red cap rolls. To complete the outfit I also wore cowboy boots. The only thing missing was a horse.

I was so proud of my cowboy outfit that I wanted to wear it all the time even when I wasn't playing. I also practiced my quick draw every day and I became very fast on the draw: so fast in fact that I could beat any kid around in a quick draw contest. Every time that I would pull my gun and pull the trigger my cap gun would "pop" first. I was the fastest gun around.

One evening after supper I went down to the wharf at the harbour and most of my friends were there as well. Of course I was fully decked out in my cowboy outfit. I was demonstrating my quick draw for my friends and when I pulled the gun's trigger you could hear the "pop" of the cap exploding. Everyone marveled at how fast I was on the draw and I let some of the guys try their luck at it as well. It was determined that none of the kids was as fast as I was. I was happy about that.

My happiness didn't last very long. There was this ten year old girl there who was visiting from Barachois, a community about eighteen miles away. I did not know her but apparently she was a distant relative of mine. I figured that she must be Catholic because she didn't go to the same school as I did. Anyway it appeared that she didn't like me because she started giving me heck. I guessed she thought I was showing off when I started drawing my pistol, twirling it around and around with my finger and flicking it up in the air, catching it and quickly reholstering it. She started pushing me around right up to the edge of the wharf. I tripped and fell off the wharf about seven or eight feet into the water below. I was lucky that there wasn't a boat docked in the spot where I fell because I could have been seriously injured. When I swam out of the water I was really angry with the girl. She was three years older than me and I felt like punching her but I would not hit a girl. Instead to show my defiance I approached her, squared myself and pulled my gun. I aimed it at her and pulled the trigger but the gun would not fire. The caps were all wet.

20. Granny Dies And Comes Back To Life

I wrote about my great-grandmother Angelina Leggo De Vouge in a preceding chapter. I and other family members knew her as Granny and she passed away in 1957 at the ripe old age of ninety-two. I had lived on the farm with Granny from the age of ten months until I was seven years old and moved to the town of Murdochville eighty miles away.

I would like to tell you the story of how Granny died and then came back to life. I do not remember this happening but will repeat it as it was told to me.

It appeared that when Granny was around ninety years old one day she wasn't feeling well and she told my grandmother that she was going to take an afternoon nap. After a while Nanny was a little worried about Granny and decided to look in on her. Nanny came running out of the bedroom and yelled to my father and uncle Denzil that she thought that Granny had died. When my dad and uncle Denzil entered Granny's bedroom they found her lying on the bed apparently not breathing and appearing dead. Not knowing what they should do in this situation they quickly grabbed her by her shoulders and feet and lifted her up off of the bed. They dropped her on the bed and then did this once again. This time Granny gasped, opened her eyes and started breathing again. She had come back to life.

When she was taken to the doctor it was discovered that Granny had a serious case of diabetes. In those days the treatment of diabetes was not what it is today and many people considered it a death sentence. I was still living on the farm at that time but moved away a short time later. My family did not tell me about that incident or the state of Granny's health because I was young and they thought that it would upset me too much. Knowing what I do today I'm pretty sure that Granny had been in a diabetic coma and my dad and uncle Denzil shocked her out of it.

By the time my great-grandmother was ninety-two years old years old her diabetes was getting progressively worse and eventually she had to have one of her legs amputated. She passed away at the age of ninety-two in 1957 when I was eight and a half years old.

I am very thankful that my great-grandmother lived so long and I got to spend so much time with her. Most people never get to meet their great-grandparents and I consider myself to be extremely lucky to have lived with two, her and her husband Elias my great-grandfather.

21. Granny (Angelina De Vouge)

My great grandmother Angelina Leggo was born in Brilliant Cove (L'Anse-a-Brilliant) in 1865 two years before Canada became a country. She married my great grandfather Elias De Vouge in 1889 and they started their married life on the farm that I moved to sixty years later.

When I moved to L'Anse-a-Brilliant in 1949 I lived with my mom and dad in the old end of the house and Granny lived in the new end with my great grandfather Elias (Gappy), my grandparents Ruby and Leslie and my uncle Denzil.

I don't believe that I ever heard anyone call Granny by her given name Angelina. Everyone, relative, friend or stranger addressed her as Granny.

She already had three other great grandchildren by the time I moved to the farm but two of them were in Ontario and the other one lived in Truro, Nova Scotia. She took to me right away the moment I arrived on the farm. She was eighty-four and still in good health. I remember she was still energetic enough to churn the butter that we made on the farm with my help of course.

Granny was a very giving person and a collector much like I am today. She collected various things but her pride and joy was the fine bone china and teapots that she had collected over the years.

On my first birthday Granny did not buy me a toy. I guess that I had enough of them already. She gave me a 1939 silver dollar or I should say she gave it to my mother to hold for me and told her to give it to me when I became a man. She was obviously worried that I might spend it if it was given to me when I was a child.

On my second birthday Granny gave me a fine bone china cup and saucer. It was a Castle brand hand painted set with a dragon on the cup. The dragon has glass eyes with two little glass beads moving around inside. Whenever you move the cup the eyes move and the dragon is always looking at you. It is quite unique and beautiful. Over the next few years Granny gave me more beautiful and rare bone china cup and saucer sets as well as a fancy teapot. Once again she asked my mother to keep them for me and give them to me when I was a man. My mother collected fine bone china as well and treasured these items that Granny had given me.

When I grew up and left home my mother was loathe to give them up so I left them with her and retrieved them when I was fifty-eight years old after my mother passed away in 2007. My three sons will each get one of these valuable bone china sets and it is my hope that they will pass them down as well.

In 1953 when my sister Donna was born Granny was eighty-eight and now had two great grandchildren living on the farm with her. The fact that she had lived long enough to have a part in her great grandchildren's upbringing set well with her. She adored us and the fact that we were a four generational family all living together.

The feeling was mutual. It is one of the pleasures of my life that I got to live with two great grandparents when I was a child.

Granny's health started to deteriorate when she was ninety-one and she had to have one of her legs amputated because of her diabetes. She passed away in 1957 at the ripe old age of ninety-two. She was sorely missed.

22. Mom Makes Me Dance

Growing up on the farm in the fifties we didn't have any television or other forms of entertainment in our home. Our sole entertainment was listening to the radio, which was turned on from morning till night. The music that was being played was country and western as well as a new thing called rock and roll. I loved both types of music.

My mother had moved to Montreal from Newfoundland in 1940 when she was sixteen years old. In the big cities in the forties the big thing was dance contests.

I'm sure you've seen some of them on those old black and white movies from the forties. There were the dance marathons where couples danced for hours and days on end to be the final couple and there were the skills completion where couples danced and the most skilled couple won a prize.

My mother and her dance partner entered the jitterbug contests and sometimes they even won. My mom was quite a good amateur dancer. I think her jitterbugging days ended when she met and started dating my father. My dad being from the country was a square dancer and maybe after a few beers he might even be a step dancer but he was definitely not a jitterbugger. I can't, as hard as I might try, picture my father doing the jitterbug to a fast rock and roll song.

It was 1955 and a fast rock and roll song came on the radio. My mother turned to me and said "Bryan, let's dance."

"No," I said. "I don't want to dance."

Mom grabbed me by the arm and started twirling me around and around. I didn't know how to dance but mom was doing all the work pulling me towards her, pushing me away from her and all the time high stepping and twisting. My little sister Donna who was only two years old was sitting there in amazement watching us dance or I should say watching my mom dance while dragging me around. What could I do? I was just seven years old and could only pray that the song would end soon.

These incidents occurred several times over the next three years but by the time I was ten years old I became a fast runner and when one of my mother's favorite rock and roll tunes came on the radio I started running to the nearest door to get out of the house.

23. Valentine's Day And Girlfriends

When I started school in January of 1955 I was six years old and four months behind all my classmates who had started in September of 1954. I quickly became aware that most if not all of my classmates were in love or at least had a strong liking for their classmates of the opposite sex. For example, each guy had at least three girls that he liked and it was no secret because he would tell everyone that he liked Judy, Jane and Janet in that order. On the other hand the girls had the same system going of their three favorite guys. If a guy were not aware that a certain girl liked him someone would approach him and tell him that Judy liked him. Of course it was also vice-versa with the girls.

Of course being a new student in the class some of the girls put me on their list: several of them in fact. There was this young six-year-old brown haired beauty named Jean and she put me down as number one on her list. I knew a good thing when I saw it and I quickly developed a strong liking (love) for her as well. She became number one, two and three on my list. I know this because I have no memory of any other girl in that class or having a number two or three as I write this fifty-four years later.

When someone told my mother about this she teased me a bit and described it as puppy love. Frankly I didn't know what puppies had to do with it. Today I would describe it as kiddy romance and it lasted only six months because at the end of the school year my family and I moved to the town of Murdochville eighty miles away from our farm.

A year later we moved back to the farm and I started grade three at Belle Anse School renewing all my old acquaintances that I had missed the past year. Unfortunately it appeared that Jean had moved away and I needed to make a new list. For the next five years until I became a teenager there were three girls on my list and I was definitely on their list as well. They were Irma, Faye and Madeline and they were all good examples of what a young lad should look for in a girl. They were cute, pretty, beautiful and gorgeous and they all liked me. Over the years they all took turns being number one on my list but I know that Irma dominated being number one for several years. She had the advantage in that she lived in L'Anse-a-Brilliant less than a half mile away from our farm and I saw her every day. I only saw the other two young ladies at school.

At the age of nine or ten Irma and I got serious about each other and one day she approached my mother down at the beach and said "Mrs. De Vouge, when we grow up Bryan and I are going to get married. You're going to be my mother-in-law."

I knew that my mother really liked Irma and she replied "That's fine Irma and I would love to have you as my daughter-in-law."

Of course the marriage did not happen. I moved away for good when I was thirteen and rarely saw Irma after that.

In those preteen years Valentine's Day was a very special day for my classmates and myself at Belle Anse School. I would buy at least three packs of Valentine cards because I needed a lot. There was a system in place passed down from year to year and we all had to adhere to it. If there were eight girls in your class you had to give at least one Valentine's card to each one of them. Even if you didn't like a certain girl you still had to give her a Valentines card. After all the fact that all young girls are such beautiful creatures means that they all deserve at least one card. So you looked at all your cards and gave her the least desirable one.

For example you simply gave her the card that said "Be My Valentine". The card that said "I Love You, Please Be My Valentine was of course reserved for the girls on your top three list.

And here's where it gets tricky. I gave multiple Valentine cards to the top three girls that I liked. I remember giving number three five cards, number two six cards and my number one girl got a record seven cards. I also received multiple cards back from these three girls.

On Valentines Day, February the fourteenth our teacher would put a box on her desk and during the day they would sign Valentine cards and insert them in the box. At some point in the afternoon the teacher would announce that it was now time to hand out the valentines. She would stand at the front of the class and would take one valentine card out at a time and would announce the recipient and the sender. The smiling boy or girl amongst jeers and cheers would go up to the front of the class and receive their valentine's card. The teacher would sometimes also add comments such as "Gee, I think that's the forth valentine that Irma has received from Bryan" and the other kids would make snide comments like "He really loves her" much to my embarrassment.

This procedure would continue until the box was empty and then the teacher gave us time to admire the cards we had received. We would count them up and it usually turned out much like everyone had predicted. The most popular girls and boys got the most cards and sometimes there were a few surprises. For example I dreaded the fact that some other boy might give more valentines to my sweetheart than I did. That was an infringement on my territory and might result in the girl at the top of my list changing her mind about where her affections should be directed. After all the young ladies were oftentimes influenced by the number of cards that they had received from a certain boy. To counter this we had our spies and when someone came and told me "I think Ben sent Madeline five cards you can be sure that I would send her six. Also I lived in fear that my sweetheart would send another boy more cards than she sent me. That would have been a heartbreaker, especially on Valentines Day. However things usually went as planned and I would go home on the school bus happy in the knowledge that many of the girls in my class had sent me multiple valentines and I hoped that they would still like me as much next year. Puppy love or kiddy romance was still in effect.

24. Singing to Nanny, Singing To The Animals

As long as I can remember I've enjoyed singing when listening to the radio or while playing a record. However as a child I was much too shy to sing in front of other people solo. I did sing in choirs at school and at Christmas concerts singing Christmas carols with my classmates. At home I would sing along with Hank Williams, Johnny Horton, Johnny Cash and others when they played their songs on the radio but I was a little shy and would not sing when my mom or dad were around.

One thing I remember doing was singing to the farm animals. I was not shy with them. I would go up to the sheep barn to visit and start singing away. The ones in the sheep pen would watch me and the other sheep in the barn would come out to listen to me sing. They would all watch me and I think that they enjoyed my singing because they were very attentive and would stand there completely captivated by me as long as I sang to them. Of course when I finished singing they did not applaud (they have no hands) and they did not yell for encores (they can't talk) but I knew that they appreciated my singing to them. I told them that I would come back on another day and perform for them once again.

I believe the cows also enjoyed my singing. They were usually grazing in the field and when I started singing to them they would raise their heads and watch and listen to me. After a while they would start grazing once again but still listening as I went through my repertoire of songs.

The pigs were a little different story. When I approached their pen they would all come up to the fence and when I started singing to them instead of being attentive like the sheep and the cows they would start grunting and carrying on. It appears that they were more interested in me providing them with food than singing to them. I stopped singing and informed them that their supper would not be served for another hour when I would be back with my grandfather to feed them. They just kept grunting at me begging me for food. It appears that the pigs were always hungry and were not interested in my singing, not even one song. After all pigs are pigs. I would not be back to sing to them again.

When I sang to the chickens while they were pecking away at the chicken feed that my grandmother had thrown on the ground for them they simply ignored me and went about their business.

It must be no secret that my favorite animals to entertain were the sheep. They were a captive audience and I sang to them many times.

There was one human being who I was not too shy to sing for and that was my grandmother. When I visited Nanny in her end of the house sometimes she would be listening to hymns on her record player. Nanny was a religious lady and she did this when my grandfather wasn't home. I would sing along as the hymns were the same ones that I sang in church. The only popular singer that Nanny liked to listen to was Perry Como who appealed to the older people but not to us younger folk. She had one of his albums and I listened to it many times with her.

One day when I was about ten years old I started singing a Johnny Cash song to my grandmother. She asked me to sing something else.

I asked my grandmother "Why don't you like Johnny Cash, Nanny? He's the number one singer on the radio."

"He's a criminal" Nanny replied. "He's been in jail and he sings songs about prisons."

I explained, "I don't think that he's a criminal. He just sings some songs about prisons. Most of his songs are about other things such as girls and also about riding on trains."

"Bryan, Why don't you sing a Perry Como song for me? You must know some of his songs by now."

I decided to sing one of her favorites for her. It was called "South of the Border".

> "South of the border
> Down Mexico way
> That's where I fell in love
> When the stars above
> Came out to play.
> The mission bells told me
> That I mustn't stay
> South of the border
> Down Mexico way."

I haven't heard or sang that song for over fifty years but I still remember the words and singing it to for my grandmother.

25. The Boston Bruins, Irma and Jerry Toppazzini

I became a hockey fan when I started school in grade one. It seemed all the other kids, both boys and girls were already hockey fans and they all had their favorite teams and players. Although my father was a Montreal Canadiens fan I don't remember he and my grandfather ever talking hockey. That and the fact that there wasn't any television as of yet in L'Anse-a-Brilliant meant that I had not been exposed to the world of hockey as of yet.

In the mid-fifties there were only six teams in the National Hockey League, the Montreal Canadiens, the Toronto Maple Leafs, The Chicago Black Hawks, the Detroit Red Wings and the Boston Bruins. They are now known as the "Original Six" as now due to expansion there are thirty teams in the NHL.

I quickly became a Boston Bruins fan for several reasons one being that they had a big "B" on their jersey and I used to tell the other kids that was because they were actually Bryan's Bruins. The other main reason was because my friend Irma Leggo was a strong Boston Bruins fan as well. That's right, a seven-year-old girl who was a very big hockey fan. One would think that Irma would be a Detroit Red Wings fan like her older brother Wayne who adored Gordie Howe but Irma for some reason loved the Bruins.

In the 1950's the NHL was dominated by two teams the Montreal Canadiens and the Detroit Red Wings. During that decade the Canadiens won five Stanley Cups and the Red Wings won four. The Toronto Maple Leafs snuck in and won one cup. The Boston Bruins were a good team and made it to the playoffs eight times. They managed to make it to the Stanley Cup finals three times in 1953,1957 and 1958 and each time they lost to the mighty Montreal Canadiens. In fact the last time the Bruins had won the Stanley Cup was in 1941, a little before my time.

But that didn't matter to Irma and me, as we still loved our Boston Bruins even though most of the other kids cheered for the Habs or the Red Wings.

When the new hockey season started in the fall of 1955 I was seven years old and in grade two. We received the Eaton's and Sears Christmas catalogues and I quickly went to the sports sections where I found the NHL jerseys in both home and away colours. I decided that I wanted the Boston Bruins home jersey, which was white with yellow trim, and it had the big yellow "B" on it. I showed it to my mother and informed her that that I wanted this jersey for Christmas. I told her that it was the number one item on my list and that I wanted it really bad. I asked my mom to order it early because I was worried that it might sell out and I would be very disappointed if it wasn't under the tree Christmas morning.

About six weeks later on Christmas morning I got up really early and low and behold I did receive the Boston Bruins jersey that I wanted. I tried it on and it was a little big on me. I was a little disappointed but when I mentioned it to my mother she replied, "You'll grow into it. You want to wear it for one more than one season, don't you?

"Yes" I replied. "I'll be able to wear it for at least two years before I grow out of it."

When January of 1956 arrived and school started up once again future winter and spring days were very predictable. My mom would wake me up in the morning and she had breakfast ready for me and when I came downstairs to the eat-in kitchen she would already have the radio on. As I ate I listened for the sports scores and when the Boston Bruins won I would wear my Bruins jersey to school that day. When I got on the bus I knew that in less than a minute Irma would be getting on as well and I would give her the great news. When the bus stopped Irma would be the first to run up the steps into the bus to find me. I would say "Irma, the Bruins won. They beat the Rangers four to two." Irma in a very excited voice would say, "Yes, I know and Toppazzini scored."

You see Irma's favorite Bruins player was Jerry Toppazzini a young right-winger from Sudbury, Ontario. Irma knew everything there was to know about Jerry Toppazzini, all his stats and the fact that in his young NHL career he had already played for three teams, Boston, Chicago and Detroit. But now he was back in Boston once again. I used to call him by his nickname "Topper " but Irma always referred to him as "Toppazzini". He was one of the Bruins best players and certainly one of the most popular players on the team.

For several years Irma and I remained loyal Boston Bruins fans and she always talked about Jerry Toppazzini. Sometimes it seemed that he was the only player on the Boston Bruins as far as Irma was concerned.

In 1960 my family visited one of my dad's old friends in Montreal who worked for the Montreal Canadiens as an executive, I believe. I also found out that my father had been friends with a few of the Canadiens players when he lived in Montreal and that he had sold our cottage that he had built it Lac Echo in the Laurentian Mountains north of Montreal to one of the Habs players when we moved to the Gaspe. So I became a Habs fan. Meanwhile Jerry Toppazzini retired from the NHL after playing twelve seasons. He did not retire from hockey however as he played a few more years in the minor leagues. When he eventually retired as a player he became a coach also in the minor leagues.

In 1968 at the age of twenty I moved to Sudbury, Ontario to work at INCO and I became a fan of the Sudbury Wolves when they joined the Ontario Major Junior Hockey League. In the mid-seventies I became a season ticket holder.

Jerry Toppazzini had moved back home to Sudbury and now was a businessman here as well as the new coach of the Sudbury Wolves who were one of the best junior teams in Canada.

It was the spring of 1977 and the Wolves were in the playoffs. One afternoon I took one of my friends to my swim club at the Sheraton Caswell Hotel, which was right across the street from where I lived. After a swim and sauna we cozied up to the bar, which was just a few steps away from the pool. As we were having an alcoholic beverage and chatting with the bartender the local sports broadcast came on the television. All three of us stopped talking and were listening as a reporter was interviewing Jerry Toppazzini about the prospects of his team winning in the playoffs. Suddenly I heard a loud voice behind me saying, "Don't believe a word that guy says."

I turned around to see who had uttered those words and my mouth dropped open when I discovered that it was no one other than Jerry Toppazzini himself. The only thing I could think of to say was "Gee, he's in two places at once."

Jerry said, "I taped that interview about a half hour ago just before coming here."

Jerry Toppazzini joined us at the bar and we talked hockey. I told him about how my friend Irma and I were strong Bruins fans in the 1950's and how Irma had idolized him and that she could recite all his stats for every year he played in the NHL. I told him what a pleasure it was for me to meet and talk to him. I only wished that Irma could be there to meet him as well.

Jerry asked, "When will you be seeing Irma again?

"Gee, I don't know" I said. "I saw her last summer when I was on holiday in Gaspe but I don't know when I will see her again."

Jerry said, "When you see Irma again tell her that Jerry Toppazzini says Hi."

Although I've seen Jerry Toppazzini from afar several times since then I have never met him or talked to him again. Also I have not seen Irma for the past thirty-two years. So Irma, if you read this your childhood hockey idol Jerry Toppazzini says "Hi".

26. *Falling Through The Ice*

It was the spring of 1957 and I went for a walk with two friends on the road outside of Murdochville. It was a beautiful day, the sun was shining and the snow and ice were slowly melting away, However it was still kind of cold out.

My friends and I were walking along the road to Gaspe playing catch with this red rubber ball that we had found. I was eight and a half years old and my friends were about the same age.

One of my friends missed catching the ball and it rolled into this pond that was next to the road. The pond was perhaps half open water and half ice covered. The ball floated right up to the ice covered part of the pond and stayed there. I suggested that one of us go out on the ice and retrieve the ball. The other two guys were obviously smarter than me because they both refused to go out on the ice.

I checked the ice at the edge of the pond and it seemed ok to me. I decided to go get the ball and very slowly and carefully I walked the fifteen feet to the end of the ice. I bent down and grabbed the ball, got up and turned to go back. The ice broke underneath me and I fell down into the water, which was deep, and over my head. In a moment the freezing water had saturated my winter clothes and I was shocked by the cold. I called to my two friends to help me but they looked at each other in panic and ran away towards the town.

I was left alone in a life-threatening situation with nobody around to help me. I tried to climb back onto the ice that wasn't broken but was unable to do so. The ice was now wet and very slippery. I tried again but was still unsuccessful so I had to try something different. Because I was such a good swimmer I decided to swim my way unto the ice. I flattened out and by kicking my feet like crazy I got my forearms on the ice and I slid on to the thicker ice. Instead of getting up and walking I crawled over the ice on my belly until I reached solid ground.

Back on the road I started walking the half-mile back to town. I was hoping that someone would drive by and pick me up but nobody came. My two buddies were nowhere in sight.

Being totally wet my clothes quickly froze and my pants became as stiff as a board. I walked home very slowly and I was very cold. When I arrived home and opened the door my mother was shocked and yelled, "What happened to you?"

"I fell through the ice" I replied. Mom said "Let's get you out of those wet clothes."

She tried to get my winter coat off but she could not unbutton or unzip it because it was frozen solid. Being a smart lady my mom did not panic but decided to run a hot bath for me. As weird as it seems it was a good idea because soon after I got in the bathtub my frozen clothes melted and became pliable once again. Mom got my coat off and I took off the rest of my clothes. I got back into the bathtub to thaw myself out. I was so cold. I was fortunate that my toes and feet had not been frostbitten and that I was ok. After the hot bath my mother had hot chocolate waiting for me.

The rest of my youth and adulthood I have never fallen through ice again. Once was enough for me. I became very cautious and smarter as I grew older. I attribute the fact that I am alive today to my swimming ability. Thank God that I am such a good swimmer.

27. A Cure For Bullying

It was the winter of 1957 and I was a little over eight years old. This was the year my family and I had moved from the farm to the town of Murdochville eighty miles away. It was a brand new town built in the interior of the Gaspe when copper was discovered there and a new mine was developed and a new town built. By now there were a few thousand people living there and half were English and half were French.

This should have been a good time in my childhood but unfortunately it wasn't. You see, I was being bullied by a bigger French kid who was a year older than me. He would wait for me when I was coming home at noon for lunch and beat me up. He would punch me and knock me down and then he would put handfuls of snow down my back. He would also wash my face with snow.

This happened several times over a period of two weeks and I was getting tired of it real quick. For every problem there's a solution and I had to come up with one to deal with this bully real fast.

Just up the street from me lived a classmate of mine, a young lady who had a tough older brother. At that time I considered Conrad Jones to be the toughest ten-year-old kid in town. He was a nice guy and he was definitely not a bully. I decided to tell him about my problem with T'Guy the bully and asked for his help. Since I was a good friend of his younger sister he agreed to help me.

The next day I was walking home from school at lunch hour and sure enough the bully T'Guy approached me. After hurling a few insults at me in French he started pushing me around. I resisted him but he was too big and strong for me and once again I ended up down on the snow. Before the bully could do me anymore harm Conrad Jones popped out from behind a car where he had been hiding and quickly approached us.

"Hey T'Guy what are you doing with my friend Bryan?" he asked.

The bully T'Guy didn't answer but he looked kind of scared of Conrad.

Conrad looked at me and said "Bryan, what would you like me to do?"

"Knock him down" was my reply.

He then tripped the bully T'Guy knocking him down in the snow. That was all the help I needed. I immediately jumped on top of him and started pummeling him with punches to the head. Of course he started to cry so to wash away his tears I washed his face with snow. I then let him get up and he ran home still crying.

After lunch when I returned to school I was called into the principal's office. He told me that he had received a call from the principal of the French school informing him that I had beaten up one of his students on his way home for lunch. The principal then asked me for an explanation.

I told him the whole story of how T'Guy was a year older than me and that he was bigger and stronger and how he was bullying me almost every day. I explained how he punched me, knocked me down in the snow, washed my face with snow and put snow down my back.

The principal asked me why I had not come to him or told my parents about the bullying.

"I'm not a tattletale" I replied.

There was no punishment and I figured that was because the principal was on my side.

The next time I saw T' Guy the bully walking down the street I stopped and waited for him. I was no longer afraid of him. I considered him a bit weaker now because he cried and was a tattletale. Instead of approaching me he changed direction and cut between two houses to avoid me. In the next five months that I lived in Murdochville before moving back to the farm he never bothered me again.

In 1962 when my family once again moved to Murdochville T'Guy was still living there but now was known as a gifted athlete rather than a bully. This shows you how people can change.

I mentioned before that "For every problem there's a solution." Now fifty-two years later as an adult I wonder if I came up with the right solution to the bullying problem. As a child it may not have been the right solution but it worked.

28. Skiing In Summer,
I Don't Think So

The story I am about to tell may be hard to believe in the present days of 2009 but it did happen over fifty tears ago when I lived in the mining town of Murdochville for one year in 1957 when I was eight years old.

It was a beautiful sunny summer day in the middle of July 1957 and my friends and I were walking along the sidewalk on 5th. Street probably on our way to play a pickup game of baseball at the ball field. We noticed this thirty something couple standing next to their car looking at a map and they appeared to be bewildered. They were looking all around at the mountains, which surround the town of Murdochville. I noticed that there was a roof rack on the top of their car on which there was two pair of snow skis. I also looked at the license plate on their car and saw that they were Americans from the state of Virginia.

When we were walking by the man asked us "Is this the town of Murdochville?"

"Yes" was our reply.

"It shows on this map that there's a ski hill here," he said.

I pointed to the end of 5th. Street to the mountain and said, " There's the ski hill. You can see the ski hill, the rope tow and the trails from here."

"But where's the snow?" the man asked.

We kids looked at each other and we all exclaimed together in one voice "It's the middle of summer. We don't have snow in the summer. It's warm here in the summer."

The man was puzzled and said that he had been told that there was snow here all year around. I figured that someone must have been pulling his leg, in fact even stretching it.

Later that summer of 1957 we moved back to the farm in L'Anse-a-Brilliant where we lived for the next four and one-half years. We moved back to Murdochville after Christmas in 1961.

When the summer of 1962 arrived I was thirteen years old and I had pretty much forgotten about the people who had wanted to snow ski five years before in the summer of 1957. And then it happened again.

One of my friends and I were walking to the recreation center on 2nd. Street when this car bearing a USA license plate pulled up and stopped next to us. There were three young guys who were in their twenties and yes, there were three pairs of snow skis on their roof rack.

The young man came right to the point. "So where's the snow?" he asked. Somehow he didn't seem as puzzled as the other couple was five years before.

"It all melted away," I said. "We only have snow here from December to April. There's the ski hill over there and because the snow gets really packed down this year people were able to ski on the hill well into May. There was one day it was so warm that some guys were skiing in bathing suits and I saw one lady in a bikini."

"Well I guess we're a few months late" The guy chuckled to his friends.

"You should have brought water skis," I said. York Lake is only five miles from here and it's a nice calm lake perfect for water skiing."

The young man asked, "How far will I have to drive until I find some snow?"

"Maybe two thousand miles" I responded. "If you could drive all the way to the North Pole you might find some snow but there's no ski hills there."

The young man looked over at the ski hill and said, "That looks like a really good ski run over on that mountain. You are lucky to have such a good ski hill right on the edge of your town.

"I have skied from half way up" I told him. I'm not a good enough skier yet to ski from the top. Maybe I will be in a few years. There are skiing competitions here in January and February and you guys should come back then."

"Maybe we will," he said. "Maybe we will."

As strange as it may seem on at least two other occasions I have seen snow skis on roof racks in the middle of the summer.

However in these modern days of 2009 I doubt you will ever see this happen again. Nowadays people are much more educated and knowledgeable about the world than they were back in the 1950's. At least I hope so.

29. Community Discipline

I have coined the term "Community Discipline" to describe the way children or I should say misbehaving children experienced growing up in the 1950's in L'Anse-a-Brilliant.

Of course our parents disciplined us all, more harshly I might add than the children growing up nowadays in the new millennium.

When your parents were not around to monitor your behaviour other adults in the community would and sometimes they would give you a stern lecture if you were misbehaving. Other times you ran the risk of getting your rear end kicked by an adult male if he deemed it necessary to do so. Of course in 2009 this could never happen because in these days of political correctness the person doing the discipline would get themselves in all kinds of trouble and even threatening to kick a child's butt would result in criminal child abuse charges and a civil suit by the child's parents. Not so in the 1950's in L'Anse-a-Brilliant.

One beautiful mid-summer day when I was about nine or ten years old my friends and I were down at the harbour watching the fishermen unload their catch of cod fish up unto the wharf from their boats docked below. After watching them go about their work for a while we started to get bored and started running around on the wharf playing tag. After a while a fisherman approached us and said, "Don't run around on the wharf. Go over towards the beach or go to the beach to do your running around. You're making me nervous. You might fall over the wharf into the water."

"I can swim" I replied.

"Yes, but I can't" he said, "and you might hit your head on the boat below and knock yourself out. Then I'd have to try and save you and I would probably drown myself because I can't swim. So go somewhere else to play."

The fisherman was right of course and he wasn't angry but just informing us of the dangers involved. He was concerned for our safety.

"Yes sir" I replied and my friends and I left the wharf and went over to the beach to play.

A few weeks later some other kids were fooling around on the wharf and one of the fishermen yelled at them to stop fooling around on the wharf because someone was going to get hurt. One of the boys talked back to the fisherman telling him "I can do anything I want and you can't stop me."

The fisherman took a step towards the boy and said "I can kick your rear end if you don't stop fooling around right now."

The boy looked up at the fisherman in a brazen manner and said, "If you kick me I'll tell my father and he'll beat you up."

The fisherman said, "I know your father young fellow and when you tell him it won't be me that he'll be beating up. It'll be you and when he kicks your rear end it's going to hurt a lot worse than if I kicked it."

Of course the fisherman was right. I know that if that was I misbehaving my father would have reacted just as the fisherman had said. Community Discipline was in effect in L'Anse-a-Brilliant.

30. A Skunk Under The House

One nice sunny day when I got home from school I noticed my grandfather down on all fours poking a shovel into the crawl space under our end of the house. His end of the house had a basement, which we called the cellar, but our old end had only a crawl space under it. I wondered what grandpa was doing and asked him.

"There's a skunk under there and I'm trying to get it to leave," he replied.

"You better watch out the skunk don't squirt you." I said.

Grandpa said, "I got to get it out of there before it takes up residence. I think that it's a female skunk looking for a place to live. We don't need a family of skunks living under our house."

My grandfather Leslie was a big man and I figured he was too big to crawl into the crawl space under the house. Being ten years old and skinny as a rake I knew I could do it however there was no way I was going to volunteer to do this job.

I didn't know how grandpa was going to get rid of that skunk. I said, "See you later grandpa" and went into the house to tell my mother about grandpa and the skunk.

The next day I went to school and I was in no way worried about the skunk under our house. I was hoping that it would just decide to move out. After all skunks lived and belonged in the woods and not under our house.

Later that day when I got off the school bus nothing seemed to be amiss. As I walked up to the front of our house however I knew something drastic had happened. I smelled this ungodly stench, which was a lot stronger than the smell's of the dead skunks we had driven by on the highway.

"Phewh, Phewh," I yelled out. "What a stink!"

I quickly went into our house and was relieved to find that it didn't smell bad inside. Of course, my mother had all the windows and the doors closed to keep the stench outside.

I knew that my grandfather must have been after the skunk again and it must have backfired on him. I went into my grandparents end of the house to see what condition my grandfather was in. He seemed normal and he didn't stink.

I asked my grandfather what had happened with the skunk. He didn't give me any details. He just said, "There's no more skunk under the house and the smell will clear up in a few days."

31. Grandpa And Rupert

My grandfather Leslie De Vouge and Rupert Leggo were cousins and lifelong friends. Rupert lived three farms over with his wife Nora and he was a semi-retired farmer like my grandfather. When you live on a farm you never really retire but scale back a bit when you get your old age pension on turning sixty-five years of age.

On our farm when the chores were done and Nanny had fed Grandpa his supper my grandfather would say "I'm going over to Rupert's for a while" and he would go visit his best friend for a few hours. Likewise some days Rupert would come over to our farm and visit Grandpa. If either one of them needed a hand to complete any farm task he could rely on the other to come over and help.

In those days back in the 1950's most of the food we ate was grown right on our farm. We did not buy steak, pork chops or chicken in a grocery store but grew animals for our own consumption. Small animals like chickens could be slaughtered at any time but the big animals like pigs and cows were always slaughtered in the fall when we were starting to get freezing temperatures. That was so they could be hung up and frozen in the big shed between the barn and our house.

Grandpa and Rupert slaughtered these animals and they were a team, a tag-team so to speak. I watched then in action a few times and I would describe them as tag-team champions. One time I watched as my grandfather shot a pig in the head with his old 32 caliber single shot rifle. Rupert, who was then in his mid-sixties vaulted over the fence and quickly, stuck the pig in its jugular vein with his long knife. The pig then just stood there grunting with blood pouring out of its neck like water pouring out of a tap. The task was completed quickly and efficiently because they didn't want the pig to suffer needlessly. They then cut the pig open and removed the offal and after cleaning and dressing it they hung it up in the shed to freeze.

This may seem offensive to some that read this but it was not so to me when I was a child. I grew up on a farm and this was a natural occurrence to me.

One day I accompanied my grandfather when he went over to Rupert's farm to slaughter one of his cows. I remember that the cow was brown and it was one of Rupert's older cows. It was out in the field grazing when we approached it and grandpa raised his rifle, aimed it at the cow and pulled the trigger. Instead of the usual loud bang when his rifle discharged this time there was only what I can describe as a very quiet bang. The bullet hit the cow between the eyes and the bullet fell to the ground, as it did not enter the cow's head. The old brown cow shook her head and then looked at my grandfather and said "Mooo," a very loud one in fact. In cow language she was saying "Hey mister, don't do that again."

The cow then went back to grazing on the grass evidently no worse for wear. I did notice a small drop of blood had appeared where the bullet had struck her between the eyes.

"Grandpa, are you going to shoot her again?" I asked.

"No, the same thing might happen again" he replied. "I don't want the cow to suffer any. I'll go home and test fire this old rifle to see if the problem is the rifle or the shells. It could be the firing pin but I think that it was a bad bullet. We'll let the cow live another day.

I was not there the next day but I gather that things went better the second time around and Rupert and Nora probably had fresh beef liver for supper that night.

I do not remember but I think Grandpa and Rupert helped other people in our community slaughter their farm animals as well.

My father and grandfather were moose hunters and I do remember them bringing home a moose although it was already quartered. All the dirty work had been done back in the woods where they had shot it.

I moved away to Murdochville after Christmas of 1961 and on to Montreal in 1966 to attend MacDonald College of McGill University. My grandparents also moved to Montreal that fall to spend the winter months with my Aunt Leona. During the winter Grandpa's life-long best friend Rupert passed away back in L'Anse-a-Brilliant. Grandpa took it hard. My grandfather Leslie De Vouge passed away less than a year later in 1967.

32. Grandpa (Leslie De Vouge)

My grandfather Leslie De Vouge was born on the farm in L'Anse-a-Brilliant in 1892. He was a farmer/fisherman and he spent all of his life on the farm except for a short time when he was a police officer in Northern Ontario.

For many years I was closer to my grandfather than my own father because dad worked eighty miles away and only came home on the weekends. Grandpa and I worked together on the farm doing chores such as feeding the animals and cutting, sawing, chopping and piling firewood. I also helped him pull his lobster traps many times the few years that he was a lobster fisherman.

Grandpa never asked me for help or asked anything of me. He never ordered me to do anything. He appreciated the help I gave him. When I felt like going swimming in the summer or sliding in the winter he never said, "I need you to help me do this work." He knew that I was a big help to him and that I also needed to have some fun. After all I was a child and all work and no play would make Bryan a dull boy.

Grandpa taught me to look after tools and to keep them in good condition. Before he had a chainsaw we sawed the firewood with an old Swede saw and when I broke the blade he told me that I had to buy a new replacement saw blade. It cost about a dollar and thirty-five cents, quite a sum for me at that time. He was not being mean, he was just teaching me to be more careful the next time I sawed some firewood.

Many times after doing farm chores Grandpa would invite me into his end of the house for a few slices of raisin bread that we both loved so much. Sometimes he would bake his favorite cookies, which were molasses cookies. He made them so big they were at least three times the size of a normal chocolate chip cookie. When they were fresh out of the oven and we buttered the backs of the cookies we ate them while they were still warm. We drank the beverage that we both liked the most, cold water pumped from the well. I could have as many of those delicious cookies as I wanted. That was my reward for my hard work helping Grandpa on the farm.

My grandfather was a big muscular man. He stood six foot, two inches tall and weighed around two hundred and thirty pounds. There was no fat on him. He was very strong like his father Elias. He looked like a professional wrestler. Even when he was in his seventies he still worked hard on the farm and was very strong. I remember when I was about sixteen years old I brought a few of my friends over to see how strong my old seventy-two year old grandfather was. I was a strong sixteen year old and I challenged grandpa to an arm wrestling contest. Sitting at the kitchen table we locked arms and I tried with all my strength to put his arm down. Grandpa was showing no effort and he said "Whenever you're ready Bryan" and when I said, "I'm ready" he slammed my arm down on the table. Even at the age of seventy-two he was much too strong for me. My friends were amazed.

The first time Grandpa went to see a doctor in his life was when he was seventy-four years old and didn't feel well. He was diagnosed with diabetes and had to take oral medication for his illness.

When I moved to Montreal in 1966 to attend MacDonald College of McGill University my grandparents moved to Montreal as well to spend the winter months with my aunt Leona. When I visited on the weekends Grandpa loved to watch the rock and roll shows on TV with me. I was surprised he liked watching "Top Ten Plus" so much as I never knew him to be a music lover. But he would be sitting there reclined in the lazy boy chair moving his feet to the rock and roll beat.

A year later in 1967 my grandparents decided to fly from Montreal to Halifax at Christmas to visit my uncle Glen and his family in Truro, Nova Scotia. He had a blood lot in his leg, which moved to his brain, and he passed away. He is buried in Truro, Nova Scotia. It was not a good Christmas.

33. Pizza Pie for Supper

One day at Belle Anse School when I was in Grade four or five the teacher asked us what we had eaten for supper last night. I guess she was trying to teach us about nutrition.

Several of the children said that they had codfish for supper. This was no surprise since the main industry in this part of the Gaspe was fishing and many of my classmates' father's were fishermen. Some of the other kid's stated that they had hot dogs, chicken soup with homemade bread and butter and other foods like beef stew.

The teacher turned to me and asked "Bryan what did you have for supper?"

I replied "pizza pie."

The class erupted in laughter. I kind of knew that this would happen, as most kids in my school had never heard of pizza. You see there was no such thing as pizza in any of the restaurants or grocery stores in 1950's Gaspe. The restaurants served fifties style meals like fish and chips and hot chicken sandwiches.

The teacher told the class to settle down, turned to me and said "Bryan, do you like pizza pie?"

"I love pizza pie" I replied. "We have it at least once or twice per month."

"Bryan, I know you were born in Montreal and moved here when you were one year old. Is that where your mother is from?"

"She moved to Montreal in 1940 from Newfoundland and lived there for nine years until we moved here" I replied.

The teacher then addressed the class and said "I had pizza pie when I was in Montreal this past summer. My husband and I went to an Italian restaurant one evening for supper and guess what? I had pizza pie and it was delicious. Now since we can't find pizza pie here in Gaspe you have to make it yourself. Bryan, can you explain to your classmates how your mom makes pizza pie?"

I had watched my mother make pizza pie and had actually helped her several times. So I explained the process to the class.

"My mom puts flour on the counter and makes dough likes she does when she makes bread. She spreads the dough out in a circle and rolls it out with a rolling pin until it's completely flat and round. She puts it on a round cookie sheet. She then opens a can of tomato sauce and spreads it on the dough and grates cheddar cheese on it. She slices a pepperoni or sausage into thin slices and puts them on top of the cheese. She also puts chopped onions on it and then puts it into the oven and it cooks for about twenty minutes. When she takes it out of the oven she cuts it into slices like a pie. That's why it's called pizza pie. My sister and I love it."

The teacher thanked me and joked to the class.

"Maybe we should all go over to Bryan's house and have some pizza pie."

A few years later in the early sixties mom came home from grocery shopping with a new product. It was a Kraft Pizza Kit and everything was there to make your own pizza at home. It had the dough, cheese, pepperoni and a packet of spices that gave the pizza a distinctive taste that I liked very much. You may notice that pizza pie was now simply called pizza.

In 1966 at the age of eighteen I left the Gaspe and moved to St. Anne de Belleview, a suburb of Montreal where I attended MacDonald College of McGill University. I ate my first restaurant pizza at a good quality restaurant near the campus. It was fully dressed with cheese, pepperoni, onions, mushrooms and green peppers and man it was good.

I would like to have a dollar for every pizza I've consumed since that day.

34. Rabbit Stew

One of the greatest things about living on a farm in the Gaspe was the wide variety of food we ate. One of my favorite all-time meals was rabbit stew. We did not buy the rabbit in a grocery store but snared them in the winter months when there was snow on the ground.

There's an old adage that you don't eat wild rabbit in any month that does not have an "R" in it. This means that you shouldn't eat rabbit in May, June, July and August and nobody has ever explained to me why.

My grandfather set his rabbit snares once the snow came in December and we had rabbit to eat until sometime in April when spring melted the snow away.

The snares were set on the part of our land that was wooded on the other side of the L'Anse-a-Brilliant River, which divided our property between farmland and woodland. In the fifties there weren't any snow machines like today so my grandfather and I would use snowshoes to walk in the bush. Grandpa would loan me a child's pair of snowshoes to accompany him and I often wonder why he just didn't just give them to me as he ended up loaning the snowshoes to me many times. The snowshoes were identical to grandpas but smaller and designed for a child.

Once in the bush you would see the different animal tracks in the snow. For example a fox places one paw in front of the other when walking and this leaves a trail like a straight line. You could easily identify the small paw prints of the rabbits and you would tie a wire snare to a branch of a tree so that the snare would be directly above the rabbit trail. Since rabbits always use the same trail over and over again eventually one would come and stick its head into the snare and strangle itself when the wire tightened around its neck. Nowadays you may find that cruel but it was how we obtained our food. Remember that the meat you buy at the supermarket today was once a live animal that had to be slaughtered so that you could enjoy it on your dinner plate.

My grandfather checked the snares a few times a week and usually came up with two or three rabbits. He would bring them home and skin them, which was real easy to do.

You didn't cook rabbit by itself like a chicken but cut it up to make rabbit stew using the same recipe as beef stew only without the beef. It was so delicious and when one rabbit stew was finished I couldn't wait to go back into the woods with my grandfather to see if we had more in the snares.

I believe the last Gaspe rabbit stew I ate was in 1962 when I moved with my family to Murdochville, which was eighty miles from the farm.

I did however eat a rabbit stew cooked by a New Orleans chef in 2001. It was ok but the Cajun recipe was way too hot and spicy for my liking. How I long for the rabbit stews that my mother and grandmother used to make.

35. Summer Fun, Winter Fun

When you were a child in 1950's Gaspe having fun meant doing something outdoors as there were no televisions or computer games to keep you in the house. Although we had fun in all four seasons my favorites were summer and winter in that order.

By the time the school year ended late in June summer was already in full swing. There were so many fun things to do I cannot list them all here. I'm positive that my number one fun activity was swimming down at the beach. Any summer day that was even close to being sunny and warm you would find my friends and I swimming and splashing around in the frigid water. The water was so cold that after fifteen or twenty minutes our feet would become so numb that we would start to lose feeling in them. We would start turning blue and start shivering and shaking like crazy. That's when we came out of the water, dried off and wrapped ourselves in a towel or blanket. What we were experiencing was the early stages of hypothermia but we didn't care because we were having fun. We rested, warmed up a bit and then we would go back in the water.

When visitors or tourists came to our beach and saw us in the water they would see us swimming and having fun. When they walked into the water however they would exclaim, "Oh my God, That's cold!" Most of the people would turn right around and head back to their towels or blankets on the beach. I remember one lady asking me "How can you swim in water that cold?"

I replied "We all live here and we're used to it but we have to come out and warm up once in a while."

"But still, you were having lots of fun out there" she said.

I readily agreed with her.

Once in a while I would go fishing along the river for trout, sometimes with Reid De Vouge and sometimes all by myself. On one occasion I remember going fishing with the three Leggo brothers Lance, Denver and Zane. After catching some small trout we decided that we were going to build a small fire, clean the fish and cook them by placing them on sticks and holding them over the fire. We discovered that this was a bad idea because we either burned the fish or undercooked it. A few mouthfuls were all I could stand. How I longed for trout dipped in egg and flour and cooked by my mother in her frying pan.

The next time we went for a hike in the L'Anse-a-Brilliant woods I took a snack with me in case I got hungry. We could always find water to drink if we got thirsty because there were springs in the area as well as the river. All in all it was great fun going on half-day hikes in the woods. We could not get lost in the woods because we all lived by the ocean and when you walked into the woods you walked uphill and when you returned home you walked downhill. There were wild animals in the woods but we weren't very afraid of them. I had my trusty pocketknife in my pocket and if we ever met up with a bear and it chased us I figured it might get the slowest runner and that wasn't me.

We played cowboys and Indians and hide and seek in the woods and we also built little houses where we could hang out. We chopped fir boughs from trees to use as walls and roofs for our houses or forts as we used to call them. We had picnics and great fun times in the woods.

Summer days seemed endless and when I laid my head down on my pillow at night and fell asleep I couldn't wait to wake up in the morning to do it all over again. When you're a ten-year-old child the summer months of July and August seem to go on forever. Adults feel that they disappear too fast.

I considered spring and fall to be the interlude months between the fun of summer and winter and I was more dedicated to doing farm chores in those months than having fun. Of course I considered farm work to be fun.

There were also many things to do in the winter months as well. I guess my favorite fun was sliding either on my toboggan or on someone's sleigh. There certainly was no shortage of places to slide in L'Anse-a-Brilliant as it was two big hills with a river flowing between them down at sea level. When I went sliding by myself I stayed on our property and went up on the head above our house. It would take me between fifteen and twenty minutes to walk up the field and only about a minute and a half to slide back down to our house. Was it worth it? You bet it was.

When I went sliding with a group of friends some of them had tin signs to slide on. These tin signs were usually found on the front and sides of stores and usually advertised soft drinks such as Pepsi Cola, 7 Up and Kik Cola. If you ripped one off the side of a store and turned up the end you made a big toboggan on which you could seat several kids. The only problem was that these tin signs were almost impossible to steer and when you got on one and went down a hill you had no idea where you were going to end up. If you found yourself heading towards a fence or a tree sliding at breakneck speed sometimes it was better to abandon ship and jump off the tin sign to avoid breaking your neck or worse. But it was exciting and great fun.

I also did a lot of skiing mostly on our farm in the field above our house. I could ski straight down like a downhill skier or from side to side like a slalom skier. Our farm was quite long and wide making for a lot of choices. Sometimes my downhill skis also served as cross-country skis when my friends and I went in the woods for a winter picnic.

We also skated on the river and played shinny down below the bridge under the highway. That was great fun until the ice broke but the water was only about six inches deep and I got my feet wet once or twice. It was no big deal because I had an extra pair of dry socks in my coat pocket.

I remember one cold winter when Gaspe Bay froze over and we went skating out on the Atlantic Ocean. I was more than scared, in fact I was terrified. I asked the Leggo's "What if we fall through the ice?"

"We won't " was their reply. "The ice here is very thick. Don't worry."

We made it safely back to land that day. I was very relieved and did not want to skate out on the ocean again. Skating on the river was good enough for me.

In the winter I also enjoyed going snow shoeing with my grandfather when he went into the woods to check his rabbit snares. Grandpa had this old set of children's snowshoes that my dad and my uncles had probably used when they were children. Grandpa did not give me these snowshoes but let me use them sometimes. When we checked his snares it was always nice to find a few dead rabbits in them. I loved rabbit stew.

I remember one winter morning when I looked out our kitchen window over towards Cecil De Vouge's farm and saw his son Reid doing something outside. He was working at something but he was too far away for me to see what he was doing. That afternoon I went over to Reid's and discovered that he had built an igloo. I found him in it and he invited me in. Reid was about three years older than me and about thirteen at the time. He was mechanically inclined and was obviously good at making igloos because it looked perfect, just like the pictures I'd seen in books. After blocking the entrance way and spending about an hour inside the igloo it got warm enough in there that we took off or winter coats. It appears that snow is quite good insulation. I was also surprised to find that it was not dark inside the igloo because light penetrates the igloo somewhat. Now I understand how the Inuit in the Artic had lived in the old days. I only wish that I had been there to help Reid build the igloo and learn how to do it. I certainly didn't have the skill to build one by myself.

These are some of the fun things I did as a child. Sometimes I wish I could go back to those fun days in the 1950's and do them all over again.

36. Is My Dad Bud OR Herzil?

My father's name was Herzil Leslie De Vouge. He was born in L'Anse-A Brilliant in 1917 and died at his home in Port Mouton, Nova Scotia in 1996.

I had no doubt about who my father was but some others did. I would discover that in the 1950's when meeting certain adults for the first time.

One day I encountered a school friend with a man I believed to be his father. My schoolmate (I don't remember his name) introduced me to his father.

"Dad, this is Bryan De Vouge from L'Anse-a-Brilliant"

You're one of the L'Anse-a-Brilliant De Vouges" he said. "Which one is your dad?"

"My dad is Herzil De Vouge"

"I don't know him" replied my friend's father.

"My grandfather is Leslie De Vouge" I replied.

He looked at me and said, "I know all of Leslie's sons. There's Cyril, Bud, Glen and Denzil but I don't know any Herzil.

"Well Bud is my dad's nickname" I replied.

"Gee, I thought Bud was his name. I didn't know that his real name was Herzil. Everyone always called him Bud. I never heard anyone call him Herzil."

"My mom calls him Herzil" I replied "but all of his brothers and his sister Leona call him Bud. All my cousins call him uncle Bud."

"Is Bud still working in at Murdochville?" he asked me. "Say hi to him for me."

From this I determined that people wanted to call my dad Bud. I don't know when people started calling my father Bud. It probably started when he was very young and stuck with him. Maybe his brothers and sister didn't like the name Herzil and started calling him Bud instead. Who knows?

In all of my sixty years I have never heard of or met another man with the name Herzil. I really don't know how my dad felt about his name or why my grandparents called him Herzil. I now regret not having asked my grandparents or my dad how he came by that name. Years after my dad passed away I asked my mother and she said that she wasn't sure but she thought that dad was named after an old Jewish peddler who travelled through the Gaspe peninsula door to door selling and sharpening knives and scissors. Apparently in the early 1900's my grandfather or great grandfather had befriended him and would invite him in for a good meal when he passed by our farm.

When he moved to Murdochville and later to St Catharines, Ontario new found friends called my dad Herzil. In the 1980's when my parents retired to Nova Scotia he was Herzil. However when he visited Gaspe on vacation he was once again known as Bud.

I sort of like the name Herzil, even if others found it a bit weird. However, I didn't name any of my three sons Herzil.

37. The Gas Is Going Up To Thirty-Seven Cents A Gallon

As I write this in 2008 one of the main topics of conversation you hear anywhere you go is the price of gas. You will hear someone say that at one dollar and forty-two cents per litre ($6.45 per gallon) the price of gas is as high as it's going to be. Someone else will state that it's predicted to be one dollar and sixty cents per litre next month and two dollars per litre by the end of the year. Someone else will say that the price of gas will have to go back down to below one dollar per litre or the world's economy will crash. Who to believe?

In the early fifties Henry Snowman had a single solitary gas pump out in front of his store. It was obsolete even before I was born in 1948. It was so old that there were no other gas pumps anywhere around like it. It was tall and had a see-through gas tank on the top of it. It had a crank on the side and you had to pump gas from the underground storage tank up into the small gas tank above the pump. If you wanted to buy ten gallons of gas you manually pumped ten gallons of gas into the tank and then had Henry check it. You then put the gas nozzle into the gas tank of your car, squeezed and gravity did the rest. Henry would then say "ten dollars at thirty-five cents per gallon. That's three dollars and fifty cents please."

However if you only needed seven and one- half of the ten gallons there was a graduated scale on the side of the tank showing that there was still two and one-half gallons left. Henry would charge you accordingly. Of course getting your gas at Henry's was old fashioned and time consuming as well as being labor intensive. People started going elsewhere to the newer electric gas pumps, which showed you, how much you owed right at the pump. Henry eventually retired the old gas pump and decided not to replace it.

I remember one year when the gas price rose to thirty-seven cents per gallon. I don't remember which year it was exactly but it was somewhere in the mid-fifties. There was a hue and cry at how high the price of gas was going. Because we lived in a rural area without any bus service people had to drive long distances on a daily basis. Gas was also used in farm tractors and in other farm equipment. People were saying that they couldn't afford to drive as much as they used to. They would have to cut back on driving to save money.

This was how it was over fifty years ago in the fifties. Have things changed that much today?

Nowadays if you want to see a pump like Henry's you'll have to go to a museum or maybe watch an old black and white movie from the thirties or forties.

38. Swivel Head

I acquired my first nickname when I started school in grade one. It was "Sweetpea" and it was given to me on the school bus by Verna Leggo, a second cousin who was about five years older than me. This nickname stayed with me for a while until I acquired the next one, which is now long forgotten.

Five years later when I was in grade six I acquired the most unusual nickname of "swivel head". This nickname was given to me by my teacher who I think may have been the only male teacher in our school.

I don't remember the teacher's name but I remember that he was very strict and did not tolerate students talking to each other when they weren't supposed to. This was different because most of the lady teachers I had in the past were fairly lenient and we could get away with a little talking in class.

One day in class I was whispering to the girl sitting directly behind the teacher and me caught me.

"Bryan!" he yelled. "Stop talking in class. I want your shoulders straight and your eyes front. From now on I want to see you keep those shoulders square."

Now there are some people who can contort their bodies into various and weird impossible positions like touching the back of their head with the bottom of their foot etc. I can't do that. What I can do is sit or stand straight and turn my head around to see directly behind me. I have the ability to turn my head around enough that I can place my chin behind my shoulder and therefore I have three hundred and sixty degrees of vision.

The next time the teacher caught me talking to the girl behind me he once again told me to keep my shoulders straight. I informed him that my shoulders were straight. He walked over to my desk and asked me to demonstrate how I was able to talk to my classmate directly behind me while keeping my shoulders straight ahead. I turned my head and showed him how I could put my chin behind my shoulder and look behind me.

"Bryan, you have a very flexible neck," he said. "From now on I'm going to call you "swivel head" and I want you to keep your head and shoulders straight ahead."

From that day onward there was not a day that I did not hear the teacher yell! "Swivel Head" when he caught me talking so the new nickname stuck with me at least to the end of that school year.

While writing this at the age of sixty I demonstrated my uncanny ability to look behind me to one of my adult sons, Jesse who still lives with me. He tested me on it and was amazed. Although I hadn't demonstrated this flexibility of my neck for many years I can still do it. However now my neck is sore.

39. Mom, Please Cook Me Liver.

Throughout my youth one of my favorite meals my mother made was liver and onions.

When it started to get cold in the latter part of the fall my grandfather Leslie started slaughtering animals for meat for the winter. One of the first parts of a cow or a pig that we ate was the liver, in part because it doesn't keep well and it's better when eaten fresh. I also liked the other organs like the heart and kidneys but liver was my absolute favorite.

My mom and sister liked liver but my father absolutely hated it so we could only have liver and onions when dad wasn't home. Since dad worked eighty miles away and only returned home on weekends this meant that we could only have liver Monday to Thursday's as dad would return home Friday evening and even the smell of liver seemed to make him ill. I found it strange that someone could get so queasy from the smell of liver that they would almost throw up. But that was my dad.

My grandfather would bring us some fresh liver and joke that we better eat it up fast before my dad got back home on the weekend.

My mother cleaned it up, dipped it in flour and fried it in a frying pan along with onions. Since I loved liver so much I didn't want many side dishes, just boiled potatoes to go along with it. It was so delicious I could eat it every day but of course it was unavailable every day because we would run out of farm animals.

Our enjoyment of liver and onions continued until we moved to Murdochville to live with dad. Unfortunately mom had to stop cooking liver even for lunch as dad would come home from work hours later and almost get sick from the smell.

But mom picked her spots. When dad went hunting for moose in the fall with his friends he was usually gone for four or five days. Mom went to the grocery store and bought liver, which my sister and I were eagerly waiting for.

Later in life my wife cooked me liver and it was just as delicious as my mother's. Although our three sons would not eat it they never complained of their mom cooking liver or the smell.

Now that I am retired and single I have liver only once or twice a year here at home in Sudbury, Ontario. However when I spend the winters in Panama City Beach in northwest Florida I have discovered "Lynn's Country Kitchen" a buffet restaurant, which serves liver and onions along with many other delicious foods on Friday's. Guess where I go for lunch on six or seven Friday's in winter? Miami, Orlando, Tampa and Daytona Beach are exciting places to visit but Panama City Beach has all you can eat liver.

40. Collecting Bottles & Hitting The Jackpot

Growing up in the fifties I never had enough money to buy the everyday things I wanted. By everyday things I mean pop, potato chips and chocolate bars etc. I didn't receive any payment from my parents or grandparents for doing farm chores as that was expected of you. I had to rely on the generosity of my mom to give me a dime once in a while when I was broke.

The only time I earned money for my labor was when I did jobs of short duration for non-relatives. I plucked chickens for Basil Leggo for ten cents per chicken. In the spring I picked gum (sap) from fir trees and sold it to Raymond Leggo, a middleman who in turn sold it to pharmaceutical companies. In the spring I planted potatoes for Garfield Leggo for three hours after school for twenty-five cents per hour. And in the fall I harvested potatoes. All of these occasional jobs contributed to but was not the main source of my income.

In the fifties you had to pay a two-cent deposit on small pop and beer bottles and a five-cent deposit on the larger ones. The main source of my income was collecting these bottles and delivering them to Basil Leggo's store to cash them in.

During the summer I found these bottles in the ditches and in winter in snow banks along the highway, Route 132 that is the main highway that encircles the Gaspe Peninsula. It passes right through L'Anse-A-Brilliant and actually divided our farm in two parts, farmland and woodland.

In those days in the Gaspe people used to get thirsty when they drove in their vehicles and after finishing a pop or a beer they would roll down their window and throw the bottle out into the ditch or snow bank. Since the ditches were usually soft ground and grass the bottles did not break. In those days, believe it or not some people thought it was cool to drink while driving as long as you didn't get drunk. Then they would throw the empties out the window, as they didn't want the empty bottles cluttering up their car.

Every few days I would patrol the half-mile of L'Anse-A-Brilliant that was on my side of the river and I left the half-mile on the other side to the kids who lived on that side. I would start by going up the hill facing traffic and searching the ditch and then cross the road and come back checking the ditch on the other side. I usually came up with five bottles or more and then I would take them to Basil's store and lay them on the ground outside the shed where he stored them. Basil would come out and check them and pay me. Sometimes I took the cash and sometimes I spent my earnings in the store.

The worst time to collect bottles was in the winter because when someone threw a bottle into the snow bank it sank into the snow where you couldn't see it and also it seemed that people didn't drink as much in the winter. Therefore I didn't do much bottle collecting in the wintertime.

Surprisingly the spring was an excellent time to collect bottles. When the warmer weather came the massive snow banks on both sides of the highway would melt away and expose the bottles that had been hidden there. It took at least a full month for the snow banks to melt away and they contained a lot of bottles.

Of course the summer was the best time to collect bottles as the weather was warm, people were thirstier and there was more traffic on the highway.

In the fall of 1958 the Anglican congregations of our area got together and had a "Harvest Supper" at the Mal Baie Hall, which was located next to St Peter's Anglican church in Mal Baie. This was an annual event, which celebrated the bounty of the fall harvest of our community. It was actually a Thanksgiving Dinner followed by music and a dance. My parents, my sister and I would get dressed up in our Sunday best and attend every year.

After everyone was finished eating and the tables and chairs were stored away a few fiddlers would go up on stage and start playing. There would be square dancing and we kids would watch the older generation dance.

A few of my friends and I went outside and discovered several men drinking beer out behind the hall in the dark. They had open cases of beer in their vehicles and after they drank the beer they would throw the bottles away behind the hall. You see, there was no alcohol allowed in the hall at "Harvest Supper".

I went back into the hall and located my dad. I told him about the men drinking out behind the hall and throwing their bottles away. I wanted to collect them and put them in the trunk of his car.

My dad said, "No, you're not going to stink up my new Mercedes with beer bottles."

I was disappointed because I knew I could have made a lot of money.

Dad said, "Hey next year we can bring the old Jeep and we can fill her up with bottles if you want."

One year later in the fall of 1959 dad drove the old Jeep to the Harvest Supper instead of the Mercedes. After the meal was over and the men started to go out behind the hall I joined them and started picking up empty bottles and putting them in the back of my dad's Jeep. After some of the men realized what I was doing one of them said, "Collecting bottles eh, good idea young fellow."

When I made a return trip to the back of the hall men were handing me empties and I didn't even have to go looking on the ground for them.

By the time the celebration was over and my family were ready to leave my father could not believe I had filled up the back of the Jeep with beer bottles. Of course we had to put up with the stink of beer on the twelve-mile drive home,

but of course it's a pleasant smell.

I hit the jackpot in that fall of 1959 because when I counted the empties I had one hundred and eighty of them, which brought me three dollars and sixty cents when I cashed them in. What a haul. It was the biggest of my life.

Unfortunately the next year when I returned to "Harvest Supper" several other kids had decided to collect bottles as well and I only managed to collect thirty or thirty-five which was a good haul but no jackpot.

After I became a teenager in 1961 I gave up collecting bottles and left it to the younger kids. And then the no deposit, no return glass bottle came out followed years later by the throwaway plastic pop bottle. The collecting of returnable bottles was good while it lasted.

41. Aunt Minn Gives Me A Tip

Aunt Minn was my grandmother Ruby's older sister, which made her my father's aunt and my great-aunt but everyone in L'Anse-A-Brilliant called her Aunt Minn even if they weren't related to her. She was a gracious older lady and she was a widow. Every spring she came down from Montreal and moved into her small cottage, which was located next door to Arnold Johnson's house. Her son Billy Smith lived in Montreal and would come down in the summer to visit her for a few weeks. He would be accompanied by his wife Gertie and some or all of their four sons.

My grandmother had several siblings but most of them had passed away or lived elsewhere. I knew a few of her sisters but I knew that her favorite was Aunt Minn.

Since most of the people in L'Anse-A-Brilliant were relatives of some sort help was available for Aunt Minn any time she needed it. When she needed a small favor done like going to the store for a loaf of bread or a can of condensed milk she would get one of the local kids to do it for her and she usually gave them a ten cent tip. Since there were several children that lived real close to her on that side of the river and I lived a half mile away I wasn't asked to run any errands for her.

One day my grandfather came back from the store and I went out to the truck to see if he needed any help to carry groceries into the house.

Grandpa said "Bryan, Aunt Minn wants you to go over to her house to do her a favor."

"I'll go right now, as soon as I tell mom" I replied.

I told mom that I was going over to Aunt Minn's to do her a favor and my mom said "Bryan do not accept any tip from your Aunt Minn. She is an old lady and you should be happy to do a favor for her."

I said "ok" and I was off.

When I knocked on her door Aunt Minn invited me in and I sat down at her kitchen table.

"Bryan, I would like you to go to the store for me" she said.

I said "ok" and she gave me some money and told me what she needed. I went to Basil's store and got the items Aunt Minn wanted and returned to her cottage. It didn't take me long as Basil's store was just a few minutes walk away.

When I put the groceries on Aunt Minn's kitchen table I handed her the change from her order. She picked out a dime and handed it to me.

"I can't accept that" I said.

"Why not?" she asked.

"I'm happy to run errands for you for free, anytime" I replied.

"I know that Bryan but I give your friends a dime when they do me a favor and I want to do the same for you."

"But my mom will get mad at me if I take the money" I replied."

"Here's the dime and tell Frances that I insisted that you accept it. You deserve it. You came all the way over here to help me and now you have to walk all the way back home. All the other kids accept it so you should to. Your mother will understand."

I took the dime, thanked her and went back to the store and bought a five cent chocolate bar and a five-cent bag of potato chips. That's how far a dime went back in the fifties. It was the first tip that I had ever received. But I would have been happy to do the favor for Aunt Minn for free. And when I told my mom she wasn't mad.

42. Henry Snowman

Henry Snowman was another resident of L'Anse-a-Brilliant. He lived in a big white house, the only one built on the flat down by the harbour and beach. Henry had immigrated to Canada from Jersey of the Channel Islands to work for Hyman and Sons at their store in Grand Greve, which was almost directly across Gaspe Bay from L'Anse-a-Brilliant. He eventually moved to L'Anse-a-Brilliant to work in Hyman's store here and married Jenny Leggo, a local girl. They had two sons Gary and Lorne who were several years older than me. In fact when I started school they were almost finished.

He was one of two retailers in our community, the other being Basil Leggo who was basically a grocer. Henry's store, the larger of the two was more of a general store selling some hardware and other items as well as groceries.

Basil Leggo's store was the more popular as he was very popular and people came from other communities such as Seal Cove, Bois Brule, Bougainville, etc. to shop at his store. Henry did manage to get some business and I remember my mother telling me that "we have to give Henry some business but we'll buy most of our stuff from Basil."

As a fairly aware child I got the impression that most people didn't care for Henry much but shopped at his store because he was married to Jenny who was related to many of the local people.

Henry did not treat children with much respect and as a result we didn't like him very much either. For example when I was sent to his store by my mother I would enter his store and he was almost never at his counter, but hung out at his desk in his office at the back of the store. When he heard me he would come out of his office and ask me what I wanted.

I would reply, "a loaf of white bread."

Henry would then turn around and instead of getting me the bread, he would go back into his office for half an hour. He would eventually emerge and get me the bread and I would pay him and leave the store. When I got home my mother would ask why I took so long and I would tell her what happened and request that the next time I be allowed to shop at Basil's. Mom would say that "Henry has his ways" and that things might be different next time.

I was about eleven or twelve and one day when I got home from school, did some chores and had supper I would run over to the field between Basil's and Harry's stores to play baseball with all the Leggo's, Lance, Denver, Zane, Wayne, Irma and sometimes others such as Reid De Vouge would be there. My mother asked me to pick up a loaf of white bread at Henry's and to do it before I started to play baseball. She was worried that the store would close before I got the bread.

I ran the one-third mile to Henry's store and on entering the store I noticed Henry had no customers and that he was in his office. He came out and asked me what I wanted.

I replied, "a loaf of white bread."

He immediately turned and went back into his office. I figured that he must have been reading a book or something. After five minutes I was so impatient to get playing baseball that I decided to leave and buy the bread at Basil's store next door. When I entered Basil's store of course the purchase and payment were completed in less than a minute. I got to the field and played baseball with my friends until almost dark.

After the baseball game I headed home and on passing Henry's store he came running out and he was furious. He started yelling at me about buying the bread at Basil's. He gave me crap and said that my mother would hear about it and that I would be in trouble. I had always been taught to respect my elders but on this occasion I told him that I had been in a hurry and Basil was a lot faster in serving me than him. I told him that I didn't have time to wait for a half-hour for service when I could be playing baseball with my friends. I then continued on home and that was the last I heard of the bread issue.

On another occasion my sister Donna accompanied me to Henry's store. She was seven years old and had just learned to ride her new bicycle. Mom didn't want her to ride her bike on the road unless I was with her. Being twelve years of age I didn't always like my sister tagging along when I rode my bike but in this case I relented.

We entered Henry's store and on this occasion he came directly to his counter, looked at us and let out a humongous fart. I think he was trying to shock us or something. I was almost ten feet away from him but Donna was right at the counter closer to him. She twitched her nose, looked up at him and said "Pheuh, Henry you stink worse than a buck goat."

Henry looked back at her but was speechless. Now, you wonder where a little seven-year-old girl would pick up this expression and also have the moxie to say it to an adult. Well it's an old Newfie saying that she heard our mother say to my dad several times. By the way Henry never repeated this performance again, at least never while we were in his store.

A few years earlier when I was nine or ten I was in Henry's store with a friend. I noticed that he had placed a rack of potato chips on the counter. They were the small five-cent bags of Humpty Dumpty chips. Yes, in the fifties a small bag was only five cents and a large bag was ten cents. I grabbed a bag from the rack, paid for it, opened it and discovered a small piece of paper in with the potato chips. I took the paper and read the message out loud. It said, "You have won a free bag of Humpty Dumpty chips. Present this to your retailer to receive your free bag."

I gave it to Henry and immediately he got angry. He accused me of cheating, saying that I had seen the paper through the bag as there was a small frosted window on the bag where you could see chips inside.

I replied, "No, I saw it after I opened the bag. I didn't even know that there was a contest."

Henry told me that he wasn't going to give me a free bag. I told him that I was in the right and that I would get my mother to write a letter to the Humpty Dumpty company to complain. He reluctantly gave me my free bag.

Later I told Lance Leggo about this and he told me there were five free bags in a rack of fifty. He knew this because his dad Basil owned the other store in L'Anse-a-Brilliant. Lance also told me that if you looked through the little frosted window carefully, sometimes you could see the paper message.

Now, what I'm about to tell you may come as a complete surprise. Nobody I know ever won a free bag of chips at Henry's store again. However when you bought a bag of chips at Basil's store you had a ten percent chance of winning.

Before you get the impression that Henry was a bad man I would like to say that he was not really. He was just a little different than most. He did have his good side. In the winter one of the best places to go sliding with our toboggans and sleighs was Henry's hill, which was the old road down from Henry's store to the river and harbour. Henry's house was at the bottom of the hill and across the river. It got dark real early and there were no streetlights there in those days. We could not slide there without some lighting as it would be too dark and dangerous. Henry would put his front outdoor light on and we could see quite well. When there were four or five of us kids there we could be quite loud at times as we were having so much fun. When Henry thought we should be on our way home he would simply put the light off and we would head home. We were thankful to him for letting us slide for that long.

43. Basil's Store

In L'Anse-a-Brilliant also known as Brilliant Cove we were fortunate to have two grocery stores. Although we were a small community the two stores also served communities such as Seal Cove, Bois Brule and Bougainville as well. The smaller of the two stores was my and everyone's favorite. It was owned by Basil Leggo, who was my father's cousin and one of his best childhood friends. Basil's three oldest sons Lance, Denver and Zane were also my best friends.

When my mother sent me to Basil's store with a list of things to buy I would say hello and stroll up to the counter and start reciting the items required. Basil would retrieve each item from the shelves behind the counter and write the price down on a piece of paper as he didn't have an adding machine. As he put the groceries on the counter in front of him Basil kept adding numbers to his list and when it was complete he added it up and wrote the final cost or the items down. Basil then added the numbers once again to make sure his addition was correct. He really didn't have to because he was always right the first time. I would pay him cash and he would bag the groceries into a brown paper bag as in the fifties the plastic bag was not available as of yet.

Many people paid for their groceries with cash and many people paid "on tic", a fifties slang expression for buying on credit. There was no such thing as credit cards in the 1950's but there was credit. People who received government checks once a month took them to Basil and when he cashed them he deducted what they owed him and gave them back the remainder in cash. People on welfare and on pensions benefited from this service.

When I think back to the fifties I remember that Basil's prices were cheap as compared to prices today. In fact the prices were miniscule. A small chocolate bar such as a "Caramilk" or "Oh Henry" cost only five cents while a large one was only ten cents. Also a small bag of "Humpty Dumpty" potato chips cost five cents and a large bag cost ten cents. A bottle of Coke, Pepsi, Orange Crush or other soft drink cost only eight cents, which included the two-cent deposit on the glass bottle. If you bought a bottle of pop and drank it in the store it only cost six cents because you didn't have to pay the deposit. What a bargain. You could get a two pack of "Chicklets" chewing gum or one "Double Bubble" bubble gum for just a penny. I find it ironic that after all these years I can still remember the cost of these items but I don't remember what a loaf of bread cost. That tells you what was important to me fifty-five years ago.

Sometimes when you went to Basil's store there would be a few men there sitting on the wooden pop cases that were stacked up against the far counter. They would be drinking a warm pop because there wasn't any cooler for the pop and they would be discussing the latest news and gossip. At election time there would usually be an animated discussion damming the Liberals and their pork barrel politics. I would just stand there listening and not say a word hoping that the topic of sports would come up so I could exhibit my knowledge of such things as hockey and baseball.

I can also say that I worked for Basil's store at least once. One year he grew chickens for sale and when his sons Lance, Denver and Zane and I got home from school Basil had killed several chickens and we got to pluck the feathers off the dead chickens. I think Basil paid me ten cents for every chicken that I plucked so I made around thirty or forty cents after school. With these wages I thought that I had hit the jackpot as that seemed like a lot of money in those days.

These days both stores in L'Anse-a-Brilliant are long gone; closed many years ago. Nowadays people drive twenty miles up to Gaspe to two modern supermarkets where you can buy pretty much anything under the sun. I must tell you however that when I visit L'Anse-a-Brilliant from time to time I really miss Basil's store.

44. On Thursdays Nanny Bakes The Bread

In the fifties my grandmother Ruby De Vouge always did her weekly baking on Thursdays. She fired up the old wood cook stove with the proper wood to get the oven up to the right temperature as there was a temperature gauge on the oven door.

Nanny usually baked seven loaves of white bread, a loaf of raisin bread for my grandfather, maybe a layer cake and then cinnamon rolls as a treat for my sister Donna and me.

Six of the loaves went into the freezer and one was taken out each day. In those days in Quebec it was a tradition to have bread on the table for every meal. A slice of fresh buttered bread went well with a bowl of homemade soup at lunchtime or with a plate of beef stew at suppertime.

When my mother baked she made layer cakes and raisin pies but she didn't usually bake bread very often. She preferred to buy sliced white bread at the store. But I preferred my grandmother's homemade bread especially when I toasted a few slices up for breakfast to go along with our homemade raspberry jam, or at lunch when spread with molasses.

My grandfather did some baking of his own and he made these gigantic brown molasses cookies, which were so delicious. I often wonder why my grandmother didn't make them for him but he preferred to make them himself. He usually made them once a week in the evening and he would call me to come and have a few with him. We would butter the bottom of the molasses cookies and enjoy them as our evening snack.

On Thursday's during the school year my sister Donna and I endured the fourteen-mile bus ride home from school. When the bus stopped we ran up our long driveway and entered my grandparents part of the house, Our grandmother had it timed just right as she was just taking the cinnamon rolls that she had made for us out of the oven. Nanny would coat them with homemade white icing and sprinkle cinnamon on them and serve them to us hot. What a treat. They were definitely the favorite dessert of both my sister and me. No store bought dessert could compare with them. I have never ever tasted anything as delicious as those cinnamon rolls my nanny used to make.

45. Salt Fish, Fresh Cod And Smoked Herring

When you grow up in Quebec's maritime region the Gaspe Peninsula one might assume that we ate a lot of fish and other seafood. I can only say that you were one hundred percent correct in your assumption. In any given week in the summer we ate fish at least four days out of seven: in winter months two days out of seven. There were so many different species of fish for us to eat, cod, halibut, sole, herring, mackerel, smelt, caplain, trout, salmon and of course shell fish such as clams and lobster. They were all there for the taking and all you had to do was go out and catch them except for clams and salmon, which we had to buy. It also helps if you're a seafood lover and all of my family was.

Since my grandfather was a cod fisherman I would estimate that ninety percent of the seafood we consumed was cod and we loved it. During the fishing season of spring to early fall we had fresh cod cooked in many different ways but my favorite was cod fillets dipped in egg and flour and fried in a frying pan. I also loved it when my mother made fish cakes combining potatoes and onions with the cod into small cakes that she fried. That was "some good" as my uncle Glen used to say.

In the summer my grandfather dried a lot of salted cod on the flake to preserve them for the winter. The flake was a raised platform built about two and a half feet above the ground and covered with chicken wire. After grandpa cleaned and flattened out the cod they were placed on the flake, course salt was applied to them and they were left to dry and cure in the sun. The cod needed a few weeks of long sunny days to dry and cure properly. They had to be re-salted from time to time and turned over every few days as both sides had to be exposed to the sun. I used to enjoy helping grandpa turn the drying cod over because we had hundreds and hundreds of them to turn. You did not want the drying cod to get wet so if it got real cloudy and was expected to rain we stacked the cod up and covered them up. At first the cod were soft and pliable and as they were re-salted, dried and cured in the sun they became hard and very stiff. That was when they were ready and my grandfather then removed them from the flake and stored them and started drying a new batch. Grandpa sold salted cod to customers and kept some for our use. I love salted cod and several times every summer when I felt like a snack I would grab a cod off the flake and tear a six inch strip off. Of course it was extremely salty but I liked it like that.

When my mother served up salted cod with boiled potatoes and fried fat pork she first soaked the cod in water overnight to dissolve most of the salt out of it. Then the next day she boiled more of the salt out of it. The longer you boil it the less salty it becomes so it can be cooked to your taste. Although this is one of my favorite meals you will never find it on a restaurant menu here in Canada. It is popular in Europe especially in Portugal. In fact five hundred years ago French, Basque and Portuguese fishermen came to the Gaspe Peninsula to fish for the summer. They had camps on shore where they settled and dried their catch and in the fall they returned to Europe with their ships filled with salted cod. Now since cod fishing is practically dead in Eastern Canada it is ironic that this year I bought salted cod imported from Portugal.

We also filleted fresh cod and froze them in our big freezers to last us throughout the winter until the next fishing season. It is sad that these days there is no cod fishing industry in Eastern Canada and the cod were fished nearly to extinction.

One of the other things I liked doing was helping my grandfather when he smoked herring. He built a smokehouse right next to our driveway between the highway and our house. It was about half the size of an outhouse and grandpa built a fire pit a few feet away. The smoke from the fire went through a stovepipe to the bottom of the smokehouse and then up through the fresh herring, which were pinned to steel rods with clothespins. The end result was smoked herring, which was very delicious.

With all the different species of fish we had available to us there was one that I absolutely hated to fish for or go near. That cursed fish was a mackerel, which I liked to eat. What I would not do was clean a mackerel because although it was a small fish of twelve to fourteen inches long when you inserted a knife into it to clean it then it seemed to contain about a gallon of blood. The much bigger cod only had a small amount of blood in it and was easy to clean. If someone put a cooked mackerel on a plate in front of me I would gladly eat it but that was the only contact I wanted to have with it.

I had eaten so much fish during my childhood that when I moved to Ontario in 1967 at the age of nineteen I didn't want to see another one. But less than a year later I started craving fish and started eating it once again. The bad thing is now I have to pay for it.

46. Homemade Jams

Growing up on the farm one of my favorite breakfasts was homemade bread toasted and covered with homemade wild raspberry jam.

We had our own very large raspberry patch on our property which was located up on the head, a term we used to describe the area at the top of our farm where the cliff fell a few hundred feet to the Atlantic Ocean below. This raspberry patch was fenced in so that the grazing farm animals could not get in. It also kept out any wild animals living in the area.

When the raspberries were ready for picking my grandmother, mother, sister and I would walk up to the head with our containers and pick raspberries for hours. When I got tired I would ask my mother if we could go back home now.

She would reply "No Bryan, not till you pick your picker full."

The picker was the small container you used to wander through the raspberry bushes picking berries. When it was full you dumped its contents into the bigger container and then returned to pick some more. When we filled our containers we started back to the house and the walk was a pleasant one as it was all downhill.

Mom and Nanny would then make the raspberry jam boiling the raspberries on the stove along with pectin, which you had to add as well as white sugar. When the jam was ready it was poured into jam jars while it was still hot and the lids were put on. Although there seemed to me to be more than enough raspberry jam to last us until next year's crop we always seemed to run out by springtime. Did we eat too much jam? No, I don't think so! My mother gave too many jars away to friends and relatives as gifts because they loved her homemade jam. When we ran out and we had to buy store bought jam we most always bought Kraft Pure Raspberry jam and it was delicious. We also bought strawberry jam and orange marmalade a well.

There were also other berries on our farm, which were made into jams. There were a few gooseberry bushes along the fence with the neighbouring farm. They were located half way up to the head and I used to pick them for my grandmother who would make gooseberry jam with them. Since gooseberries weren't very plentiful she didn't get very much jam from them. Actually I didn't care for gooseberry jam and I think my grandmother was the only one that ate it.

We also had wild strawberries on our farm. I remember a good patch about one hundred yards up the hill from our end of the house where the land was flat. These wild strawberries were very small compared to the ones you buy in the store. They were only about the size of a raspberry or blueberry. However they were better tasting than the tame cultivated strawberries and my grandmother made delicious wild strawberry jam with them. Unfortunately there weren't enough of these wild strawberries on the farm to satisfy my longing for them.

I also loved blueberry jam but we didn't have any blueberries on our farm. The year that we moved to the mining town of Murdochville up in the mountains we were very close to some excellent blueberry patches. After dad got off work and we ate supper the whole family would get into dad's car and we would drive about ten miles to get to the blueberry picking area. We would pick several six-quart baskets of them. While we picked the blueberries we also had to keep our eyes open for bears as they loved blueberries as much as we did.

We picked so many blueberries that my mom made blueberry jam, blueberry pies, blueberry muffins and the extra blueberries were frozen for future use.

Back on the farm my grandmother had some plum trees located adjacent to the apple trees. She made plum jam which I don't remember eating. Nanny also made apple pies with the apples from the orchard.

One year when I was about ten years old I needed to make some money for a school project so nanny suggested that I pick some of the remaining raspberries and we could make jam to sell to raise the money. She also sent me to Basil's store to buy pectin and after I got back we made the jam and bottled it. The next day after I got home from school I took four jars of the wild raspberry jam down to the end of our driveway. I did not make a sign advertising wild raspberry jam for sale but simply held up a jar so the drivers passing by on the local highway would know what I was selling. Several cars passed by before one stopped and I made my first sale. However I sold all four jars in less than twenty minutes and earned the two dollars I needed for my school project.

As an adult living in Sudbury, Ontario I have gone to a pick-your-own raspberry farm and my wife and I made jam the way my mother and grandmother used to do on the farm. I did it mainly so my three sons could experience homemade raspberry jam. They loved it.

47. Catalogue Shopping

Back in the 1950's on the farm most of the things we needed other than groceries were purchased from a catalogue, usually Eaton's or Sears.

Although we had two small grocery stores in L'Anse-a-Brilliant we had to go elsewhere for anything else we needed. There were several shops and small stores in the town of Gaspe twenty miles away but selection wasn't the greatest.

Most of the clothing we all wore was ordered from either Eaton's or Sears. Eaton's which at that time was known as the poor man's store because it had cheap prices had a catalogue shopping depot in Moncton, New Brunswick which served the Maritimes and eastern Quebec. When we ordered something from the more expensive but reasonably priced Sears catalogue our order went to their office in Toronto, Ontario.

In those days all the orders were done by mail as there was no such thing as a 1-800 number. Besides even if there was we didn't have a telephone. It took around ten days before our parcel arrived at the post office five miles away in Douglastown. The mailman would then leave a card in our mailbox located at the end of our driveway informing us that he would be delivering our parcel COD (cash on delivery) the next day. The amount we owed including taxes was listed on the card and the next morning my mother would leave an envelope with the amount owing in our mailbox for the mailman. When he delivered our mail and parcel that day he would put the parcel into the mailbox if it fit and give us a few toots on his car's horn to let us know that our parcel had arrived.

From Eaton's and Sears we would receive the rather large "Spring and Summer", "Fall and Winter" catalogues and the somewhat smaller but eagerly awaited Christmas catalogue. Through the year we also received small spring, summer, fall and winter sale catalogues as well.

When we received any catalogue we all wanted to be the first to look through it and my mother usually let my sister and I have the first gander. If my sister Donna had the catalogue first I kept my eye on the clock and if I thought she was hogging it I would complain to our mother.

"Hey" I would say. "She's had the catalogue for twenty minutes. That's long enough. It's my turn now."

My mom would say "Donna, let Bryan look at the catalogue for awhile."

Donna after complaining that she didn't have it long enough would reluctantly hand the catalogue over to me and then she would check the clock. Of course twenty minutes later she demanded the catalogue back once again.

If by chance the Eaton's and Sears catalogues came on the same day then there wasn't any fighting as we each had one to look at and we could trade them with each other at intervals.

When I looked through the Eaton's or Sears catalogues I would put check marks next to things I really liked. If I discovered something that I absolutely had to have I would put two check marks next to it. If it was an article of clothing I wanted I would also circle the size and underline the colour I wanted. In the fall when we received the Christmas catalogues I would also circle the items I wanted as well (toys). Isn't it ironic that on Christmas morning I received many but not all of the items that I had checked and circled. Obviously Santa had checked our catalogues, noted my selections and decided to give me these gifts.

I think my mother's favorite catalogue was the Avon cosmetics one. We didn't have an Avon Lady in our area so my mother ordered a lot of Avon products to give as Christmas and Birthday gifts. My mother always gave my teachers Avon products. I remember some of my lady teachers were overjoyed at receiving the Avon talcum powders and perfumes. My mother also liked the Regal catalogue especially for buying her Christmas cards and the nice stationary that she liked.

My father was always waiting for the new Canadian Tire and the Princess Auto catalogues to arrive. He received some others as well but I remember those two as being his favorites. He was always looking for new tools to order. I thought that he had enough tools already but he said "a man can never have enough tools."

My grandfather had catalogues that sold items for the farm however I think he liked the Eaton's catalogue the best because I remember him ordering a new water pump and his first Teco chainsaw from there.

My grandmother ordered all her material and remnants she needed to make herself housedresses and the aprons she made to sell. Once again it was either Eaton's or Sears.

In those days in 1950's Gaspe the catalogue was a godsend to us for it provided us with the majority of the things we needed.

48. *Before Frisbee's Were Invented*

I don't know exactly when frisbees were invented. My earliest memories of playing with them is sometime in the late 1960's. I do remember buying my first frisbee around 1970 when I was in my early twenties. It was a big black one and I took it everywhere with me for years. Its normal place of residence was the trunk of the car I was driving at that particular time. When I was on vacation whenever I arrived at a beach wherever it was the frisbee was retrieved from the trunk and the flying disc flew through the air. This included L'Anse-a-Brilliant beach when I went there on vacation in 1973.

As a child back in the 1950's I did throw black flying discs through the air but they were not frisbees. They were my mom's old 78 rpm. record collection from the 1930's and 1940's. They were obsolete because you could not buy a record player that played them. All the new record players played both the small 45 rpm records, which had one song on each side and the 33-rpm long play records which usually had six songs on each side of it. My grandmother had a newer model record player and she played her hymns and Perry Como records on it. But we could not play the old 78 rpm records.

One day when I was about ten years old my mother was doing some spring cleaning and came across her old record collection. She asked my dad "What should I do with these old records?"

Dad replied "Throw them out. You can't play them anymore. They're no more good for anything."

Mom gave me quite a few of them and asked me to throw them out. I took them outside but I didn't feel like throwing them out but I did feel like throwing them. I went to the top of the little hill beside our house and took a few of the records out of their protective sleeves and started throwing them sideways so that they flew through the air like a flying saucer. I wanted to see how far I could throw them and I marked where the furthest one had landed and then went back to throw the old records again. Then I would throw the old 78 rpm record harder this time to try and make it go farther. One thing that became apparent very quickly was that these old records were very fragile because several of them broke when landing on the hard ground.

Although these 78's were large and heavy they were not at all durable like the newer vinyl 33's and 45's. were and they shattered very easily.

Not far from where I was throwing the old records Geraldine Hodgins lived in the old schoolhouse that had now been converted to a home. Geraldine lived there with her mother Almear and when she saw me throwing the records she came out and asked me what I was doing.

I replied "I'm throwing my mom's old 78 rpm records to see how far I can throw them."

"But you're breaking them" she said "Doesn't your mom want them anymore?"

"No" I replied. "She told me to throw them away because we can't play them anymore. The new record players won't play these old 78 rpm records. These records are no more good."

"Could I have them?" asked Geraldine. "We have a very old gramophone that only plays 78's and we can't use it anymore because all the old records we had were broken and thrown out."

We gathered up all the old records that I had not broken and the others that I had not thrown and took them to Geraldine's house. Almear was delighted to receive the old records and she started to set up the old gramophone so that we could play them. I had seen the cabinet there sitting underneath the window but had not known what it was. Almear opened the top of the cabinet and which exposed the actual record turntable. She swung out the gramophone which looked like the one that the dog is listening to on the old RCA Victor logo and then she turned this big crank on the side of the cabinet to wind up the old gramophone.

"Where's the plug in?" I asked.

"There's none" Almear replied. "It's not electric. It's so old it runs by winding it up with the crank."

She also had this box with hundreds of needles in it. She said that after she played a few records she had to change the needle on the record player. Almear then put on a record and we listened to Harry James and his Orchestra play a fox trot with vocals by someone I had never heard of. Almear was over fifty years old at the time and she seemed really happy to be listening to this old music, this big band sound of the 1930's and 1940's. Geraldine and I looked at each other and we didn't know what all the fuss was about. We obviously weren't impressed with the music. Give us Elvis Presley any day.

Almear told me to be sure and thank my mother for the records and she also told me that "anytime I wanted to listen to them she would play then for me." I didn't think that I'd be taking her up on that offer very often.

Now due to the nostalgia craze over fifty years later in 2009 I was able to purchase a record turntable which plays the 33 rpm. 45 rpm and 78 rpm records. Also before she passed away a few years ago my mother gave me seven old 78 rpm records that she had saved with names such as Harry James, Benny Goodman, Charlie Spivak, Freddy Martin and Vaughn Monroe and their Orchestra's accompanied by vocalists of the day. These seventy year old records are very rare and maybe valuable.

Today I played a Harry James and his Orchestra recording with vocal chorus by Kitty Kallen. It was a fox trot style recording of the big band sound popular in the 1940's. It sounds good on my new turntable and I enjoyed listening to it but I tell you it ain't rock and roll.

49. Grade Five ------
I'm number One

In the 1950's at the Belle Anse Consolidated School each student was rated at the end of each term. This ranking was listed on your report card at Christmas, Easter, and at the end of the school year in June. The top student was rated number one and of course was praised by the teacher along with numbers two, three, and four. The student that was ranked fifteenth in a class of fifteen was shamed and usually faced ridicule from his or her classmates. Being teased as the class dummy was not a pleasant experience. The student that was ranked last was usually a big strong boy for some reason.

In the present day of political correctness this system of ranking students is gone the way of the dodo bird (extinct) and rightly so.

All the years that I attended Belle Anse School until I moved away in grade eight I was consistently ranked in the top three. Every year the top three students were Carol Hotton, Lance Leggo and myself. Carol and Lance were very smart and they took turns being the number one ranked student. I was always number three, sometimes just a fraction of a percentage point behind the other two. I was happy being number three and was never obsessed with being number one or two. I believe Carol and Lance felt the same way about being number one or two.

In the fall of 1958 when I was in grade five I received my report card at the end of the first term which was at Christmas break. Once again I was ranked number three and when I got home I presented my report card to my mother.

Mom studied my report card and was very pleased with my marks. She noted that I was tops in the class in subjects such as History and Geography and ranked lower in subjects I didn't like. She said that I should work a little harder on those subjects. She was right of course. I loved History and Geography so much that I would go beyond the current curriculum and do further research on them by taking books out of the school library. I didn't want to wait until grades six, seven, or eight to find about Argentina, Brazil, or Cambodia etc. I wanted to know about them right now. At the age of ten I could name almost every country in the world and tell you their capital cities. Most people found this amazing.

I decided that I would take my mother's advice and spend more time on the subjects I disliked and study a little harder. When school started again in January I put this plan in effect and in the next two and one half months I worked very hard until the pre Easter exams.

When the exams were all completed and we were ready for Easter break our teacher presented our report cards to us. I was ranked number one. The hard work had paid off.

The teacher of course praised me in front of the class telling them that I had worked very hard this past term to achieve the number one ranking. I was sort of embarrassed at the praise as I knew there wasn't much of a difference between being number one and being number three; maybe one percentage point.

In the third term between Easter and June I realized how much I missed all the non-curricular reading I used to do. I figured that education was more than what you learned in school. When I read the newspaper every day and read my dad's Mechanix Illustrated and Popular Mechanics magazines cover to cover I knew that I would not be writing exams on them in school but I would be learning things that would be useful to me later in life.

I decided that the number one ranking was not all that important to me. I was getting good marks and advancing to the next grade every year. That was important. So I started to do the things I used to do like reading books not related to school.

At the end of the school year when I received my report card I was once again ranked the number three students in the class. Being number three was good enough for me.

50. I Loved School

Way back in the 1950's when I went to elementary school I didn't understand why some people hated school and today in 2009 that feeling still exists in some people.

The summers seem endless when you're a ten year old and when the middle of August rolled around we children of L'Anse-a-Brilliant started to talk about the upcoming school year slated to start once again a few days into September. Some of my friends dreaded even the thought of having to go back to school and they complained about it but I couldn't wait I was so excited to get back to school.

I wanted to dig into all the new school books I would be getting and read them all front to back as fast as I could. I had a thirst for knowledge that I could not quench. I especially wanted to start on the History and Geography text books as they were my favorite subjects.

Because I attended Belle Anse Consolidated School which served a rural area my school friends were spread out over a twenty-five mile area and I did not get to see most of them all summer. I was anxious to get back to school and renew old friendships.

Perhaps there would be a few new students in the school this year to make friends with. Perhaps there would be a new girl in my class to fall in love with. In the past it seemed that all the guys in my class fell in love with her at the same time. She did not have to be as beautiful as the girls that were already there. She was a new girl and that's what did it.

At home in the summertime we were always short of players when we played baseball. Now at school we had enough players to cover all the positions and we played at every recess and lunch hour in the spring and early fall.

When we started school we would have a track meet to determine who would be representing our school in the regional track meet against other schools. I was always on the tract and field team and I loved participating in these events.

Learning new things was what I loved most about school. Because my class had only fourteen or fifteen students most years we would be combined with the next grade up. When I was in grade five we were at the side of the classroom closest to the window and the grade six students were on the other side. When the teacher was teaching grade six History of Geography and we grade fives were having a study period I would listen intently and sometimes the teacher would ask her class a question and they would not know the right answer. I would raise my hand and thinking that I maybe wanted to go to the washroom or something the teacher would say "Yes Bryan, what is it?"

"Ankara is the capital of Turkey and not Istanbul I said. "Most people think that the capital is Istanbul because it was the capital for almost four hundred years until they made Ankara, the second largest city in Turkey the new capital."

"How do you know that Bryan?" she asked. "Not all that information is in our grade six textbook."

"I have an encyclopedia at home" I replied. "I like reading about other countries and their history and geography."

This answering the question happened a few times and then one day one of the grade six students asked the teacher a geography question that the teacher surprisingly did not know the answer to.

"That's not in our grade six geography book" she said. 'So I'll have to look it up and get back to you."

The grade six student said "Maybe we should ask Bryan. Maybe he knows the answer."

I don't remember what the question was but I did happen to know the answer and I volunteered it. The teacher did not look too pleased that I had upstaged her and later suggested to me that I should spend more time concentrating on my grade five curriculum than on grade six subjects. I kind of liked the fact that in this case I knew more about geography than she did.

When the school year progressed and the June final exams approached most students were getting anxious for the school year to end. The last day of school was a celebration of the school year, basically party time. No work was done on this day. We played most of the day and report cards were handed out.

On the school bus ride home all the children were singing "No more pencils, no more books, no more teacher's dirty looks" over and over again. I sang along although not enthusiastically because I had mixed feelings about the end of the school year. Although I knew that I was going to enjoy the summer I was going to miss my access to the school library and all those glorious books and seeing many of my friends as well. But I knew that in a little over two months September would arrive and I would be back at school. I loved school.

51. Lord, Don't You Buy
Me A Mercedes Benz

In the 1950's cars were on the minds of every member of the male species and many of the ladies minds as well.

Cars were big and beautiful, long and sleek, finned and chromed. They were gorgeous. They were works of art. And every year styles changed. The 56, 57 and 58 Chevrolet Bel Air's were vastly different from each other. For example in 1957 the Chevy had great fins at the back of the car that the 1956 model did not have. These cars are now called "Classics" and rightly so.

I as well as most of my friends knew the styles, makes and models of all the big three, Chevrolet, Ford and Chrysler. Also many kids liked the cars of smaller companies such as Studerbaker. There were very few imports in those days although the Volkswagon Beetle from Germany and the Austin Cambridge from England became popular when they came out.

My dad was always partial to Buick's but in the mid-fifties had bought a used lime-green Austin from the local Anglican minister. It had these little signal ears that popped out from the body when the turn signal indicator was deployed. It was kind of weird and cool at the same time.

In 1958 dad decided to buy a brand new car but was undecided on which car to buy. My uncles Cyril and Glen drove Chevies and my uncle Denzil always drove Studebaker's which I liked better than Chevies. However I liked Pontiac's better than the others and strongly lobbied my dad to buy one. I told him that Pontiac made the best car and that it was superior to Chevs, Fords and Plymouths etc.

My father worked eighty miles away in Murdochville while my mom, sister and I lived on the farm in L'Anse-a-Brilliant. Dad worked and lived in Murdochville Monday to Friday and came home on the weekends.

This one spring day in 1958 when I was nine and one-half years old I noticed this sort of ugly but new black car pull into our driveway and drive up to the house. I approached the car to see whom the visitors were and was surprised to see my dad exit the driver's side door. He was accompanied by another man who I did not recognize. Dad asked me to go and get my mother.

I told mom that dad was home with another man and we both went back outside to see him. Since it was the middle of the week she had not expected him home.

My mom looked at dad and the stranger and said "Herzil, you bought a new car."

Dad replied "Yes but we have to drive to New Carlisle to pay for it. Go get Donna and we'll all go.

My heart almost sank to my knees as I had an immediate hatred for this car, this ugly black car. I turned to my dad and said "I thought you were going to buy a Pontiac. What is this car?"

It's a Mercedes Benz 180 D model which has a one hundred and eighty cubic inch diesel motor," he replied. It' imported from Germany and it's the only car with a diesel motor on the Gaspe coast.

I asked "What's a diesel motor?"

Dad replied " It runs on diesel fuel or fuel oil like we burn in our cook stove. It doesn't burn gas and it doesn't have spark plugs for ignition. The heat of compression provides ignition instead."

I didn't know what he was talking about. After all I was just a kid. I looked at the car a little closer and noticed that it had these gigantic round headlights and it had a hood ornament like a three prong star enclosed in a circle. It also had a very unusual grill. It had four doors but it had no fins. Its shape was somewhat like some of the cars or the early fifties. I was so disappointed that my dad was buying this car, this Mercedes Benz. I had my heart set on a brand new two-tone Pontiac Strato Chief.

We all piled into the car and the salesman insisted my mom sit up front with my dad and he sat in the back seat with us kids. The first thing I noticed was that it had a standard transmission which was a no-no with me. I considered an automatic transmission a must have in an automobile. I was in complete shock when my dad turned on the ignition and the motor let out this God forsaken roar. How could a fairly small car like this be so loud?

We started on our way and I figured it was less than one hundred miles to New Carlisle which is further down the south coast of the Gaspe Peninsula towards New Brunswick. When we passed Corner Of The Beach and started climbing the mountains to get to Perce I was in for another major disappointment. This car was as slow as a snail. I had doubts that we would get to the top of the mountain in this vehicle. It had absolutely no power, no way near the horsepower of a Pontiac. However we did finally make it to our destination where dad completed the deal. He had traded in the old Austin and I missed it already. The Austin was certainly better than the Mercedes

Benz. The return drive home was completed and I went to bed that night thinking about how my friends were going to tease me about my dad's ugly car.

A few days later I asked my dad why had he bought this Mercedes Benz instead of a Pontiac. I said "If you don't like Pontiac's you could have at least bought a Chevy like uncle Glen's."

Dad replied that "this car costs twice as much as your uncle's Chev. The Mercedes Benz cost three thousand six hundred dollars while a new Chev cost's around eighteen hundred dollars. I couldn't believe this but dad explained that the Mercedes was considered a luxury car and that it was so well built it would last for many, many years. Wow, I thought, he could have bought two Pontiac's for the price of one Mercedes.

In the next few years I came to like this car and was proud of the fact I was being driven around in a Mercedes Benz. I went through grade school, high school and went to college and dad was still driving his Mercedes Benz. He drove it for eleven years and put almost five hundred thousand miles on it. It never let him down. Nothing went wrong with it and it always started on the coldest days in the winter when the neighbour's cars wouldn't. I have come to realize that way back in 1958 dad did most certainly make the right decision.

52. The Mercedes Benz And Trouble At School

The preceding chapter explained that much to my dismay my dad had bought a brand new 1958 Mercedes Benz. In this chapter I will explain how this Mercedes car got me in trouble at school.

It all started when the kids on the school bus asked me about my dad's new car. I told them that it was a diesel and run on oil instead of gas etc. They looked at me and chuckled. I had the distinct impression that they did not believe me.

Arriving at Belle Anse school I got settled in at my desk with my other grade four classmates and wasn't prepared for what happened next. One of the boys told the teacher that I was telling a bunch of lies about my father's new car.

As this happened more than fifty years ago I'm afraid I don't remember my teacher's name but she was young, probably around late-twenties or thirty. She asked me about my dad's new car and I explained to her that it was a 1958 Mercedes Benz 180 D model and it was a diesel car which burned fuel oil instead of gasoline. When I mentioned that it had no spark plugs she stopped me right there and said "Bryan why are you telling your classmates these false things? Everyone knows that all cars have sparkplugs."

I replied, "Yes, all the other cars did but my dad had the first one with no spark plugs on the Gaspe Coast." I was one of her top three students but I could see that she was getting her dander up and that she was aggravated with me. She raised her voice at me and said "Bryan, unless you apologize to your classmates for this nonsense you can go stand in the corner for the rest of the class."

Now, having been made to stand in the corner was the second worse form of punishment those days. The worst was a strapping by the principle but you had to do something really bad like stealing to get the strap. I had never stood in the corner before but I was in the right and would not submit. My teacher was wrong. So I got up from my desk and stood in the corner at the front of the class with my back to the class. I knew I would be ridiculed and teased and get a few punches from the older kids because that's what used to happen in those days. But I was right and I knew I was right.

At recess and lunch hour I was teased and laughed at and it continued on the fourteen mile bus ride home that afternoon.

On Friday evening when my dad got home from work I couldn't wait to tell him what had happened to me at school. I blurted it out and told him about having to stand in the corner as punishment. I expected him to get angry and do something about it.

Dad asked mom for pen and paper and he sat down at the kitchen table. He wrote a letter, placed it into an envelope and sealed it. He handed me the letter and told me to give it to my teacher on Monday morning.

Arriving at my classroom on Monday morning I handed the envelope to my teacher. She sat at her desk and read the letter. The school bell rang and we did the morning activities singing "Oh Canada" and reciting the Lord's Prayer.

She addressed the class and said "Good Morning children, I have a letter here from Mr. Herzil De Vouge who is Bryan's dad and I would like to read it to you." She read the letter and it explained in language we all could understand the workings and operation of the diesel motor. He gave his reasons for buying this car and asked that the teacher read the letter to the class. My dad did not give the teacher heck or ask her to apologize like I wanted but simply taught the teacher and my classmates a lesson. I was vindicated and now everyone knew I was right. I felt a foot taller than I actually was however I also felt because of the standing in the corner that the teacher owed me one.

53. *A New Indoor Bathroom*

The year was 1958 and my grandfather Leslie De Vouge who was a fisherman and farmer decided to end his cod fishing career and continue with some small time farming. He turned sixty-six years of age and was already receiving his old age pension check every month. Grandpa would keep busy by raising some animals and cutting some wood on his woodlot for the woodstove and wood furnace.

My grandfather sold his beautiful fishing boat the "Herzil" named after my dad who had built it. The "Herzil" was only five years old and grandpa got a pretty penny for it and he was suddenly awash with money and wondering what to do with it.

I don't remember grandpa ever asking me for my advice but if he did I had a few suggestions for him, well at least one in particular. Here we were in 1958 and we did not have an indoor washroom. I would estimate that more than fifty percent of the houses in L'Anse-a-Brilliant already had indoor facilities. We were still using the old outhouse which was out behind the house. Also we used the chamber pot in the house at night which I had to carry out to the outhouse in the daytime and dump. It certainly wasn't one of my favorite chores on the farm. But at least I only had to dump my family's pot and not my grandparents as well.

My grandfather decided to put in a new bathroom, washroom or restroom. Whatever you want to call it was fine with me. It was going to be in a former bedroom that my great-grandmother used before she passed away the previous year. It was located on the main floor of the house in my grandparents' end of our large farmhouse.

One day when I got home from school my mother informed me that the new bathroom was in service. I was now ten years old and had been waiting for this day all my life. I wasted no time in going and checking it out. There it was, a new bathroom with the traditional toilet, bathtub and vanity sink with a mirror above it. Because the new bathroom was a former bedroom it was much larger than most and had room for a dresser to store towels, washcloths, soaps, shampoos and bathroom tissue. It was all new so it was gleaming, shining and sparkling clean. There was something unusual about it however and that was its colour. The vast majority of bathrooms that I had seen were white but I had also seen some that were a mild gold colour and a few that were a light green shade. I had never seen a bathroom with a pink toilet, pink bathtub and a pink sink. It was a first for me and I don't remember ever seeing a pink bathroom again. Maybe it was one of a kind or maybe my grandfather got it on sale. I don't know and now over sixty years later I'm wondering why I didn't ask him.

Over the years when people came to our house and used the washroom some of them would ask me why we had a pink toilet. I would reply that I didn't know why it was pink but what I did know was that when I sat on it and then flushed it, it worked. Pink toilets were fine by me.

54. Relatives Visit From The USA

The year was 1958 and we had relatives from the USA visit us at our farm in L'Anse-a-Brilliant. When they got out of their vehicle I saw an older lady who looked very much like my grandmother Ruby. I knew her to be Norma, one of my grandmother's sisters who had moved away to the USA in the early 1900's. My grandmother's brother Curtis Leggo also emerged from the car along with two grandsons; one around my age and the other a year or so older. I had never seen them before and didn't know their names but I knew that they were my second cousins just like the Leggo kids who lived here in L'Anse-a-Brilliant. I remembered that my dad had told me that most of his cousins in the USA worked designing cars for Ford and General Motors in Dearbourne and Pontiac, just outside of Detroit, Michigan. I figured that these guys were rich and they would probably find us country folk in the Gaspe a little backward or behind the times.

I took my two American cousins on a small tour and one of the first things they noticed was our outhouse which was located next to our apple trees.

"Is that your outhouse?" cousin "A" asked me.

Both cousins looked at each other and snickered.

Cousin "B" said, "Our grandfather told us the farms here had outhouses. Oh my God, do we have to go to the bathroom in there?"

"No," I replied, "We have a brand new modern washroom in the house."

"Then why is that old outhouse still there?" asked cousin "A". "You don't need it if you have a washroom in your house."

"It's our spare washroom," I replied.

We continued around the back of our house and I showed them the apple trees, the plum trees and the lilac trees. Further along they noticed my dad's brand new shiny black 1958 Mercedes-Benz.

"Oh my God!" cousin "A" exclaimed, "Who owns the Mercedes?

"That's my dad's new car," I replied. "He just bought it last month. I wanted him to buy a new Pontiac but he wanted a new Mercedes-Benz. My dad says that he could have bought two Pontiac's for what he paid for his Mercedes- Benz. Now he wants to buy a Jeep for moose hunting and for running around on the farm."

"Gee, you guys must be rich," one of the cousins said.

I just smiled at them. I think my American cousins were impressed.

55. The Tramp Ate A Whole Loaf

Summers in the Gaspe Peninsula were almost perfect. "Just right" as many people would describe them. "Not too hot, not too cold, just right."

In the fifties the term "homeless person" had not been invented as of yet. However "tramps" wandered through the Gaspe in the summer looking for a free meal and a barn to sleep in. They weren't local and they came from elsewhere to enjoy the beautiful Gaspe coast in the summer. I guess they were called tramps because they tramped around from place to place and didn't stay in one place. They were penniless, sometimes dirty and were usually dressed in shabby clothes. Some people were afraid of tramps and didn't like to see them coming up the driveway. Most women would not answer the door if they were home alone and the tramp would move on to the next farm.

One beautiful summer afternoon when I was about ten years old my sister Donna and I were playing outside when we saw this man walking down the hill along the highway from the direction of Seal Cove.

The man spotted us playing in front of our house and he started walking up our driveway. I did not recognize him.

"it's a tramp" I said to my sister. "Go tell mom that a tramp's coming."

Donna ran in the house to tell mom. The man approached me and asked me if my mom or dad were home.

I replied "Yes" and my mom stepped outside and said hello to the stranger.

The man looked at my mother and asked "Maam, Do you have something I could eat, some leftovers or something? I haven't had anything to eat all day. Please can you spare something for me?"

Mom said "I don't have any leftovers or anything on the stove right now but I can offer you bread and butter with homemade raspberry jam if you want it."

The tramp replied "Yes, thank you very much."

My mother put the loaf of bread, the butter dish and a jar of homemade jam down on the kitchen table and asked me to pump the gentleman some cold water from our well.

The stranger buttered the slices of bread and covered them with the homemade raspberry jam. He must have been very hungry and he must have liked my mom's homemade jam because much to our astonishment he ate the whole loaf of bread.

When the man finished his meal he got up from the table and he turned to my mother .

"Thank you very much" he said. " May God bless you and your family for inviting me into your home and feeding me. I will pray for you and your family."

The man left, walked down along the highway and we never saw him again.

This past summer, fifty years later I called up my sister Donna in Toronto and informed her that now that I was sixty I was going to write about our childhood growing up on the farm in L'Anse-a-Brilliant . I mentioned the stories I was going to write about and mentioned the tramp that ate a whole loaf of bread.

Donna was only five when the tramp came to our farm and she still has vivid memories of it. She said that she would never forget how scared she was when the tramp came into our house.

Back in the fifties these homeless people we used to call tramps didn't cause our community any problems. They didn't hitchhike but walked along the highway along the Gaspe coast. I think they actually enjoyed the lifestyle. They were free.

56. You Want Trout For Supper? Go Catch them

Living in the Gaspe Peninsula you have so many varieties of seafood available to you to catch or to purchase. If your father or grandfather was a fisherman then it became a major part of your diet. We had cod, halibut, herring, mackerel, salmon, smelt, lobster and other more rare species. Some people also dug clams in the sand bars, and some people salted cod and cured them in the sun.

Our small community of L'Anse-a-Brilliant (also known as Brilliant Cove in English) was a mile in length and consisted of two long hills with a river dividing them in two. The river was only about thirty to forty feet wide and not very deep. Its banks were wooded on both sides except on one corner of our property where the cattle could walk down to the river to drink. The river originated in the interior of the Gaspe Peninsula and emptied into the Atlantic Ocean at our harbour.

Now what I loved about the L'Anse-a-Brilliant River was that it was full of brook trout or speckled trout as some people called them. These trout were kind of small and most of the ones I caught were only four to six inches in length. Sometimes if you were lucky you might catch a seven or eight incher. Trout was the only fresh water fish available to me.

When I was very young I usually went trout fishing with friends but when I was around eleven I started trout fishing by myself. The reason for this is I didn't want the river fished out of trout. The vast majority of people didn't fish the river for trout because it was very time consuming to catch only a small number of small fish. The only adult I remember who fished the river was my aunt Dot who came out from Murdochville on the weekends in the summer and enjoyed fishing for trout. In fact I think she was better at catching trout than I was.

One summer day my mother asked my sister and me what we wanted for supper.

"Trout" I said.

"You want trout for supper, then go catch them" she replied.

"I'll be back in an hour with trout " I replied as I ran out the door with my fishing rod.

First, I had to get bait so I grabbed a shovel and went out behind the house to our apple trees. That was the best place to dig up worms. Ten minutes later I was putting a worm on my hook at my favorite fishing hole which was located on our property. This fishing hole was the best and my favorite for catching trout when I was in a hurry. It was partially surrounded by dense trees and was well shaded. It was a mini cove with a five foot long sandy beach where you could stand and drop your line. The water was still here and a few feet deep making it a small pool. There were always trout here because it was a favorite spot for them. This fishing hole was never fished out because as soon as I caught several trout here others were ready to move in and take their place.

I was back home within the hour with five trout and I presented them to my mom to clean and cook. She used scissors to cut their heads off and to split them up the middle to clean them. She rinsed them under the cold water tap and patted them dry. She dipped them in egg and flour and into the frying pan they went. When they were cooked she put them on two plates and placed them in front of Donna and me.

I said "Mom, you can have some too."

Mom replied "No they're for you and your sister" and then "Well maybe, just a little taste" and she would have a bite.

Of course, I got more than Donna as I was five years older than her and she didn't eat much. I loved these trout and I especially liked the crisp tail. Some people wouldn't eat trout tails so I would ask for their trout tails and eat them as well.

I fished the river on a regular basis until I moved to the town of Murdochville in 1962.

Maybe twenty-five years later when I was visiting Gaspe I went to check my favorite fishing hole and it was gone. Mother Nature has a way of changing things and storms, floods, and erosion had taken it away.

But I still remember the pleasure of catching my own trout in the L'Anse-a-Brilliant River and in sixty years I have never tasted more delicious fish.

57. One Raisin In A Loaf Of Raisin Bread

My Grandmother did her baking on Thursdays and sometimes if she had any raisins she would bake a loaf of raisin bread for my grandfather.

Sometimes when we had finished doing some chores he would turn to me and say "Bryan let's go in the house and have some raisin bread."

I would follow him into the house and get the butter dish out while he got the bread knife out. In those days in the fifties you had to slice your own raisin bread, even the store bought kind. Grandpa would slice a few thick slices and place them on the table. I would pump us some cold water and we would each butter our raisin bread and sit down and enjoy it. Mmmmm, it was good. This was repeated many many times during my childhood.

One day after doing farm chores my grandfather informed me that he was going over to Basil's store to get some raisin bread as we were fresh out.

I went into the house and told my grandmother that grandpa had drove to Basil's to get some raisin bread and he would be right back.

Grandpa returned shortly thereafter and after slicing three or four slices turned to nanny and said "There's no raisins in this bread."

Nanny replied " Maybe you didn't buy raisin bread."

" It says raisin bread right here on the label" grandpa replied with a puzzled look on his face. It looks the colour and it smells like raisin bread." He buttered a piece and tasted it.

"It tastes like raisin bread."

Grandpa then kept slicing the raisin bread looking for those elusive raisins. Finally when he was down to the last slice he found a raisin. One raisin in a loaf of raisin bread.

My grandmother told him that maybe he should take it back to exchange it for another loaf.

My grandfather said "No" since it was already all sliced up and although there were no raisins in it still tasted good.

Grandpa turned to me and said "I think the next guy who buys a loaf will probably get too many raisins."

Nowadays more than fifty years later the raisin bread I buy at the store is always sliced and it always has lots of raisins in it. But I still check.

58. Arnold Johnson ---
A Math Genius

Wherever you live in any day or age you will encounter adults male or female who will ignore you or not acknowledge your presence simply because you are a child and therefore not worthy of their attention. Some adults believe that children should be seen and not heard. As a child in the Gaspe I would say "Hi" to an adult I knew when I encountered he or she walking on the road or down at the harbour. Most of them would say hello and move on. Some of them would not reply and would completely ignore me.

Arnold Johnson however was a local man who was friendly with all the children in L'Anse-a-Brilliant. When he saw us he would greet us and ask us how we were doing. Unlike most adults he seemed to be very interested in what we had to say. He always treated us with respect and he treated us like we were his equals. It was always a pleasant experience when I met up with and talked to Arnold. This trait must have run in his family because his sister Lorraine Leggo, the mother of my three friends Lance, Denver and Zane was the same way with children, friendly and attentive.

In the early fifties Arnold had married Audrey Leggo who was my father's cousin and he built a small house on property next door to Henry Snowman's store. They raised their three children Mona, Wade and Trudy there.

Arnold had a water hose that brought cool spring water from up in Raymond Leggo's field down and through a culvert under the highway to the edge of his property. The hose was always running and everyone was welcome to come and get a drink of the best drinking water in L'Anse-a-Brilliant. One day on my way to visit the Leggo brothers I stopped to get a drink and Arnold came out of his house to greet me.

"How are you today Bryan?" he asked.

"I'm fine" I replied. "How are you?"

"Miserable" he replied. "Just miserable. I don't feel good at all."

"Sorry to hear that Arnold" I said.

We chatted for a while and then I was off to see Lance, Denver and Zane. When I saw Lance outside his dad's store I mentioned that Arnold wasn't feeling good today.

"Did he say that he was feeling miserable, just miserable? " Lance asked. "That's the same thing he told me yesterday. He always says that."

Arnold was being honest. I know that sometimes when I feel poorly and someone asks me how I am I usually lie and say that I feel fine. I guess that most people don't feel like explaining how bad they feel so they just say "I'm fine."

When Basil Leggo had to go away on business Arnold Johnson took over the running of the store on a temporary basis. I explained in another chapter how Basil didn't have an adding machine in the early and mid-fifties and he did his addition by hand. Basil was always right the first time but did the addition a second time just to make sure.

The first time I saw Arnold add a column of seven or eight numbers I couldn't believe that he got his addition right. He didn't do it a second time. I didn't think that it was possible to add as fast as he did. Of course when I checked his addition later it was correct. It was well known that I was good with numbers and fast with my addition at school but Arnold was much faster than me. He was obviously a math genius and I told him so. He didn't think anything of it and I guess his ability came natural to him.

In 1966 I moved away from the Gaspe first to Montreal to attend college and then to St. Catharines and Sudbury, Ontario to work. I did return to L'Anse-a-Brilliant in 1973, 1975, 1977 and 1984 on vacation. Each time I visited with Arnold Johnson to see him and his family and to get a good drink of water from his hose. Each time he was genuinely happy to see me and in 1984 when I told him that I now had three children of my own he was happy about that. When I asked him how he was somehow I knew what his answer was going to be.

"Miserable, just miserable" was his reply.

That was the last time that I saw Arnold Johnson. I didn't return to L'Anse-a-Brilliant because my parents had retired in Ontario and moved to Nova Scotia where I visited them every year or two. By the time I made it back to L'Anse-a-Brilliant in the 1990's Arnold had passed away. The place was not the same without him being there.

You will meet many good people in your lifetime. You may have several good friends but you may meet only a few people that you truly admire. Arnold Johnson was one of those. The world would truly be a better place if there were more people like him in it.

59. Nanny's Famous Aprons

My grandparents were always busy on the farm but when they retired from farming things started to settle down a bit. For example instead of milking a cow and then pasteurizing the milk now milk was purchased from the milkman. My grandfather still kept busy at times especially in the summer when he cut, hauled, split and piled firewood for the wood furnace.

My grandmother Ruby De Vouge who I called Nanny found herself with a lot of spare time on her hands. Being a religious lady she read the bible every day and she also wrote letters to her brothers and sisters some who lived in the USA. She also did knitting but how many pairs of wool socks do you need to knit for your husband, sons and grandchildren? She needed something else to do so she started thinking about a hobby.

In the 1950's if you visited a farmhouse in the afternoon chances are you would see the lady of the house attired in a plain house dress and also sporting an apron. Every lady owned several of them and they were basically plain and simple.

Nanny got out her old Singer sewing machine and started making aprons. The old Singer was not a modern electric sewing machine but was a very old model that was foot operated. Nanny sure gave her feet some exercise pumping the pedal. Sometimes when she was getting started Nanny would say "Bryan , come here and thread the needle for me. I'm having trouble seeing the hole with these old eyes."

Over fifty years later I know what she meant because I don't think it would be easy for me to see the hole in the needle these days.

Nanny started out making plain white aprons but then she added frills to them and added a pocket which was a useful addition to any apron. She also took a square white apron and rounded the corners which made the apron appear circular. Nanny distributed some of these aprons to my mother and to my four aunts who all loved them. Nanny didn't want to make the same style apron over and over again so she came up with new designs. She ordered very bright and colourful material from the Sears and Eaton's catalogues, some of which were solid colours and some of which were patterned. Nanny started making aprons using vertical stripes of contrasting colours and patterns. She used so many colours and patterns that no two aprons were the same. Sometimes my grandmother let me pick the contrasting colours and patterns.

My mother thought that Nanny's aprons were so beautifully designed that people would love them so mom bought several of them to give as gifts. Of course the ladies who received them as gifts loved them and wanted to buy more for themselves and to also give as gifts.

Nanny made many aprons of different colours and designs and as more people became familiar with them everyone wanted a Ruby De Vouge made apron. As fast as my grandmother could make them they were sold. Nanny started taking orders for them especially before Christmas. What started out as a hobby to pass the time ended up being a part time job so to speak.

One day I was visiting my grandmother and she was getting ready to make a few aprons. "Bryan" she said. "I have to come up with a new design, something different."

"Today I was studying triangles at school and you could make a triangular apron" I chuckled and said. "No, that would look stupid, wouldn't it?"

Nanny looked at me and said "You know I could make small triangles out of all the remnants I have and put four or five triangles on the bottom of the aprons. That was what she did and they quickly became the favorite Ruby De Vouge designed aprons.

I remember one day when my family visited one of our friends and the lady brought out one of my grandmother's aprons that she had received as a gift to show us. It was one of the aprons with the triangles on the bottom and it was all folded up neatly. Obviously it had not been used.

"You don't use it," mom asked?

"Oh no, it's much too nice an apron to wear when cooking or baking" the lady said. "Maybe I'll use it on a special occasion or put it on to have my picture taken. But I'm not going to put it on to make pies or anything. It's too nice to get it dirty."

I piped up and said "I helped my grandmother design that apron and pick the colours."

"Good for you" she said "You both did a terrific job."

Over the past fifty years I'd almost forgotten about Nanny's famous aprons. I did not have any of them and only saw one when I visited my mother in St Catharines, Ontario and later in Nova Scotia. I surmise that the wearing of aprons has gone out of style in this modern age when a lot of cooking and baking is not done from scratch but simply food bought at the supermarket and placed in the oven or microwave.

In the summer of 2007 when my mother passed away in Liverpool, Nova Scotia my sister Donna and I went down to Nova Scotia for our mother's funeral. We had to settle her affairs and administer her estate. Because we were unable to transport much of our mother's belongings back to Ontario my mother had requested that we donate everything that we could not use to charity. I took about eight truckloads of donations to the Liverpool Salvation Army Thrift Store as my mother had requested. One day I was loading several bags of light stuff into my truck when one of the bags ripped open and several of the beautiful aprons that I had helped my grandmother make fell out. I kept five of them and donated the rest. I will give then to my daughter-in laws at the appropriate time and keep one for myself. I am overjoyed that I now own a "Ruby De Vouge" apron.

60. *Nanny (Ruby De Vouge)*

My grandmother Ruby Dell De Vouge who I called Nanny was born in L'Anse-a-Brilliant in 1895. She married my grandfather Leslie De Vouge and they spent the rest of their lives on the farm raising five children.

I spent a lot of time with her doing many diverse things such as picking raspberries to make wild raspberry jam and helping her design her famous homemade aprons.

Nanny was a religious lady but did not attend any church in our community. She was a follower of Pastor Charles Taze Russell who was a Christian Restorationist Minister from Pittsburgh, Pennsylvania. He was prominent in the late 1800's and early 1900's as the founder of the Bible Student Movement.

Nanny was a bible student and follower of Pastor Russell. She studied her bible every day and corresponded with her like minded brothers and sisters as she called them all over Canada and the USA. As a bible scholar she also welcomed the local Anglican minister into her home for a bible study. He had great respect for her knowledge of the bible and her religious writings which were read by her fellow bible students.

Although I am not an overly religious person and I do not attend church on a regular basis I believe that Nanny had a profound positive effect in the makeup of my character.

As a child Nanny always gave me children's religious books as Christmas presents. I think that I may have preferred to receive a toy but being a book lover I gratefully accepted them and read them cover to cover. I had to because Nanny would eventually ask me religious questions about them and she expected me to know the right answers. I made sure that I did.

When my grandfather passed away during a Christmas visit to Truro, Nova Scotia in 1967 Nanny returned to Montreal alone and spent the rest of the winter with my aunt Leona. In the spring she wanted to return to the farm in L'Anse-a-Brilliant. I think that my aunt Leona, my dad and my uncles would have preferred that she stay with aunt Leona in Montreal because she would be all alone on the farm, but she wanted to go back to her home and that was what she did.

Unfortunately one day in that summer of 1968 Nanny was walking across the local highway to collect her mail at the mailbox on the other side and was hit by a car and she was killed instantly. She is buried in the L'Anse-a-Brilliant Anglican cemetery. She will never be forgotten.

61. *Fishing Lobster & Lobster Feasts*

My grandfather Leslie was a fisherman/farmer for most of his life. He owned his own fifty-two footer and fished mainly for cod. He and his crew would be out on the water for three or four days at a time before coming into harbour with a load of cod fish. He was in his mid-sixties and wanted to be home at the farm. When he retired he sold his fishing boat the "Herzil".

Grandpa decided to fish for lobster as it would take only a few hours per day to pull and reset his lobster traps. You only needed a small boat for this as the traps were set fairly close to shore in water that was about thirty to fifty feet deep. He used the flat (a smaller wooden boat) that my father and uncle Glen owned which was driven by a seven and one-half horsepower motor.

Lobster season was a short one and in our area I believe that it only lasted from six to eight weeks. It started in the spring and ended during the summer. My grandfather could do it by himself but I helped him on the weekends and when school was finished I accompanied him some days Monday to Saturday. He did not check his traps on Sunday.

In those days the lobster traps were all homemade of wood slats and twine. They were baited with herring which were fresh or ones that were preserved in brine.

Since there were several lobster fishermen based in L'Anse-A-Brilliant and most set their traps in the same area the buoys which floated on the surface and indicated where the traps were on the bottom had to be of different colours to indicate whose trap it was. The buoys were homemade of wood and were usually brightly painted in two colours. For example fisherman A had white and yellow buoys , fisherman B had white and green buoys and fisherman C had red and black buoys etc.

In the mornings when we went to check the lobster traps I would be in the bow of the boat while my grandfather ran the outboard motor in the stern. The first buoy was located about one-quarter mile from the harbour wharf and when I spotted it I would yell back to my grandfather.

"First buoy one hundred feet ahead on the port side (left side).

Grandpa would slow the boat down and shut the motor off when we approached the buoy. I would snag the buoy rope with a gaffe (a long stick with a hook on the end) and we would haul the lobster trap into the boat.

There were usually two or three lobsters in the trap along with seven or eight crabs. There wasn't any market for these small crabs so they were just thrown back into the water. Everyone hated these crabs and some fishermen bashed them against the side of the boat before throwing them back in. The lobsters were placed in a wash tub and we placed new bait fish in the trap and dumped it back over the side. We continued on to the next buoy which was usually between one and two hundred feet away. We repeated this procedure for all of the twenty-five or so lobster traps. On a good day we would end up with about fifty lobsters which would partially fill two wash tubs.

When we got back to the harbour and tied up at the wharf the lobsters would be weighed by the buyer and shipped to market. My grandfather was paid thirty-five cents per pound so on a very good day he would make up to twenty dollars. In the late 1950's that was a lot of money.

My much appreciated reward for helping my grandfather came on Saturday when the lobster catch was not sold but was cooked up for the whole De Vouge family.

My aunts, uncles and cousins drove eighty miles out from the mine (Murdochville) to visit and there would be around twenty or more of us present.

Nanny, my mom and aunts Edna, Dot and Ina would have several pots on the stove and they would cook up all of the fifty or so lobsters. The end result would become what I called a "Lobster Feast" where everyone ate as much lobster as their heart desired or I should say "as their stomach desired."

Of my eleven cousins only three were older than me and eight of them were younger. Some of my very young cousins didn't eat much lobster and usually there would be quite a bit left over. Now, I would have liked to repeat the all you can eat endless lobster feast the next day however my grandfather had other ideas. You see, he had this canning machine and he would can the leftover lobster.

The canning machine was a manual one with a crank. After the tin cans were scalded in boiling water and filled with lobster meat they were placed on the canning machine. A lid was placed on top of the can and the crank was turned. This crimped the lid unto the can thereby sealing it.

At the end of the lobster season grandpa would keep some for himself and split the remainder of the canned lobster between his four sons. Therefore we had lobster to eat all through the winter if mom opened one can every two weeks or so. The cans were fairly large and one can could feed our family of four.

I must admit that I didn't like the canned lobster as well as fresh just cooked lobster. It simply just didn't taste as good. I would have preferred to have two lobster feasts per week in the summer and none canned for the winter. However I was grateful for any lobster my mom put on a plate in front of me in summer or in winter.

62. Bilingual Curser

Throughout your life you will hear some people swear or curse and you will meet people who will never utter a cuss word of any sort. You cannot identify a curser by looking at him or her and saying "that person looks like a curser". Some people will curse or swear on a daily basis while others curse only when they are angry with someone or if a hammer falls on their foot. There are cursers who are profane and take the Lord's name in vain and then there are cursers who are vulgar and utter a string of nasty vulgarities.

I spent the first nineteen years of my life in Quebec and then my adulthood in Ontario. I have found that there is a big difference between the two provinces in the way they curse. In Quebec cursing or swearing is almost always religious in nature while in Ontario it's mostly vulgar.

I am not a swearer but I do admit that I have done so on some rare occasions when the need arose. Perhaps the fact that I do not curse as a rule is because of my upbringing. In all the time I spent with my grandfather on the farm I never did hear him swear. My father was also not a swearer however I did hear him utter the word "tabernac" a few times, once when he hit his thumb with a hammer and again when he cut his finger while sawing with a hacksaw. This is a very mild cussword and it's in French. It's comparable to saying "damnit" in English.

The vast majority of the people living in my community of L'Anse-a-Briliant were English speaking and the ones that swore did so most often in French instead of in English. Somehow I guess they felt it was ok to swear in a different language than their own.

Cecil De Vouge was L'Anse-a-Brilliant's champion curser. Cecil owned the farm two farms over and he was a distant relative of ours. He was one of those fellows who only cursed when he was angry and he was a bilingual curser. Cecil swore in both official languages, English and French.

When chain saws came out in the fifties it made cutting firewood for the winter much easier than the old Swede saw. However to have them work to perfection you had to do proper maintenance on them. My grandfather had a Teco chainsaw and he knew how to maintain it very well. Cecil, however always had trouble with his chainsaw as he was not very good at maintaining it.

One day I went over to Cecil's to visit his son Reid and I noticed Cecil was behind his house attempting to start his chainsaw. He was pulling on the pull cord over and over again and his chainsaw would not start. He put the chainsaw down and I could see that he was angry as he was getting very red in the face. He raised his voice and let out a string of curses in French that almost lasted a half minute. He took a break to catch his breath and he attempted to start his chainsaw once again. Of course once again it would not start so Cecil put the chainsaw down and uttered a string of curses but this time in English.

I said "Your chainsaw won't start. What's wrong with it?"

"I flooded it, eh" was his sort of out of breath reply.

"Maybe you need to change the spark plug" I advised.

Cecil just looked at me.

Cecil De Vouge was obviously a horse lover because when all of the other farmers had got rid of their farm horses in favor of farm tractors he kept using a horse on his farm. Over the years I remember he had traded his horse in two or three times because they didn't work out for him.

I've always have loved horses and I considered them to be the most beautiful animal on the farm. At that time we didn't have a horse on our farm so I would often go over to Cecil's to visit his horse and I would sometimes feed it a treat of a carrot that I had pulled from our garden or an apple from our apple tree. The horses that he bought were always really beautiful horses but he was never satisfied with their work habits. Maybe an ugly horse would have worked out better for him.

Cecil would swear at his horse and when asked what was wrong he would say that the #*&%$&^% horse was balky and that it would not work. So he would trade it in for a new horse.

One day after observing Cecil swearing at his chainsaw I went over to Basil's store where a few of the local men were sitting down on the pop cases drinking Coke's, Pepsi's and 7 Up's.

I told Lance Leggo that I had just come from Cecil's and that he was swearing a blue streak. One of the men looked over and asked.

"Hey Bryan, Is Cecil cursing at his horse again?"

"No" I replied. "His chainsaw won't start."

"So he's cursing a blue streak, eh" he said.

"In English and in French" I replied.

"Cecil is a bilingual curser" he said as everyone had a chuckle.

63. *The Hottons*

In the 1950's when my father, mother, sister and I went on a Sunday drive to visit friends it was most always the Hottons who lived at Mal Baie close to where I went to school in Belle Anse. We would visit them about once every two or three weeks. Mr. Percy Hotton was one of my father's best friends and a cousin as well. Percy's wife Camelia used to live close to our farm in L'Anse-a-Brilliant before she married Percy and moved to Mal Baie. They had two children, a very pretty girl named Beverly who was about five years older than me and Percy Jr. who was three years older than me.

It was more than friendship that drew us to visit the Hottons every few weeks. In the 1950's men and boys liked to be well trimmed and Mr. Hotton was our barber. I remember that dad would step up to the chair first and later I would follow him. Mr. Hotton used the old manual hand clippers which made for a slower hair cut than the newer electric clippers that professional barbers used, but they got the job done and Mr. Hotton always said the same things to me while he was cutting my hair.

"Bryan, you have nice black hair. It's very fine and easy to cut."

After he finished cutting my hair he would say "Bryan you look so handsome all the girls at Belle Anse School are going to be after you tomorrow."

Percy Hotton was a cod fisherman and he owned a nice white fishing boat which was named "Beverly" after his daughter. He fished with his brother Tommy Hotton, a bachelor who lived with Percy and his family. As well as his sideline of barbering Percy had another unique talent. He used to build these beautiful model boats and I'm not talking about those plastic boats that come in a box that you simply assemble and paint. Percy would find a suitable piece of wood and with his carving tools and sandpaper produce a beautiful model of the fishing boats that plied the Gaspe coast. He would outfit them with masts, sails and all the rigging required to make them identical to the real thing. Percy made them of different sizes and I remember a few of them that were about two feet long and magnificent. In fact I considered them to be masterpieces.

I must confess that the number one reason that I wanted to visit the Hottons so often was because of Camelia's baking. The layer cakes that she baked were without doubt the best that I've ever eaten in my life. Her cakes were not made from a cake mix taken out of a box. They were made from scratch the old fashioned way that her mother had taught her. She also made her own icing sugar and when applied to her cakes the combination made her cakes almost to beautiful to eat. However I did eat and savor Camelia's cakes many times over the years. I don't know how often she baked her cakes but every time we visited on Sunday's over the years she always offered us tea and cake after our haircuts were completed. Camelia knew how much I loved her cake and always offered me a second piece after I gobbled down the first generous serving. Of course I always accepted and thanked her.

To go with the cake Percy and Camelia made tea and I also loved the tea they served. I don't remember which brand they used but I suspect it may have been Red Rose as it was most people's favorite brand back in those days. The Hottons did not use tea bags but measured loose tea in the teapot to steep. I used to emulate Mr. Hotton because he didn't wait for the tea to cool before he started to savor it. He poured some of the hot tea from his cup into his saucer and then blew on it to cool it a bit before drinking it right from the saucer. Most of the others waited for their tea to cool a bit but I drank and enjoyed the hot tea from my saucer just like Percy did. Sundays at the Hottons drinking tea and eating the world's best cake is one of the most pleasant memories of my childhood.

Percy Jr., the son was a good friend of mine. Like his father he loved boats and used to carve some small ones himself. I especially remember the time one winter when he hitched up a sleigh to his big dog Roxie and we went on a long sleigh ride on his property in the field behind his house and up into the woods. It was very easy for Roxie to pull us around on the sleigh and I could not believe a dog could be so strong. Actually Roxie was strong enough to haul firewood from the woods back to the house in the winter. Roxie was a large but gentle and friendly dog of mixed breed. She was very smart and the Hottons had trained her to do certain things. Roxie would shake a paw with me when I asked her. Percy Jr. could place a piece of bread or cookie on Roxie's nose and she would balance it there without moving patiently waiting until Percy Jr. said "ok." Then Roxie would flip the bread or cookie up into the air and catch it in her mouth and of course eat it. What was amazing was how patient she was in waiting until she was given the ok to flip it into the air. She was truly an amazing dog.

The last time I saw the Hottons was in 1961 before I moved to Murdochville and they moved away to Montreal. The few times I drove by their house in Mal Baie the times I went back there on vacation there were no vehicles in the driveway and nobody home. Over the years I asked my mother in Nova Scotia about the Hottons and she told me that Mr. Percy and Mr. Tommy Hotton had passed away. About ten years ago she told me she had heard that Camelia had passed away as well.

In August of 2008 I took my oldest son Zac on his first ever visit to Gaspe to show him where I had grown up. One day we visited Lloyd De Vouge, a distant cousin who informed me that Percy Jr. had retired and was spending his summers at Mal Baie. We drove to Percy's and he came out to greet us not knowing who we were. After forty-seven years we didn't recognize each other but when I introduced myself and my son he invited us into his house where we met his wife Leona. A few moments later an elderly lady slowly walked into the room with the aid of a walker.

Percy said "Bryan, do you remember this lady?"

I was shocked momentarily as I recognized Camelia but my mother had told me that she had passed away ten years before. I was speechless and then I said "no" as I thought it might be Percy's aunt.

"It's my mom Camelia" Percy said. "Mom this is Bryan De Vouge and his son Zac. Do you remember Bryan?

"Yes" she said. "I remember Bryan"

"And I remember the most delicious cake you used to serve me when I was a child" I said. "It's good to see you. How are you?"

"I had a stroke a few years ago" she said.

"But you're still alive" I thought. "Thank God."

On this occasion Percy's wife Leona served me a toasted bacon and tomato sandwich. Just as I could have predicted it was simply delicious.

64. Conservative Or Liberal

Are you Conservative or Liberal? One day at school that question was asked of me and honestly I did not know the answer. It was 1957 and a federal election had been called in Canada. I was only nine years old and didn't know much about politics so I asked my mother about it.

My mom said "There's six teams in the NHL. Are the Montreal Canadiens your favorite team or are the Boston Bruins your favorite team?"

"The Boston Bruins" was my reply.

"Well politics is like that" my mom said. "There are four or five parties and each one of them want to win the election. Each party has a team of people that want to run the government of Canada."

"What are we, Conservative or Liberal?" I asked.

"Go ask your father" she replied.

"When my father got home from work for the weekend I asked him "Dad, are we Conservative or Liberal?"

"Neither " was his reply.

"Well whom do you vote for?" I asked.

"The third party" was his response.

I didn't know who the third party was but I was determined to find out.

The next day after school my mother sent me to Basil Leggo's store for something and there was quite a few men there standing around or sitting down on the pop cases. The topic of conversation was the upcoming election and as I listened to what the men were saying I learned a lot about politics. I found out that almost all of L'Anse-a-Brilliant was voting for the Conservatives. The lone exception was Cecil De Vouge, a distant relative of mine who was a committed Liberal. I found out that he stood close to the pork barrel whatever that meant. It appeared that because the Liberals were in power Cecil was the only L'Anse-a-Brilliant man hired to work on the government dredge that came in the summer to dredge out our harbour. This plum summertime job was only available to you if you were a Liberal. All the men sitting there that day were Conservative and would not be hired. This made them a little hot under the collar getting their blood pressure up and forced them to utter a few cuss words. So there was a little tension in the air and a little ill will towards Cecil De Vouge.

When I got home I sought out my grandfather and asked "Grandpa, are you voting Conservative or Liberal in the election?"

"Conservative" was his strong reply. "The Liberals have been in there too long and it's time for a change. They're not paying enough in the old age pension and if the Conservatives get in they are going to give the pensioners more money. When he retires how's a man supposed to live on what they're paying now?"

I knew that my grandfather was sixty-five and was about to retire from being a fisherman so increased money in his pension was important to him.

By reading the newspaper I learned that The Liberals had been in power for a very long time indeed, twenty-two consecutive years in fact starting in 1935. Our existing Liberal Prime Minister was Louis St Laurent and the new Progressive Conservative leader was John Diefenbaker who was from Saskatchewan. He was described as an underdog which meant that people didn't expect him to win.

One day I heard a loudspeaker outside and ran outside on our gallery to listen. I saw a car with two loudspeakers attached to its roof driving slowly down the highway and when the man spoke into his microphone all of L'Anse-a-Brilliant heard his message. "Come one, Come all to the Hallimand Hall. Liberal party rally tonight at seven o'clock" and the message was repeated several times.

"I don't think any of us will be going" I yelled at the car. "We're all Conservatives here."

A few days later the car returned and this time the message emitted from the loudspeakers was "Come one, come all to a Liberal Party Rally at Cecil De Vouge's in L'Anse-a-Brilliant at seven o'clock."

"That's not going to go over well" I thought. "All the Conservatives in L'Anse-a-Brilliant are not going to like this at all."

When seven o'clock rolled around I looked over towards Cecil's farm and counted only four cars parked there so I concluded that not many Liberals were attending the rally which was fine by me.

At about this time I found out that like hockey teams political parties had different colours attributed to them. The Conservatives had the colour blue which I absolutely loved and the Liberals had the colour red which I absolutely hated. I was happy that the Conservatives had chosen blue as their colour because most of my clothing was blue and I was right in sync with my favorite political party. Election Day came and when the results were announced over the radio we learned that the Liberals had been booted out of office and the Progressive Conservatives had won the election and would take over governance of Canada. Most people were very happy at this good news but then they found out that it wasn't a big victory after all. The Progressive Conservatives had won only one hundred and twelve seats in the House of Commons while the Liberals had won one hundred and five. There were also twenty-five CCF party members along with nineteen Social Credit and four Independents. This was a minority government situation and I read in the paper that this was not a desirable situation for the ruling Conservatives as they could not accomplish all the things that they wanted to change under those conditions.

At this time the Liberals decided to change their leader and Lester Pearson, a Liberal Member of Parliament from Ontario was chosen as the new leader of the opposition.

The Prime Minister John Diefenbaker called another election to be held on March 31, 1958 as he was fed up with his inability to govern with a minority government. He wanted Canadians to elect a majority government so that he could accomplish what he had set out to do in the first place.

So the whole election process started all over again so soon after the last election. The campaigning and the rallies and everyone talking politics once again made this forthcoming election a very important one. I listened to the radio and one day I heard our new Prime Minister John Diefenbaker speaking in French this time. He said in a heavy accent "Mes cher amis, je suis ici ce soir pour vous addressez sur la situation de Quebec et sur la situation du Canada."

I knew that he had learned French so that the French speaking people would vote for him. After all he was not only representing English speaking Canada but all of Canada and the French speaking Canadians would like him for speaking their language.

I found the way he spoke French funny however and I would recite his speech in French imitating him. This always got a chuckle out of my friends at school and on the school bus. It's funny but I performed that speech so many times back in 1958 that I still remember it now fifty-one years later.

All the people in L'Anse-a-Brilliant except for Cecil De Vouge were overjoyed when the election results of 1958 were announced. John Diefenbaker and his Progressive Conservative party won the largest majority in Canadian history up to that point. They had two hundred and eight seats in the House of Commons while the other political parties only won fifty-seven seats between them. John Diefenbaker had won the majority government that he had wanted so badly.

Eighty percent of Canadians eligible to vote did so resulting in the largest voter turnout in Canadian history.

I was happy that my blue team had won and my grandfather was happy that he was getting a good increase in his old age pension. I still don't know how my mother and father voted in that 1958 election. They never told me.

65. I'm a Good Runner,
Nanny Says Slow Down

By the time I turned ten years old in 1958 I had become a runner. Everywhere I went I almost never walked. When my mother sent me to Basil's or Henry's store for a loaf of bread I ran there, bought the bread and ran the half-mile back home again. When I went to play with my friends I ran to their house and when I wanted to go to the beach to go swimming I ran there as well. It was like I had discovered a new talent, something that I was good at so naturally I wanted to become a better runner. Just a few years earlier I had been sickly and found it hard to keep up with the other children but now I was healthy and discovered that I could run faster and further than most of the kids my own age. I truly enjoyed running and I didn't seem to get tired at all.

For the next few years that I attended Belle Anse Consolidated School I competed in the track and field competition at my school and always did well in the running events. I would always make it on the roster to represent my school in the regional track meet that took place up in Gaspe and if I didn't win I usually placed second or third.

Now looking back over fifty years later The only thing I regret about those track meets is that the top three runners in any event were presented with these small ribbons to wear and not medals that you can hang around your neck like the school kids are presented with in this modern day and age. However the good feeling of winning, placing or just competing was still there.

In 1960 I was picked to represent Belle Anse School in the regional track meet up at Gaspe and I decided to start training really hard because I was going to be competing against at least two terrific runners from the Gaspe school. Stan Vibert and Ricky Shannon were exceptionally fast runners and I did not think that I could beat them in any of the races I was entering. However if I trained really hard I thought that I could be a close third behind them and win a ribbon for my school. Our old farmhouse was a rather long rectangular duplex with my grandparents living in one end and my family and I lived in the other end. I remember one day after school when I started running around and around the house to train. It didn't take me very long to run around the house on the path that encircled the house and when I passed by my grandmother's back window I noticed that she was in her rocking chair rocking away and looking out the window at me as I ran by. I don't know how many times I ran around the house that day but after Nanny observed me for about a half-hour she came out on her gallery and said "Good Gracious Bryan, Why are you running around and around the house? You're making me tired just watching you."

"I'm doing my homework" I replied.

"What homework" she said. "Whatever happened to reading, writing and arithmetic?"

"I'm training for the track meet up in Gaspe."

"Well come on in the house for awhile Bryan. You've been running around the house for more than a half-hour for goodness sake."

"But I'm not tired yet Nanny" I replied.

"You have a lot of wind in your lungs Bryan" she said. "I wish I had your wind."

The next day when I got home from school I started running around and around the house once again as my grandmother sat there in her rocking chair watching me through her window. As for the track meet that year I do not remember the result but I probably came in third place.

These days I don't run. I don't think that I could jog very far either. I can only remember how good a runner I once was. I can only wish that I could run as fast and as far as I did when I was a child.

66. Not A Fish Story

One summer day when I guess I was around ten years old I went fishing for cod with my father and my Uncle Cyril who had come out from Murdochville to visit us on the farm.

We were using my dad's eighteen foot boat which was used solely for inshore fishing on Gaspe Bay. Dad had his favorite spots for jigging cod and we went to the closest one about one quarter mile off shore from L'Anse-a-Brilliant harbour.

The water here was about two hundred feet deep. I know because our fishing lines were three hundred feet long and two-thirds of it was let out before the jiggers hit bottom. Then we pulled our jiggers up so that they would be three feet above the bottom and started jigging for cod. Cod are bottom feeders and would be attracted to the shiny stainless steel sinker and red plastic skirt over the treble hooks. In the late 1950's there were a lot of cod in Gaspe Bay and usually it took you only a minute to catch your first one. However after fishing about ten minutes or so we still had not caught any cod. As a rule salt water fishermen are not very patient fishermen and my dad announced that we should pull in our jiggers and move to another location further down the bay.

My dad drove the boat about a mile and we decided to fish off of Bois Brule. Once again we fished here for about ten minutes without even getting a nibble. This was highly unusual that we had fished for twenty minutes and we had no cod to show for it. I could see that my father was getting more aggravated by the minute and again he announced that we should move once again further down the bay to a spot level with the St. George church.

When we started to pull in our fishing lines I could not pull up my line. I thought that it might be snagged onto something on the bottom. My father noticed this and I figured that he wasn't going to be very pleased about it.

"What have you done now?" he asked. "You got your line hung up on the bottom."

Meanwhile my uncle Cyril was looking down at the spot where my line was coming out of the water and he said to my dad, "Herzil, I don't think he's hung up. His line is moving a bit. I think he hooked a big cod or maybe a halibut."

I was not strong enough to pull in this big fish that I had hooked, whatever it was so my uncle Cyril helped me. Dad and uncle Cyril were hoping that it was a halibut instead of a big cod because cod were cheap and halibut were usually rare, big and expensive to buy. It took uncle Cyril and I quite some time to haul the big fish to the surface and we discovered that it was not the hoped for halibut but a giant cod. It was so big that my uncle and I could not haul it aboard the boat. My dad came forward with the gaffe, hooked the fish and they both lifted it into the boat.

My uncle Cyril had an astonished look on his face and said "My God, Herzil That's a big one. That's the biggest cod fish I've ever seen."

My dad agreed that it was the biggest cod that he had ever seen as well and he said "Bryan, you've caught a monster cod."

We then proceeded to another fishing spot and caught several regular sized cod before calling it a day and returning to the wharf at L'Anse-a-Brilliant harbour. When some people that were hanging around there saw the monster cod they admired it and exclaimed "Gee Herzil, that's the biggest cod I've ever seen. It must weigh fifty pounds at least."

"Pretty near fifty pounds for sure" said another man.

We didn't have a scale there to weigh the fish and no camera to take a picture of me holding it up. Although I don't think I had the strength to hold up the fish that I had caught.

One of the bystanders asked "What are you going to do with that fish?"

"Eat it" was my dad's reply.

"That's a big fish and you'll be eating it for a month" one guy said.

"I like fish" my dad replied. "Don't worry. It'll get eaten up."

We took the giant cod and the other fish we had caught home and directly to the fish cleaning table that was located behind the house. In our household you cleaned and filleted your fish as soon as you got them home and froze them in the big deepfreeze while they were still fresh.

My mother and my grandmother came outside to see the giant cod and were astonished at the size of it.

Nanny said "Save the liver for me boys. I'm going to get my canning machine ready to can it."

Later I found out that the liver filled four cans. That was a big cod liver to preserve.

You know that if someone from the big city had come to the Gaspe and caught this big fish instead of me a big fuss would have made of it. The fish would have been weighed and photographed and maybe the photo would have been put in a newspaper or magazine. After all it was almost a world record cod, but in our fishing community that didn't mean much. No great fuss was made over it. Local people didn't weigh or take pictures of their fish in those days. I have caught many cod since that day but none more than a third the size of that monster cod.

This is not a fish story of the big one that got away. It's the story of the giant cod fish that I actually caught in 1958.

67. Dad (Herzil De Vouge)

My father Herzil De Vouge was born on the farm in L'Anse-a-Brilliant in June of 1917. He was destined to be a farmer/fisherman like his father and grandfather before him. But it was not to be. His talents were put to use in other areas. He was a jack of all trades and a master of all trades. He could do anything, fix anything that was broken and design and make anything. He was a master carpenter and woodworker, a master mechanic and millwright, a master welder and a master boat designer and builder.

My father was a very smart man. He knew how to solve problems with any mechanical equipment. I remember one day in the early sixties he told me about something that happened at work that day. It was summer and they were having trouble with their big B & B centrifugal compressor in the Powerhouse at Gaspe Copper Mines Ltd. It appeared that the trust and center bearings were overheating at a certain time of the day. There was a team of engineers there who could not figure it out. Then my father was called and after he checked the tolerances and temperature readings on the bearings at different times of the day he solved the problem in five minutes. It appeared that at a certain time of the day the sun shone through a window and directly onto the trust and center bearings of the compressor drive shaft and thus overheated the bearings resulting in the compressor tripping off. My dad's solution was to put a shade on the window and to close it when the sun shone on the window. Problem solved. Dad could not understand why all the engineer's could not have figured this out. I guess they had the university degrees but dad had the common sense.

While we were living in Gaspe dad always talked about moving to Ontario and he did so in 1966. He moved to St Catharines, Ontario and lived there until he was sixty-seven and when he retired he moved to Nova Scotia where he had a new house built on ocean front property at Port Mouton on Nova Scotia's south shore.

I think his favorite work was the last ten or twelve years before his retirement when he built galleys and did other finishing work on fancy expensive yachts. He got to work with rare and very expensive woods like mahogany and teak.

Dad enjoyed his retirement years living in Nova Scotia. When he got up in the morning he could look out his living room window and see fishing boats on the Atlantic Ocean. He passed away suddenly one evening in August of 1966. He was sitting at the kitchen table having a late evening snack when he had a brain aneurysm and passed away right there in his chair. He was seventy-nine years old.

68. Sailing To Perce

In 1958 my grandfather Leslie De Vouge who had been a fisherman/farmer for most of his life decided to retire from fishing cod. He was now sixty-six years of age and was collecting his old age pension. There was certainly enough work to do on the farm to keep him busy.

Grandpa's fishing boat the "Herzil", the fifty-two footer that my dad had built for him was only five years old and since it was known as an excellent and fast boat it would fetch a pretty penny. I was a little sad when I learned that the "Herzil" was going to be sold. When it was docked in the harbour tourists and local people alike would be admiring it and taking pictures of it. When I overheard people talking about how beautiful it was and how it looked more like a yacht than a fishing boat I would step up and volunteer some information about it.

"It's my grandfather's boat." I would say. "My father built it for him and it was launched five years ago. It's named after my dad and it's the fastest fishing boat in the harbour." I was very proud of that and my father's boat building abilities.

It sold very quickly but before the new owner took possession my grandfather informed us that he was going to take his whole extended family and some friends on a short sail to Perce, the local tourist Mecca. If you drive to Perce it's about thirty miles (50 km) away from L'Anse-a-Brilliant but it's only ten miles (16 km) by water. Grandpa also told us that we were going to make use of the sails and not the big Cadillac engine unless we had to. I was overjoyed because I had never sailed before.

When the weekend arrived all my aunts, uncles and cousins came out from Murdochville for the special event. On Saturday it was a beautiful sunny and warm summer day and there was a breeze perfect for sailing. I was happy to see that save for a few of my younger cousins the ones that were around my age were there.

There were more than twenty of us and after preparations were made we exited the harbour, the sails were unfurled and we were on our way to Perce to visit the famous Perce Rock and tourist town. There was a fair wind blowing in our favor and both sails were full of wind. We sailed in almost a straight line to Plato, a small rocky island off of Point St. Peter and from there straight across to Perce.

I remember a few things that happened on the way. When the wind is strong and fills the sails the deck does not stay level as the boat cants over a little. This frightened one of my cousins who was eight years old and he started crying. Another cousin Blaine who was almost nine and a year younger than me laughed and made fun of him. I also remember that my sister Donna, only four and a half at the time sat alone right up front at the bow enjoying the sail. Our father remarked at how brave she was for such a little girl.

I went back to stand beside grandpa who was steering the boat with that big steering wheel with all the spokes and handles on it.

"Can I steer the boat for awhile?" I asked my grandfather.

"Alright Bryan" was his answer. "But keep her steady. Keep her steady."

I then took over the wheel and I didn't have to move a muscle, just holding the wheel in the same position as we sailed straight ahead to Perce. When we got a little closer to our destination my grandfather took back the wheel and the sails were taken down as we approached the wharf. When we docked and some of the men were securing the lines I noticed that there were several people taking pictures of our boat. Although Perce is a relatively small town it is always full of tourists especially on the weekend. When I climbed the ladder to the wharf a middle-aged couple approached me and asked how much an excursion in the boat cost.

I replied "This is not a tourist boat. It's my grandfather's boat and we're just out for the day. We only live thirty miles away."

"You must have a good view of the mountains and Perce Rock from out there on the water" the lady said.

"Yes, the scenery is very beautiful and it's a perfect day for sailing." I replied.

"Lucky you" she said.

After everyone had done the tourist bit and explored Perce it was time to re-board the boat and sail back to L'Anse-a-Brilliant. The sail home would prove to be quite different. You see we now had to sail against the wind which seems impossible but can be accomplished by tacking. By zigzagging your sailing path you can sail against the wind. It takes you much longer to get to where you want to go but you eventually get there. My grandfather could have done it the easy way and taken down the sails and used the engine but that would have been taking the easy way out. He had told us that we were going sailing and that's what we did.

When we were less than half way back to L'Anse-a-Brilliant it clouded over with several dark clouds. One of the men said "It's going to blow" and the wind started to gust. Now the boat was sailing faster and when it canted over my cousin Blaine got scared and started to cry. That was ironic because a few hours before he had made fun of Freddy when he was scared. This time however Freddy was not scared.

By now the sea was getting a little rougher and suddenly it started to rain. The women and younger children went to the cuddy below deck to seek shelter from the storm but I stayed on deck with the men. Besides it would have been real crowded in the cuddy with all the women and children there.

As quickly as it had started the squall ended and the sun reemerged as the clouds drifted away. The gusts of wind diminished and things returned to normal. We sailed the rest of the way to L'Anse-a-Brilliant harbour in perfect weather and our journey was over.

That was the last time that I set foot on the "Herzil" and the last time I saw it as the new owner was not local and I have no idea where it ended up. But as long as I live I will always remember that beautiful day when my grandfather took us out sailing one last time.

69. The Springhill Mining Disaster (1958)

It would not be right to write a memoir of one's youth without mentioning some of the tragic things that happened during the 1950's, news events that I still remember.

We know Springhill, Nova Scotia as the birth place of Anne Murray, one of Canada's greatest singers but it also had a tragic history in the 1950's.

Springhill was a coal mining town and on the first day of November in 1956 they had an underground bump or earthquake which resulted in many of the miners who were working underground that day losing their lives. It happened in Number Two Colliery and after the miner's bodies were recovered and the mine cleaned up the miners who had survived went back to work in the deep coal mine. I was eight years old at the time but I have no memory of that tragedy.

I do remember the next tragic event that happened in Springhill, Nova Scotia almost two years later on the twenty-third day of September 1958. It was a new school year and I had just turned ten years of age. In those days there wasn't any television reception available in the Gaspe Peninsula. We received all our news on the radio and in the newspaper.

On that fateful day in September of 1958 there was another underground bump at the same Number Two Colliery in Springhill, Nova Scotia. This time there were one hundred and seventy-four men working in the mine at the time. Rescue efforts started and they discovered many survivors in the collapsed mine. The mine rescue teams also retrieved many bodies of the miners that did not survive.

Our best source of news was the radio because our paper the Quebec Chronicle arrived in our mailbox one day after it was published. On the radio news reports were ongoing all day and when we were in class at school we were kept up to date by our school principal who was seemingly listening to the radio all day.

As the days went by the death toll had mounted to seventy-four miners and there were eighty-one survivors of the collapsed mine. There were still nineteen not accounted for and there was little hope that anyone would still be alive down in that deep mine. But still the mine rescue teams kept searching wanting to retrieve the bodies up to surface so their families and loved ones could give them a proper burial.

On September the 29th. six days after the mine had collapsed the mine rescue team heard men talking in one of the tunnels. They were trapped behind collapsed rock and rubble. They worked at clearing the rubble away and discovered twelve miners that were alive. They got them up to surface and transported to the hospital as fast as possible. These survivors had been without food and water for six days. They survived in their trapped area by punching holes in a plastic ventilation line and thus had enough air to breathe.

When we went to school the next day all that the people were talking about was the twelve miners that had been trapped in the mine for six days without food and water. I remember some children commenting "Boy, they must have been hungry and thirsty."

In our combination grade five and grade six class out teacher said "We are all very happy today but let's not forget about the seven brave miners that are still missing. We have experienced a miracle and let's pray for a second miracle. There are seven more missing miners that may still be alive down there."

Our teacher asked us to bow our heads and she said a prayer for the seven men and then she asked us to join her in reciting the Lord's Prayer. She asked us to pray for the seven men when we said our prayers that night before going to bed. I'm positive that all the students in my school did so that night.

The next day on September 31st. 1958 the remaining seven missing and presumed dead miners were found alive and they were rescued. A second miracle had occurred and our prayers had been answered.

This time that coal mine, Number Two Colliery was closed forever.

70. Milking The Cow, Not

In the early 1950's on our farm my grandmother had three cows which she milked every day. The one I remember the most was the oldest one and she was one hundred percent brown in colour. Hence she was called Brownie and she was Nanny's favorite cow. Brownie was more than just an ordinary milk cow; she was more like Nanny's pet cow.

In the winter the cows stayed in the barn and waited for the spring when they could go outside once again and graze in the field. In the spring, summer and fall they spent their days wandering around fairly close to our house and when Brownie thought that it was time to be milked she led the other two cows to the barn where they entered their stalls and waited for my grandmother to come and milk them.

When the cows "came home" as Nanny used to say she would get her stuff ready and go out to the barn to milk them the old fashioned way, by hand. Nanny would place her milking stool next to a cow and place a milking pail underneath the cow. Sometimes a cow would fidget and move around a bit before settling down ready to be milked. Nanny had to be careful because I know of one lady who had been kicked by a cow and she had suffered a broken leg. Our cows however were used to Nanny milking them and were cooperative especially Brownie who remained still and patient as Nanny milked her. When Brownie was dry Nanny would move on to the next cow until all three had been milked.

After the milking was completed the cows exited the barn and continued to graze out in the field. I helped my grandmother carry the pails of raw milk into the house where most of it was set aside to be mixed with pig meal and mashed potatoes to be fed to our pigs. The rest of the milk was for our consumption but we did not drink the raw milk. First it had to be pasteurized to kill any bacteria and Nanny had a manually operated machine to do this. I used to help by turning this crank on the separator to separate the cream from the milk. It was quite a big process because the machine had to be taken apart every time it was used and its individual parts and attachments scalded in boiling water so as to be germ free.

Thus we had lots of milk to drink, for baking, and for making into butter in Granny's churn. We never ran out of milk as we had a new supply every day. What milk we did not consume the pigs were happy to drink. My cat Timmy also got his share.

If my grandmother got ill and could not milk the cows my mother stepped in and did it but I think my mother only had to milk the cows once or twice.

The chores I did on the farm were ones that were considered manly chores like chopping and piling wood and feeding the animals. Milking cows was considered woman's work and I don't remember my grandfather ever doing it. I remember one day Nanny asking me if I would like to learn to milk the cows.

"No thank you" was my reply. "I'm not going anywhere near that thing down there." I have done many jobs on the farm but I must say that I have never milked a cow.

71. My First Coffee

Things were different back in the 1950's than they are today. In those days people drank tea rather than coffee as their hot beverage of choice. Today it is very noticeable that things have changed and more people prefer to drink coffee rather than tea. Just go to your local coffee shop any time of the day and see the long lineups of vehicles proceeding slowly through the drive through to get their favorite cup of java.

In our household my mother drank tea from Monday to Friday and when my dad came home from his work for the weekend they drank coffee. I was allowed to drink tea but didn't drink it very often at home settling instead for hot chocolate which I liked better. I usually drank tea when we visited friends and relatives when it was offered to me.

On Saturday mornings I would awaken to the most beautiful aroma of coffee perking in the coffee pot directly below my bedroom in the kitchen. When I would ask my parents for a cup of that beautifully smelling coffee I was disappointed when they would not allow me to drink even one cup. My father said that coffee was not for children and that it would stunt my growth.

When I told my friends that I wasn't allowed to drink coffee I found out that they did not drink coffee either. The few of them that had tasted coffee said that I wasn't missing much because while it smelled great it tasted terrible. I decided to take their word for it.

In the winter of 1959 when I was eleven years old Belle Anse Consolidated School organized a winter excursion for the older children in the school. We were going to visit a lumber camp deep in the woods and observe how the lumber industry operated in the winter months. We were transported by our school buses to this logging road where we were met by two big sleighs which were pulled by horses. Each class got on a different sleigh with our teachers and then we were on our way.

We were enjoying our horse drawn sleigh ride to the lumber camp although it was very cold that day and we were freezing our bottoms off. Our teacher assured us that when we reached the lumber camp the lumberjacks would have hot chocolate for us to warm us up.

Suddenly something weird happened and our driver stopped the horses and got down and inspected the sleigh. He told us that the sleigh had broken and we could no longer continue on this sleigh. It was decided that the other sleigh would take as many additional children as it could and the rest of us would have to walk the remaining mile to the lumber camp. Of course it was all the girls who were transported to the other sleigh and they were all on their way.

There were about ten of us boys including one teacher that had to walk the mile or so to the lumber camp. It was very cold and we walked as fast as we could knowing that a much needed cup of hot chocolate awaited us on our arrival.

When we reached the lumber camp and entered we found it so warm that my glasses fogged up. All of the thirty or so kids that had arrived on the first sleigh were drinking hot chocolate and obviously enjoying it. When we lined up with cups for our hot chocolate a lumberjack informed us that they were out of hot chocolate. He told us that the first group of children had arrived at the lumber camp at least twenty minutes before we did and had drank up all the hot chocolate. He informed us that there were still lots of coffee available and that it would warm us up real good.

I told my teacher "My parents don't allow me to drink coffee."

She replied "Bryan, I'm sure that your parents won't mind this time because you are very cold and the coffee will warm you up."

So I had my first ever cup of coffee on that very cold day at the lumber camp. The lumberjack and my teacher were right. The cup of coffee did warm me up. I think what I enjoyed the most about it was that it was hot rather than it's taste. In other words I did decide that day that I was probably not going to become a regular coffee drinker.

In the twenty-eight years between that day in the lumber camp and the year I turned thirty-nine I only drank about ten cups of coffee. This happened when someone made or bought me a coffee without my asking for it. When I was thirty -nine my wife and I visited one of her friends at her new home. Susan didn't ask us if we would like a coffee; she just made us each one and we sat at her kitchen table and drank it. My wife Carol also did not drink coffee but every time we visited Susan she always made coffee and placed it in front of us. We both started to like it. When I told Susan that I liked her coffee she said that it was Tasters Choice instant coffee and that she made it a little weaker than most people liked it.

So at the age of thirty-nine I became a regular coffee drinker and I drink two to three cups every day. Like most Canadians when I get up in the morning I need my morning cup or two of java. The most memorable cup of coffee I ever drank however was that very first one back at that lumber camp in the winter of 1959. I'll never forget how it warmed me up on that cold winter day.

72. Holiday To Ontario (1958)

In the summer of 1958 my father informed us that that we were going to go on a two week holiday. Just a few months before he had bought a brand new shiny black Mercedes-Benz and he wanted to take it for a drive, a long one in fact, all the way to Welland, Ontario. Dad told us that we would be visiting his good friend Dawson Baird and his family who had moved to Ontario a few years earlier. They had used to live on the farm next door to us in L'Anse-a-Brilliant.

In the fifties the province of Quebec didn't have any super highways and we had to take the small and narrow coastal highway along the north coast of the Gaspe Peninsula to get to Montreal where we were to visit and stay with relatives. It was slow going on the winding roads and we had to slow down many times to pass through small fishing villages along the St. Lawrence River. Eventually we arrived in Montmagny, a town about two hundred miles from Montreal. My dad decided that we would stay here for the night.

We stayed at the "Motel Wigwam" which was very nice and it had an Indian teepee set up right in front of the motel. In those days it only cost about ten dollars for a room with two double beds. I was nine years old and the only thing I didn't like about it was that I had to sleep in the same bed as my four year old sister.

The next morning we continued the drive to Montreal and arrived early enough that we had lots of time to spend with my mother's cousin Harold Wiseman and his family. I liked it there because there were two boys around my age to play with.

The following day we left for Ontario and were heading for Kingston where dad had served in the Canadian Army during the Second World War. He had been based at Fort Henry and when the war ended in 1945 he was discharged from the army and had decided to stay and work in Kingston for a while. However it had been about twelve years since he'd been to Kingston and we promptly got lost. It was the first time we got lost on our trip but not the last. Obviously things had changed since dad had been here before.

Ontario now had a new super highway, the 401 which went from the Quebec border to Windsor in the west.

Back on the road again dad had to stop to fill up with diesel fuel. I noticed that the gas station had a rack of free road maps and I asked dad to pick up a map of Ontario for me. He didn't and when I asked why he didn't he told me he knew where he was and where he was going.

When we arrived in Toronto we got lost again. What's worse than that was that dad was driving down a one way street the wrong way. We found this out when about ten kids in a playground ran towards us yelling "One way stet, one way street."

Dad replied "I'm only going one way."

I finally got my hands on a map and it began my lifelong hobby of map reading. With me giving directions dad did not get lost again and we made it to Wetland to Dawson Baird's house where we would be staying for one week.

Due to a divorce and subsequent remarriage Mr. Baird now had a younger family including a stepson my age. We quickly became friends and he took me to a real ballpark to play a pickup game of baseball with his friends. I enjoyed this because at home in L'Anse-a-Brilliant we played in a field and not an official ball park like this one.

As much as I loved playing baseball Mr. Baird had something in his house that was much more appealing to me than a baseball diamond. It was a television set and I fell in love with it. Television had not yet arrived in Gaspe so it was all new to me. I watched it morning, noon and night and you could not pry me away from it. My parents tried and told me to go outside and play.

I replied "I can play outside at home in Gaspe. I want to watch television here in Ontario while I have the chance."

There were programs like "Leave it to Beaver" and several westerns like "Roy Rogers", "Hopalong Cassidy" and "The Cisco Kid". I found these westerns to be outstanding programs. So when my new found friend asked me to go play baseball I went but my heart was back at his house in front of the television set.

One day our hosts took us over to Buffalo, New York in the USA. It was my first visit to the USA and we were going to the Buffalo Zoo which is a famous zoo with a wide diversity of animals. There were lions, tigers, giraffes, big gigantic elephants and I saw a most beautiful all white wolf.

The scary part was when we entered this building which housed all the snakes and I saw this big boa constrictor which I figured must have been about thirty feet long. The good thing for me was that it was in a glass cage and could not get at me to squeeze the life out of me.

Although going to the Buffalo Zoo was exciting more was yet to come. One evening after supper Mr. Les Selby (one of Dawson Baird's son-in- laws) took us to Crystal Beach which was an amusement park on the shores of Lake Erie. It was my first ever visit to an amusement park and at that time it had the largest roller coaster in North America if not the world. I wanted to ride on the roller coaster but I needed an adult to accompany me so I asked my dad if he would go on the roller coaster with me.

He said "No."

I asked dad if he would buy me a ticket so I could go on the roller coaster with someone else.

He said "No."

My first thought was that dad was too cheap to buy me a ticket. I was really disappointed because who knows when I would get another chance to ride the famous roller coaster at Crystal Beach. Then Mr. Les Selby seeing my disappointment went and bought a ticket for me and one for himself. He said to my dad "Don't worry. I'll take him on the ride. He'll be ok."

My dad said "Ok, go ahead."

I actually think that my dad thought that I was going to get killed on that roller coaster.

Les Selby and I got on one of the roller coaster's cars and were locked in. When the roller coaster started it proceeded very slowly up to the top of the loop. When we reached the top the roller coaster seemed to stop for a moment and then we plunged down the other side seemingly at a hundred miles per hour. It looked like we were heading out to and over Lake Erie and when I saw the sharp turn at the bottom of the loop I was positive that something was wrong and we were going to derail and fall into Lake Erie. Everything happened so fast I had no time to pray to God to spare me. I knew that I was dead for sure. But a miracle happened as we did not derail. We completed that impossible turn and we also survived the remaining loops, twists and turns. I could not believe that I was still alive at the end of that ride and was relieved that I had not wet my pants as I noticed one of the other kids had done. However when I got off the roller coaster for a moment I stood still and didn't think that I could walk. I felt a little weak but also tremendously exhilarated as I walked back towards my family with a smile a mile wide.

Turning to Les Selby I said "Thank You for taking me on that roller coaster. I thought I was going to die. Thank You very much."

"You're very welcome " he replied. "I'm glad that you enjoyed it."

I could see the relieved look on my dad's face and knew that he was happy to see that I was still alive.

The next day our Ontario vacation was coming to an end and we started the long almost one thousand mile drive back to the farm in L'Anse-a-Brilliant. I couldn't wait to get home because I wanted to tell all my friends about that big roller coaster at Crystal Beach.

73. Rita, A Great Lady

When you're over the age of sixty you can look back and remember your childhood friends and the adventures you shared together but how much do you remember about the adults that lived in your community and your interaction with them?

I have fond memories of many of the adults of L'Anse-a-Brilliant but there are two people that I have very fond memories of. They are Mrs. Rita De Vouge and Mr. Arnold Johnson.

Rita Leggo married Cecil De Vouge (a distant relative of mine) the day before he joined the Royal Rifles, a regiment of the Canadian Army. Cecil sailed from Vancouver in October of 1941 to defend Hong Kong in the case of a Japanese attack.

After attacking Pearl Harbour on December the 8th 1941 the Japanese also attacked Hong Kong with an aerial bombardment and an invasion force of fifty thousand soldiers of the Japanese Imperial Army. The small defending force of Canadian, British and Indian soldiers fought a valiant battle but in the end the Battle of Hong Kong lasted only seventeen days and ended when the British commander surrendered to the Japanese on December the 25th. 1941.

During the battle of Hong Kong two hundred and ninety Canadian soldiers were killed and four hundred and ninety-three were wounded. These were high numbers considering that the Royal Rifles regiment was made up of only nineteen hundred and seventy-five soldiers.

Cecil and Alva De Vouge (another distant relative of mine) were now prisoners of war and were sent to northern Japan where they were forced to work twelve hours per day and endured torture and near starvation for three and a half years until the Americans dropped two atomic bombs on Japan and the Japanese surrendered on August 15th. 1945. Another two hundred and sixty-four Canadians had died during their captivity in Japan. Now liberated Cecil came home to Rita who he had not seen since their wedding day.

I can only imagine how Rita felt not knowing the fate of her husband all those years when he was a POW in Japan. She must have been consumed with endless worry every day of the four years he was away. When Cecil came home Rita found him to be a shell of his former self, malnourished and sickly. Nevertheless she nursed him back to health and they adopted a son Reid who became one of my first-ever friends.

I remember when I was studying History in school I asked my father about the second World War and about Cecil being a POW in Japan. Dad said that "when Cecil came back from Japan he was just skin and bones. There was nothing left of him. He was as skinny as a rake."

As long as I can remember Rita played the church organ in our local Anglican church. As she played the organ and the church congregation sang the hymns you could hear her shrill voice above all others. All the years of my childhood until I moved away to Murdochville in 1962 Rita never missed a Sunday playing the organ at church.

One of the reasons all of the children of L'Anse-a-Brilliant loved Rita so much was that she was so pleasant and friendly to us. It seemed that she really cared for us and when we visited her home to see her son Reid she welcomed us warmly and she always seemed delighted to see us. Rita used to tell us stories, all kinds of stories that were of interest to children and our favorites were the ones that she told us when we visited at night.

When we asked Rita to tell us a story she would readily agree and then she would go to the light switch of her rather large kitchen/dinning room and plunge the room into complete darkness. She would then in a very haunting voice tell us a ghost story while she moved slowly around the room shuffling her feet. We could hear her but could not see her. As the ghost story progressed and we were becoming scared out of our wits her voice got a little louder and the shifting of her feet became faster. Just as the story was concluding she would take us by surprise by grabbing one of us by the shoulders. We would let out a scream and as she threw the light switch back on all of the children there had shocked and frightened looks on their faces. Our hearts would be beating a mile a minute.

But then we had another problem. We had to walk home. I had to walk two farms over and in one direction and the three Leggo brothers Lance, Denver and Zane had to walk at least four times as far in the opposite direction. In the 1950's there were no streetlights in L"Anse -a-Brilliant and we would have to walk home in complete darkness save for the little light that the moon provided us. I was so afraid to walk home alone that I would ask the three Leggo brothers to walk me home first. I could see that they were afraid as well and they would say no because they had to get home right away.

I was terrified walking home alone grimacing at every dark shadow and thinking that a ghost or goblin was going to pounce on me. However when

I reached my home safe and sound I could hardly wait until I could go back to Rita's once again to be entertained by another one of her famous ghost stories.

Another thing that Rita was famous for was her foghorn which fishing communities were familiar with in the old days. Rita's foghorn however, served a different purpose. When her son Reid and the rest of us were having a pickup game of baseball or playing elsewhere after school suddenly we would hear a few blasts from Rita's foghorn. This did not indicate foggy conditions, no it simply meant that Reid was to proceed home immediately because supper was ready. If Reid ignored this summons for supper and kept playing to finish our game then ten minutes later a louder series of foghorn blasts would ensue. This meant "Reid , get your butt home immediately."

In fact many of the mothers of L'Anse-a-Brilliant went by Rita's schedule and would always tell their children "Come home for supper when you hear Rita blow her foghorn." I know that was my mother's rule.

Even when I was a young child I had an interest in genealogy and Rita told me that the first De Vouge had emigrated here in the early 1800's and he was from somewhere in France. Pierre De Vouge had sailed here from the port of St. Malo in Northern France and settled in Pointe St. Peter. When I told my dad this he said that he had heard our ancestors were from the De Vouge Mountains in Belgium. Who to believe! Over the years I told people that I was from Belgian ancestry but I was still a little unsure of myself. So I went over to Europe in 1972 for a month. I spent about a week in Belgium but I didn't find any De Vouge's.

In fact I found that there were no De Vouge Mountains in Belgium at all. Belgium is known as one of the low countries like Holland where part of the land is below sea level. When I went to Paris, France however there were several De Vouges listed in the phonebook. Therein lies the answer. Rita was right all along. I should have known.

Over the years I have returned to Gaspe every seven years or so to visit and I always paid Rita and Cecil a visit and I even went fishing with Cecil a few times out on Gaspe Bay.

When I visited by myself in 1984 Cecil greeted me outside of his house but he hadn't seen me in seven years and he did not recognize me. You see I was sporting a full beard and at age of thirty-five I had put on a fair amount of weight.

"Come on in the house." Cecil said. "Rita will be happy to see you."

We entered the house and Cecil said "Rita, we have a visitor. Do you recognize him?"

Rita now in her late seventies looked at me and her jaw dropped. She turned a little white in the face like she had seen a ghost. She didn't say anything so Cecil said "Rita, it's Bryan De Vouge from Ontario."

"Yes, I know" Rita said. "For a moment there I thought I was looking at your grandfather Leslie. You look so much like him when he was a young man and had a beard as well."

Over the years most of the older residents of L'Anse-a-Brilliant have passed away. Last summer in August of 2008 I visited my old community with my oldest son Zac and I took him to the cemetery where many of our relatives are buried. We also visited the graves of Cecil and Rita De Vouge and I remembered her telling me ghost stories over fifty years ago. Rita was a great lady.

It is now February of 2009 and it is a rare cold day in my winter residence of Panama City Beach, Florida. I realized that it was not going to be a day to don bathing suit and suntan lotion to go for a walk on the beach. Instead I decided that I was going to stay inside today and do some writing. But first I was going to lunch at the new Olive Garden restaurant in the new and nearby Pier Park Shopping Village. While I was driving there I thought that I would write about Rita De Vouge today and I was thinking about what I was going to say about this great lady.

When I arrived at the Olive Garden I was greeted by a hostess and was escorted to a table. The hostess told me that a server would be right with me. In the meantime I was thinking about Rita and then this young, tall and slim Afro-American woman approached my table and said "Good Afternoon, my name is Rita and I'll be your server today. Here's the lunch menu and to start can I get you something to drink?"

I found it ironic that when I was thinking of what I was going to write about Rita De Vouge that this young and attractive maybe twenty-five year old server was also named Rita. I didn't say anything about it at the time and went on to give this young Rita my lunch order.

Rita checked with me several times to see if I was satisfied with my meal and if I needed anything. I noticed from her interaction with me and with patrons at other tables that she was a very pleasant and friendly person. Her beautiful and ever present smile was not a forced one but one that was omnipresent.

After my meal was finished and Rita brought me my bill I told her about this memoir I was writing and that today I was writing about a lady I once knew back in Canada in the 1950's. I remarked that Rita was not a common name these days and this was a coincidence worth mentioning.

"Rita said "Tell me a little about her."

I told her about the ghost stories and she seemed to enjoy hearing about the other Rita.

Rita then told me that she had thought about doing some writing herself but hadn't done any as of yet. I decided to give her a little pep talk, the same one that Vicki Gilhula had given me a few years before.

I told Rita to pick up a pen and paper and start writing about her childhood experiences and not worry about being perfect. I told her that her friends and relatives would enjoy her writing and the more she wrote the better a writer she would become.

I must have inspired her a bit because she thanked me and asked me if she could give me a hug. She said "I have to give you a hug."

I got up from my table and we hugged each other right there in the Olive Garden restaurant.

I had started the day with the plan of writing about one great lady named Rita and ended up writing about two.

74. Sharks And Whales

Growing up along the Atlantic Ocean you can bet that I've seen a few big fish in my day. That would include the giant cod I caught but could not haul in when I was ten years old. My father and uncle Cyril had to help me haul that near world record sized cod into the boat.

There were some really big fish swimming around out there along the Gaspe coast and I mean really, really big sharks and whales. While experts define whales as large marine mammals I still think of them as fish.

Summer in L'Anse-a-Brilliant meant long warm summer days down at the beach swimming in the cold water of the North Atlantic. Although it was said that they were more than a dozen species of sharks swimming in the waters of Atlantic Canada I'd never seen one. Most of those sharks could be found further south off of New Brunswick, Nova Scotia and P.E.I. and it was a very rare occasion when a shark was spotted in Gaspe waters.

One summer around 1957 or 1958 when I was eight or nine years old we had an unusually hot summer when compared to our normally nice and warm summers. Due to this very hot summer we spent more time at the beach swimming because the normally cold water was now much warmer. All the children in L'Anse-a-Brilliant loved it because it was so nice to swim in warm water for a change.

Some fishermen began to see sharks out on the water and suddenly our dream summer became our worst nightmare. Our parents freaked out and would not allow us to swim in Gaspe Bay any more. And then someone reported seeing a fin above water two hundred yards off our beach. My mom gave me permission to swim in the river but the river water was too cold so I nixed that idea. The sharks were ruining our summer.

One day we got the news that a basking shark had been caught in a fisherman's net and had died. The fisherman had brought it to shore and it was on display on the beach at Barachois about seventeen miles away.

Dad took us down to Barachois to see the shark and I swear there must have been almost one hundred people there. Most people had never seen a shark before live or dead. It was quite an attraction indeed.

There were several children there but most of them were too afraid to go close to the shark even though it was dead. None of my friends were there but I made friends with a local boy who lived there and we walked up onto the shark from tail to snout and we even posed while some people took photos of us standing on the shark.

My newfound friend's father yelled at him "Hey, Give the shark a kick in the head. It's probably be the only time you'll be able to kick a shark in your lifetime."

Many of the people laughed or cheered when the boy hauled off and kicked the shark. I felt like kicking the shark as well because it and its siblings were ruining my summer but I was too shy to do so in front of so many people. I just hoped that next summer the water would be cooler so that the sharks would stay away and we could go swimming in the ocean once again.

The shark was big, about twenty feet long and it was gray and dark brownish in colour. Before writing this I checked on the internet and found that the basking shark is the second largest fish in the world, second in size to the rather large whale shark. They grow up to ten meters long but the average is seven to nine meters or twenty-three to twenty-nine feet long. They have a large conical snout but their teeth are minute and numerous because they feed on plankton and very small fish. They are definitely not man eaters so we had nothing to worry about. They are sometimes seen in Gaspe in the summer months near the shore. They often get entangled in nets in fishing areas. That basking shark was the only one I ever saw during my childhood in Gaspe.

When it came to whales that was a different story because we saw many whales every summer in Gaspe Bay and Mal Bay. At our school at Belle Anse we were on a hill close to the water and in June pods of blue whales would come and hang out where they were very visible to us. We would suspend our math or history class and observe the whales and then write an essay about our observations.

There were several species of whales swimming around out there including blue, fin, humpback, minke and pilot whales. Occasionally sperm whales and killer whales also swam in Eastern Canadian waters. The North American Right whale is becoming very rare and thus rarely seen.

When I was a child I saw several whales every summer and to tell you the truth in those days I didn't know the difference between the various species. All I knew was that they were big, very big and some of them were over one hundred feet long and weighed up to one hundred and fifty tons. However I think that the majority of whales I saw were the blue whales who were a dark blue in colour. I have seen them swimming alongside our fishing boat at times and was taught not to be afraid of them as they meant us no harm.

One summer a dead whale that had been probably hit and killed by a passing ship floated ashore to the high cliff area between L'Anse-a-Brilliant and Seal Cove. It was in an area that was only accessible by water so the dead whale was left there to rot away. When the wind blew a certain way we could smell the foul stench of it decomposing. It was not a pleasant smell and I remember that at that time more than fifty years ago I wanted the Canadian Navy to come and blast it away with their ship's cannons.

On a more recent note my wife Carol and I took her parents Percy and Theda on a two week holiday to Gaspe in 1977. Cecil De Vouge, a relative of ours took my father, father-in-law and me fishing for cod early one morning. My dad noticed a big whale swimming alongside the boat as we proceeded out to the fishing area. It was swimming parallel and at the same speed as our boat and was only about fifty feet away.

I said to my father-in-law "Hey Percy, Look at that whale."

He turned and when he saw the whale he turned a ghostly white with fear and he was speechless.

I said "Don't worry Percy. That whale is our friend. He's not going to hurt us. He's just tagging along with us for a while."

Percy, a lifelong Ontario resident had seen a whale up close and personal on his first fishing trip on the Atlantic Ocean. These days there are whale watching excursions in and around Gaspe Bay and tourists get to see whales up close. But when I was young I used to see them for free.

75. Going to Church

When I think back to my childhood one of my most favorite memories is going to church every Sunday. We had one church in L'Anse-a-Brilliant and it was St. John's Anglican Church as about ninety percent of the people living there were Anglican. The three or so Catholic family's attended their church five miles away in Douglastown.

I don't know exactly at what age I started going to church but as far back as I can remember I attended church with my mother. My father did not go to church but my younger sister also attended when she was old enough to do so.

I liked everything about church such as the singing of hymns and listening to the minister preach his sermon. I liked the fact that I was dressed up in my Sunday best and that most of my friends were there as well. When the plate was passed I was proud to donate the coin that my mother had given me for the donation. I envisioned that it went to help some poor boy in a foreign land such as Africa or Asia.

Back when I was about four years old our minister the Reverend Apps asked my father to build a baptismal font for the church. My father was a master carpenter and set about the task. He built a fancy wooden frame of his own design and I remember helping him by handing him nails and his hammer. Dad then mixed up cement and added it into the frame. I helped him by adding some cement as well. When the cement had set dad removed the wooden frame; voila, there was a new font with a unique design and a basin at it's top. Dad sanded it down and then painted it white. It was installed at the back of the church and a little over a year later my baby sister Donna was baptized at the font that I had help build. I was very proud of that baptismal font.

As I grew older I envied the teenagers and adults who went up to the front of the church, kneeled down and received the holy sacrament of bread and wine. When I was twelve years old I studied the prayers required to be confirmed officially into the Anglican religion.

The confirmation ceremony took place at the main Anglican church in Mal Baie. Twelve year old children from all the Anglican congregations around were here on this day to be confirmed by a special visiting bishop. When the time came for the Bishop to lay his hands on my head and say the prayer that confirmed me into the Anglican religion I felt a strange feeling enter into me. It felt like electricity and may have been static electricity but I thought that it was the power of God entering my body and telling me to be a good person the rest of my life.

I received my first communion that Easter Sunday of 1960 at my home church in L'Anse-a-Brilliant. I was very happy and proud to receive the bread and wine symbolizing the body and blood of our Lord Jesus Christ.

By now the Reverend Apps had retired and we had a new minister, the Reverend Thomas who came to us from Wales in the British Isles. He was a bit different from the Reverend Apps in that when he gave us communion he let the wine barely touch our lips and we barely got a taste. His predecessor the Reverend Apps actually let us take a sip.

Church is a serious place but can still be humourous at times. There was a young man in L'Anse-a-Brilliant who was in his late twenties or thirty and he only came to church once a year on Easter Sunday. Derene McCoy had heard that our new minister was stingy with the church wine and he stated that if he only came to church once per year he deserved a good drink of wine. On Easter Sunday I was kneeling next to Derene McCoy and when the Reverend Thomas brought his wine filled silver chalice to Derene's lips Derene took control of the chalice and drank down all the wine before handing the empty chalice back to Reverend Thomas. I had to stop myself from laughing out loud as the Reverend Thomas gave Derene a big frown and then went into the vestry to refill the chalice with wine. When the Reverend Thomas returned I was next in line and of course he only wet my lips with the wine. However Derene McCoy had done what he said he was going to do. He had a drink of wine.

It appeared that every church going family had their own pew that they sat in every week. Our pew was located on the right side about six or seven rows back. In the summer I was dismayed that we were not located at the front but in the winter I was happy that we were located right next to the only source of heat in the church, a woodstove that had been fired up about two hours before the church opened by Mr. Dan Girard, an older parishioner who lived very near the church. The people in the front rows were cold but I was warm and toasty in our pew next to the wood stove.

When we moved away to Murdochville after Christmas of 1961 I did not have occasion to attend St John's Anglican church much anymore as I was now attending the church in Murdochville. After I moved away to Ontario in 1967 I only saw the old church when I returned to L'Anse-a-Brilliant to visit every seven years or so.

St John's Anglican church had been consecrated in Brilliant Cove (the former English name for L'Anse-a-Brilliant) in July of 1926. It was deconsecrated in June of 1985. The old church that I loved attending was demolished in 1988.

After I moved to Ontario in 1967 I have not attended church since except for weddings and funerals. However if I had lived all these years in L'Anse-a-Brilliant instead of here in Sudbury, Ontario I think that I would have been a regular Sunday churchgoer.

Now every few years when I go back to L'Anse-a-Brilliant to visit the place where I spent my childhood I visit the cemetery where many of my relatives are buried. I look at the spot where the church used to be and I am saddened. I miss that old church with its old wood stove that kept us warm in the winter.

76. My Brother Is Born Dead, Dad Builds A Box

In the fall of 1958 I was ten years old and my sister Donna was five. One day my mother announced to us that she was pregnant and in June of 1959 we would be welcoming a new baby brother or sister to our family. I was very happy about that as I had always wanted a brother. I thought that my sister Donna was hoping for a baby sister.

As June of 1959 arrived and mom was eagerly awaiting the birth of her new child I would put my hand on her rather large belly and feel the baby inside her kick my hand. I was positive that the baby would be a boy because it kicked so hard.

My mother went into labor and my dad drove her to the hospital in Gaspe twenty miles away. My brother Cedric William De Vouge was born on June the 29th. 1959 but sadly he was stillborn which means that he was born dead.

When my father arrived home from the hospital I have no memory of whether he told my sister and me about our baby brother's death or not. I do remember that there was a lot of sadness on our farm. At the time my grandparents were looking after Donna and me and I remember my grandmother sitting in her rocking chair rocking back and forth with a sad and blank look on her face. My grandfather just sat motionless staring straight ahead out the window.

Later I heard hammering coming from out behind the house and I went out to see what my dad was doing. I found him at the workbench and he was building a box.

"What are you doing Dad?" I asked.

"I'm building a box " dad replied.

"Why are you building a box?" I asked.

My father looked at me but did not answer me. He just stood there and started to cry. My father was forty-two years old and it was the first and only time that I ever saw him cry. I quickly left and went back into the house. A few days later my mother came home from the hospital and it was pretty sad around the farm for a while.

As the years went by and I got older and wiser I often wondered why there wasn't any funeral for Cedric and where he was buried. I had a baby cousin named Peter who passed away when he was three days old and he was buried in the L'Anse-a-Brilliant cemetery alongside our other De Vouge relatives. I asked my mother about this and she told me that babies that are born dead do not have a funeral. Since my cousin Peter died when he was three days old he had a funeral and was buried in the local graveyard. She didn't tell me what had happened to Cedric and I didn't ask. Other people told me that the hospital had probably taken care of it.

In 2006 when my sister Donna and I travelled to Liverpool, Nova Scotia to visit my elderly widowed mother she finally informed us of what had happened to our brother Cedric.

That box that I saw my father making on that day forty-seven years before was a small coffin. My father was a boat builder and an excellent carpenter and he wanted to make the coffin for his son himself. Mom went on to tell us that dad had buried Cedric in an unmarked grave up on the head of our farm. The head was located at the top of our land where there was a cliff rising about three hundred feet above the Atlantic Ocean. That's where Cedric's final resting place is.

77. Christmas In L'Anse-a-Brilliant

Christmas in L'Anse-a-Brilliant was magical, not the magic you pull out of a hat but magical still the same. Just look out of the kitchen window and you would see what I mean.

In the weeks leading up to Christmas my family received a multitude of Christmas cards most of which were from local friends and relatives but several were from Ontario, Newfoundland, Prince Edward Island and Nova Scotia. We even received a Christmas card from my mother's pen pal in New Zealand far away on the other side of the world. I also received a card from my pen pal in Saskatchewan.

In those days leading up to my Christmas break from school I would come home from school and I would check all the new Christmas cards that we had received that day. I would read every one and check out who had sent them. Of course Santa Claus was displayed on the front of many of the cards. I also noticed that many of the cards depicted a lovely winter scene in the country. The artists who drew these Christmas cards would put a farmhouse in the picture with bluish wood smoke billowing up from the chimney. Nearby trees would be snow covered signifying a fresh snowfall. The neighbouring house would have a snow covered roof and of course there would be a vast expanse of pure white in the fields where the "Merry Christmas" message would be written.

I picked up one card, noted the picture and looked out our kitchen window. The scene I saw before me was the same as the scene in the card.

"Mom" I said. "L'Anse-a-Brilliant is a Christmas card."

"What do you mean?" she asked.

"Just look at this card and then look out the window."

My mother looked at the card and then had a good look out the window. "You're right Bryan. It's pretty much the same isn't it?"

"Do you think the artist was ever here in L'Anse-a-Brilliant and drew the scene?"

"No" was my mother's reply. "I think he just used his imagination as to what a good Christmas scene should be and just drew it. It's just a coincidence that it turned out to look like our very own L'Anse-a-Brilliant."

As the Christmas of 1958 approached my dad and I went and chopped down a good Christmas tree on our property. Of course we had a good supply of them down in the lower valley and across the river in the woods. My mother, my younger sister Donna and I decorated it with Christmas decorations such as those colourful and shiny balls, Santa Claus ornaments and candy canes. We also added tinsel and strung on the electric lights. The tree was right inside the window so the people passing by on the highway would see it's Christmas lights. All we had to do now was wait for Christmas morning.

I was ten years old and I had asked Santa (aka my parents) for a pair of skis and I usually got what I wanted. Of course I had also asked for some lesser presents as well.

On most days of the year parents get up first and then have to drag their kids out of bed to get them up to go to school. On Christmas morning however, the kids are most often up first and have to drag their parents out of bed so they can all go downstairs and see what Santa left them under the tree.

My five year old sister Donna was the first to notice that Santa had drank the glass of milk and ate all the cookies that we had left for him on Christmas Eve before we went to bed.

The first thing I noticed were the skis that was not under the tree but propped up beside the tree. The tag on the skis said "To Bryan from Mom and Dad". Under the tree I found many other presents for me from Santa, my grandparents and all my aunts and uncles.

I received several books from my aunts and uncles because they knew how much I liked to read. I received a children's religious book from my grandmother as she was very religious and wanted to start me on the right path. I also received home-made woolen socks from my grandmother that she had knitted from wool sheared from the sheep on our farm. My mother was also an expert knitter and I received a new wool sweater in Boston Bruin colours, white with yellow and black trim.

Santa had also left me a 1959 Edsel model car. Edsel's were made by the Ford Motor Company and were only in production for two years mainly because they weren't that good a car. But Edsel cars were my favorite at the time. This Edsel that Santa gave me was lime green and for some reason it looked identical to the one my father and I had discovered in a store about two months prior to Christmas. All in all I was very pleased with my Christmas presents especially when I discovered that my three aunts did not all buy me the same book like they had done the year before.

I looked out the window and what I saw on this Christmas morning of 1958 was magical. The sky was blue and clear. The sun was shining down on a beautiful new supply of fresh snow that had fallen overnight. It was a beautiful day and the scene before me was exactly like the Christmas card that I had pointed out to my mother. I wanted to go outside right away and try out my new skis.

My mother insisted that I eat breakfast first and I gulped it down really fast. I found that my skis were a bit too big for me. They were five and a half feet long and I was only ten years old. But I was not going to complain. My parents said that I would grow into them. They also said that I should try skiing down the small hill at the end of our house at first until I got the hang of it before tackling the bigger hill down towards the neighbours. They were right because I fell several times, even on the small hill and also I couldn't make turns very well at all. After many attempts at skiing down the small hill without falling I finally succeeded and I knew that I was improving and that someday I would be a good skier. When I got tired of skiing and decided that I would go into the house and play with that green Edsel car that Santa had brought me I took one last look at L'Anse-a-Brilliant in all it's glory on this beautiful Christmas morning in 1958. L'Anse-a-Brilliant is a Christmas card.

78. *Collecting Freebies In The Fifties*

One of my favorite things to do back in the fifties was collecting the various things that came free in many of the products one bought at the store. For example when you bought tea you would find a picture card of a beautiful bird such as a Blue Jay or a Robin Red Breast in it. Because tea was the beverage of choice for my parents and grandparents my sister Donna and I managed to collect hundreds of these cards over the years. We sent in fifty cents for the album that you glued these picture cards into. Donna and I each had our own album and we still have them fifty years later.

In the early fifties I would visit my grandparents' end of the house, open the kitchen cupboard and remove this beautiful glass and then proceed to the indoor manual water pump to pump myself a glass of cold well water. The glass was clear with blue polka-dots on it. The dots near the bottom were very dark blue and further up they were medium blue. Close to the top they were a very light blue. My great-grandmother Angelina always noticed that I chose that particular glass.

"Gee Bryan" she said. "You sure like that blue glass. Don't you?"

"Yes, it's my favorite" I replied.

"That glass came full of raspberry jam like most of the glasses in the cupboard there" she said.

A few years later when I was about seven years old she gave me that glass to keep. I still have it in the back of my cupboard. I had a few others but they got broken over the years. When my three boys were growing up I told them not to use that glass and why.

In Red Rose tea we also collected these miniature ceramic figurines of animals such as cats, dogs, lions, elephants and other figures such as houses, cars and trucks etc. They were very popular and I still have around a hundred of them.

In Shreddies cereal there were these small military ships such as destroyers, cruisers and submarines. You took them apart and put baking soda into them. When you placed them in the sink and the baking soda got wet the resulting chemical reaction produced gas which exited the rear of the ship in small bubbles and therefore propelled the ship around the sink. I loved those small ships but somewhere in our many moves they got left behind somehow. I regret that I don't have one to play with today.

There were many other freebies in products such as Cracker Jack's but I don't remember being too excited about collecting them.

When the bubble gum with free hockey cards came out we bought them mainly for the bubble gum which we chewed at school. They cost about five cents a pack. We played games with the hockey cards gambling them away or we put them in the spokes of our bicycle wheels. I remember having cards of big stars such as Rocket Richard and Gordie Howe. None of the hockey cards I had in the fifties survived the fifties. I wish I had them now as they would be worth a small fortune.

I also had a collection of 1950's comic books such as Superman, Batman and other superheroes which also did not survive the several moves of my youth.

I have hundreds of beautiful marbles which I will pass on to my grandchildren some day. I used to have lots of fun playing marbles when I was a kid.

As for collecting I still do it and I collect anything and everything especially if it's blue in colour.

79. Fifties Food

One of my most pleasant memories growing up on the farm back in the fifties was the food we ate. We simply dined in luxury. Most or our food was not bought but raised, caught, grown or hunted by us. We were very self-sufficient.

When it came to the various meats we ate most came from animals we raised on the farm. We grew our own beef, pork, chicken and lamb. I remember one year when my grandmother raised turkeys but my grandmother didn't like them because they grew to be big birds who pecked at her when she fed them. My grandfather also experimented with growing rabbits one year. My father and grandfather also hunted moose every fall and grandpa set snares for rabbits in the winter. Neither of them hunted deer and I think one time I heard my dad say that a deer was much too beautiful an animal to shoot. All the animals that my grandfather slaughtered and butchered for meat for our table was done in the proper manner because we never got sick with food poisoning. The words e-coli, salmonella or listeria poisoning were unheard of on our farm. My grandfather Leslie must have being doing something right because our food was safe.

Up until I was nine years old my grandfather was a commercial cod fisherman and later a lobsterman. As well as cod and lobster we had halibut, sole, herring, mackerel, smelt and some other species that I may have forgotten about. Of course I also fished in the river for trout and I remember my father buying salmon from a fish peddler once in a while. Living in Atlantic Canada you can be assured that we ate a lot of seafood most all of it for free. Some weeks we ate fish four out of the seven days. I guess that it was an added bonus that I loved seafood.

On the farm we grew all our own vegetables, potatoes, carrots, parsnips, turnips, peas, onions, cabbage, beets and others. We had apple and plum trees out behind he house. The apples were not really good eating apples but were used for baking apple pies and desserts.

We had a large raspberry patch up on the head of our land as well as wild strawberry and gooseberries from which to make jam and other desserts.

On the farm in the fifties there were no microwaves or TV dinners. Everything was made from scratch cooked the old fashioned way which resulted in pure simply delicious food.

My mother was a wonderful cook and I had many favorite meals. Among my favorites was my mother's beef stew with her duff (dumplings) which was simply sensational. As soon as I was finished eating this meal I was already looking forward to getting hungry enough to eat some more of the left-over duff. But I had to fight off my dad and my sister to get at it. Mom also cooked a mean rabbit stew when we had rabbits that my grandfather had snared in the winter. When my mother decided to cook a roast she would often cook two of them together, a roast of beef and a roast of pork. Double your pleasure, double your fun. My mother's fried cod which was dipped in flour and egg was also a memorable meal as well as her dried salted cod cooked with fat pork and buttered potatoes. Mmmm Good. Mom's various homemade desserts were also good enough to die for but my favorite was her raisin pie. Anyone who ever had the opportunity of eating a slice would simply describe it as outstanding.

Another thing I should mention is that many ladies, especially the older ones always seemed to have a soup pot kept warm on the back of the stove. It was sort of a Quebec tradition. This delicious homemade soup was usually chicken with vegetables or pea soup and it was served at lunch time with a sandwich. When I visited friends or relatives and was offered a bowl of soup I always gratefully accepted because it was always so, so good. My favorite of my mother's soups was her beef with barley soup and I couldn't get enough of it.

In the 1950's I don't remember eating in a restaurant very often but on the rare occasion that we did I always ordered the same meal, a hot chicken sandwich with fries. It was most people's favorite restaurant meal at the time.

The delicious food we ate was one of the joys of growing up on a farm in the 1950's, Oh, what culinary pleasure.

80. Cecil Leggo Sailed His Boat

On summer days when I was down at the beach swimming and having fun with my friends I would suddenly hear the put, put, put sound of the motor of a fishing boat returning to the harbour with it's catch of cod fish. I would climb up out of the water onto the wharf and watch the boat slowly approach the harbour. When the fishing boat entered the harbour once again I wondered why this boat had two masts with sails that were not used. Since the fishermen used their motors I surmised that the sails were for emergency use only just in case the motor failed.

The fishermen who used L'Anse-a-Brilliant harbour as their home port had different sized boats but the two masters were usually between forty and fifty feet long. They had a cabin below deck in the bow which was called a cuddy. It usually slept a crew of three or four. There was a small wood stove in the cuddy for heating in cooler weather and for cooking when they were out on the water for three or four days at a time.

My grandfather Leslie was a fisherman and when he retired and sold his boat one of the men who had fished with him got his own fishing boat. Cecil Leggo's boat was a two master and it was painted a beautiful dark green. I don't remember it's name but it was a nice boat.

What made Cecil Leggo different from the other fishermen was that Cecil Leggo sailed his boat. Standing on the wharf you would see a white speck on the horizon. A while later you would realize that the white speck was actually sails and it had to be Cecil Leggo and his crew returning with a boat full of cod. Sure enough a while later you would recognize the green bow of Cecil's boat as it headed straight for the entrance to L'Anse-a-Brilliant harbour. I always loved to watch Cecil sail his boat into port and I wondered why some of the other fishermen didn't do likewise. I had already concluded that the boat was faster with the sails than with the motor. Maybe most of the fishermen were too lazy to hoist and then lower their sails. Maybe they thought that it was old fashioned to sail when they had a modern marine engine in their boat. I often wondered but I never asked anyone about this.

In the summer of 2008 When I took my oldest son Zac for his first ever visit to the Gaspe Peninsula we visited Cecil Leggo in Seal Cove. We talked about the old days when Cecil fished with my grandfather Leslie on his boat. Now eighty-four years old Cecil seemed to enjoy talking about his old fishing days.

I remarked that I remembered that he was the only fisherman who sailed his boat into L'Anse-a-Brilliant harbour and asked him why.

"That's what sails are for" was his reply. "The sails got me home faster and it didn't cost me any money for gas when I didn't use the engine."

That certainly made sense to me.

81. Five Guys On A Bike, A Bad Idea

This is one of those stories that happened in 1958 or was it 1959? I was either ten or eleven years old. I do not remember which.

The Leggo brothers Lance, Denver and Zane and I went for a walk up the hill towards Seal Cove to see what was going on up there. It was a beautiful and sunny summer day.

On our way walking back to L"Anse-a-Brilliant we were walking through the wooded area we called the portage when we met up with Billy Annett who was riding his bike.

"Where are you heading Billy?" one of us asked him.

"I'm on my way to your father's store" he said to the Leggo's.

Lance asked him "Which one of us are you going to give a ride down the hill to?"

"I'll give you all a ride" replied Billy.

"No way" I said. "You can't put five guys on one bike. Never mind. I'll walk."

"Yes I can " Billy said. I'll put Lance on the crossbar in front of me and I'll put Zane on the handlebars because he's the smallest. Denver you can sit on the front fender and Bryan can sit on the back fender."

"That's too dangerous" I said. "What if you can't steer right and we have an accident halfway down the hill?"

"We won't have an accident" Billy said. "I'm a good driver."

"What if we get caught by a cop?" I asked. "We'll get in trouble."

"When was the last time you saw a cop car down here?" asked Billy. "The nearest policeman is twenty miles that way in Gaspe and thirty miles the other way in Perce. They hardly ever come around here. We don't have anything to worry about."

We all agreed to give it a shot and all climbed on our assigned spots. I sat on the back fender and I was a little scared but I figured that if we had an accident the guys up front were more likely to get hurt than me.

L'Anse-a-Brilliant hill is about a half-mile long and it's fairly steep so if you can get a good head start you would be hitting speeds of fifty miles per hour halfway down the hill. But we wouldn't be going that fast because we were starting from a dead stop and I was hoping that Billy would go slow and put his brakes on once in a while.

When we started on our adventurous ride it was slow and wobbly but as our speed increased it got smooth. As we passed by our farm I was hoping my mother wasn't looking out the window because if she were I would never hear the end of it. We were almost to the bottom of the hill without any mishap and I was thanking God when I heard a car behind us. I turned my head to see the car and oh yeah, of course it was a police car. As we reached the bottom of the hill and started to slow down a bit I yelled to Billy "Stop the bike. The police are behind us."

I don't think Billy believed me because he made no attempt to stop. The policeman gave us two little toots on his siren.

"Stop the bike Billy!" I yelled. "he wants us to stop."

Billy did not stop but still coasted on. I think he was afraid and didn't know what to do. I was also afraid that we would be in big trouble if we didn't stop immediately so I panicked and I shoved my left foot down between the rear forks and the rear wheel to try and stop the bike. My foot got stuck and the spokes started scraping the skin off my ankle. Then the bike stopped and I got off. My ankle hurt so badly I couldn't walk and I grabbed the steel railing alongside the road for support.

The police officer got out of his car and approached us. Seeing that I was hurt he checked my ankle which was scraped and bleeding a little.

"Oh you'll be alright in a few minutes" he said.

That was very easy for him to say I thought. He wasn't the one with the hurt ankle.

The police officer then addressed us all and gave us a stern lecture about bicycle safety. He told us "You could have had an accident and could have all been seriously hurt."

I kept my mouth shut because I was afraid of the policeman. But I felt like telling him that Billy was a good driver and we did not have an accident. I also felt like telling him that he was the cause of my injured ankle because by using his siren he made me panic and do what I did to stop the bike. But of course I didn't tell him that.

The cop made us promise not to do this again and then he got back into his cruiser and was on his way. Good riddance to bad rubbish, I thought. I could hardly walk on my injured ankle. He did not even offer me a ride home and I had to hobble home on my bleeding ankle.

Nevertheless that was the last time anyone would see five guys on a bike going down L'Anse-a-Brilliant hill. A bad idea.

82. Halloween And Mardi Gras

What a difference it was in going trick or treating in Sudbury with my three young sons in the 1980's than it was when I went out on Halloween in L'Anse-a-Brilliant in the 1950's.

The community of L'Anse-a-Brilliant was about a mile long and had about twenty houses. Some of them were located quite a distance from the road so a lot of walking was involved in getting to some of the farm houses. When a group of us children knocked on a door we weren't just given a treat. we were invited into the house and the people there tried to guess who we were beneath those Halloween masks. Of course there were probably less than twenty children living in L'Anse-a-Brilliant at that time and everyone knew all the kids. But with the masks on sometimes it made it quite difficult for them to figure out who we were.

The treats that we were given were not usually what we now refer to as junk such as potato chips and chocolate bars. We received apples, oranges and an assortment of home baked treats such as cookies and date-squares. We already knew who the best bakers were in L'Anse-a-Brilliant and you can be sure that we were going to visit that lady every year. Of course we also received a few chocolate bars and a few bags of chips. While we didn't get a massive amount of loot all in all our Halloween's were very enjoyable evenings.

Fast forward to Halloween in the 1980's when I took my three young sons out trick or treating in our neighbourhood in New Sudbury. It was a newer high density area of Sudbury where the houses were very close to the street and each other. Depending on the weather we would visit between one hundred and fifty and two hundred houses Halloween night. When the boy's pillow slips were filled up with loot we would return home and drop it on their beds. Then we would go back out and they would each get their bag filled up once again. Once or twice they even got a third bag of goodies. They would sort everything out so that their whole bed would be covered with treats. Noticeably absent were apples, oranges and other baked goods, the very things I used to receive when I was a child. Times had changed and some children were told not to accept apples and baked goods etc. I saw children throwing apples away into the street that they did not want. What a waste I thought and when my boys received an apple I gave it a good inspection to make sure it was alright and if they were more attracted to the chocolate bars that they had received then I would eat the apple. We never did receive a bad apple so I guess there were a lot of good honest people in our neighbourhood.

The biggest problem with my boys getting so many treats was making sure that they didn't eat too many chocolate bars at once. I didn't have that problem back in the 1950's.

Back in the 1950's we did it all over again in the latter part of the winter. It was Mardi Gras and we did the same thing as we did at Halloween; we went around visiting and collecting treats. I actually thought that Mardi Gras was the French version of Halloween but of course now I know different. Maybe we were the only kids in Canada going out on Fat Tuesday trick or treating. Double your pleasure, double your fun.

83. *Nanny Is Charged By A Bull*

In the mid 1950's the farm next to ours burned down and for the next few years another farmer rented the vacant land and grazed his cattle on it. Initially there was a herd of ten or twelve cows and later a rather large mean looking black bull was added to the herd to protect the cows or maybe to entertain them. As a result new calves were born later to add to the herd.

There was a four foot wire fence separating the two farm properties and when I walked along the fence I would look over at the herd and observe the cows grazing in the field. It seemed like they were always eating or else sitting down relaxing. The bull was always on his feet looking at me in a very menacing manner. I knew that big bulls didn't eat kids like maybe a bear would but I sort of thought that he would like to charge at and trample me if I ever dared to venture over into his territory. So I made sure to stay on my side of the fence. Sometimes I talked to him in a friendly manner.

"Hey there, you big bull" I would say. "How are you today? I'm just passing by on my way up to the head to check if the raspberries up there in the patch are ripe enough for picking. Hey, I'll stop by on my way back home and sat Hi again."

The big mean looking bull never replied but he kept watching me and as I proceeded up the field he never took his eyes off me.

One day I was helping my grandfather pile firewood that he had chopped and we both noticed the big black bull in the next field. I told grandpa that every time I walked by the fence that the bull gave me these mean looks.

"Bryan, don't you ever tease or anger that bull" he said. "A wire fence is not going to stop that bull if it ever decides to charge you."

Since we did not have a bull perhaps grandpa had seen me pull on old Brownie's tail to tease her a time or two. When I did that old Brownie who was my grandmother's favorite milk cow would simply turn and look at me and say "Moooo". Translated into English that meant "Bryan, don't do that."

I told grandpa that there was no way I was ever going to mess with that bull and he knew that I meant it.

My grandmother had her main flower garden just beyond our end of the rather big and long farmhouse because the driveway was at the other end of the house where she lived. One day I looked out our kitchen window and I spotted nanny working in her flower garden pulling weeds. She kept the garden nice and tidy and she had several different kinds of beautiful flowers in it.

I went outside on our gallery to pump myself a cold glass of water from our well and I got the shock of my life. Nanny was kneeling down pulling weeds and about thirty feet beyond her there was that big mean black bull from next door. Nanny saw the bull and sensing that she was in danger got up to vacate the area. As soon as she started walking towards the house the bull charged her.

"Run, Nanny run" I yelled as my sixty-two year old grandmother sprinted like an Olympic runner towards the house. I thought that she would climb the steps to our gallery but she sprinted right by me with the bull right behind her. I didn't think that she was going to make it all the way to her end of the house but she did with the bull right on her heels. I thought that she had been very lucky to have made it into the house in one piece. I guess when an angry bull is chasing a grandmother you cannot imagine how fast an old lady can run.

I think that mean old bull had got tired of his cows and had decided to come over onto our farm to visit our cows. They obviously rejected his advances so he took his anger out on the only one in the vicinity, my grandmother.

When the bull's owner was informed that his bull was on our property and that he had charged my grandmother he came with a truck and took the bull back to his own farm. I never saw that bull again.

84. My Mom's A Lousy Driver

As a child growing up in the Gaspe Peninsula we had one driver in our family. That was my father who took the car with him to work eighty miles away and only came home on the weekends. When he bought a new 1958 Mercedes Benz he said he was also going to buy something for driving around on the farm and for hunting in the woods. He ended up buying an old Willys Jeep which of course was standard shift and four wheel drive. It was about five or six years old and it was navy blue in colour. It had a removable plywood top with rear and side windows. It also had a bullet hole in one of the rear side windows. It was kind of cool, a big hole with cracked plexiglas radiating out from it. I imagined someone had shot at the Jeep but my dad said someone's gun had gone off accidentally inside the Jeep and the bullet had gone through the window. It was also cool that the top came off so in the summer we could make it into a convertible.

My father figured that my mother should learn how to drive. Although she didn't have a driver's license and thus could not go on the road she could still bomb around on the farm. For instance she could drive my grandmother, my sister and me up on the head to pick raspberries.

My mom's driving lessons didn't go well and I remember my dad raising his voice a little and saying "You have to give it more gas when you let out the clutch or it will stall every time."

One day my grandmother asked me if I'd like to go up on the head to pick raspberries with her. My mother decided that she would like to come as well and she said that that she would drive us up in the Jeep. Although my grandmother was almost seventy years old and it was quite a hike up the hill to the raspberry patch (about a third of a mile) Nanny declined the Jeep ride and said that she would walk. I told my mother that I would walk as well. I guess that my mother realized that we didn't trust her driving and she didn't like that. She couldn't order my grandmother to drive with her but she ordered me into the Jeep. Of course I was hesitant but obeyed her and sat in the passenger seat. Mom started the Jeep, put it in first gear, gave it a lot of gas and let out the clutch rather fast. The end result was the Jeep starting off like a bat out of hell and smashing into and over my grandfather's old oil drum which was used to burn our garbage on the farm. We stopped abruptly finding that the front end of the Jeep was up in the air with the front wheels still turning and touching nothing but air. The Jeep was hung up on the oil drum.

When my mom and I got out of the stuck Jeep the first thing I saw was my grandfather standing there with his cap in one hand and he was scratching the top of his bald head with his other hand. His mouth was wide open and he was looking at the scene with wonder or maybe disbelief. My grandmother looked like she was thanking God that she had not gotten into the Jeep with us. After all she was a religious woman.

On another occasion Mom and Dad my sister Donna and I were driving between Murdochville and Gaspe where there's a fifty mile stretch of woods and little traffic. It was winter and my dad decided that he would let my mom drive the Mercedes. She still did not have a driver's license and I don't think that she really wanted to drive, however she said that she would.

My father stopped the car and pulled over unto the side of the road. When my mom and dad got out of the car to exchange seats I did as well and made a bee-line for the woods.

Dad followed me into the woods and asked " Why are you running off into the woods?"

"You can't let her drive" I said. "She'll kill us all for sure. With all the twists and turns in the road in these mountains we'll never make it as far as Gaspe in one piece. Mom's a terrible driver. Remember when she smashed the Jeep into Grandpa's oil drum."

My father was not ready to relent as of yet and he chased me a little farther into the woods. But he couldn't catch me, not in a month of Sunday's. When he asked me to come back to the car I made him promise that he would drive or I wouldn't get back in the car. Finally he promised and we went back to the car and he drove the rest of the way. I got the impression that mom wasn't disappointed but was relieved that she didn't have to drive on the highway.

When I was twelve years old my dad taught me how to drive the Jeep and I could drive it on the farm and in the woods. I guess he figured that I might turn out to be a better driver than my mother.

85. *Going To School In A Bombardier*

Living along the coast of the Atlantic Ocean in Gaspe we had a maritime climate that meant lots and lots of snow. We would get snowstorms that lasted for days and blizzards that would close the local highway, sometimes for days.

Normally we had a fourteen mile (thirty-three kilometer) ride on the school bus to Belle Anse Consolidated School. Sometimes when the roads were impassable we would get a day off school. We had to wait for the snowplows and snow blowers to come and clear the roads. The children of L'Anse-a-Brilliant would take advantage of this time off from school and our day would be spent sliding on our toboggans and sleighs and skiing on the fresh new snow. In fact we all enjoyed our day off immensely.

One winter morning in the mid-fifties I awoke to find that the blizzard that we had endured the previous day had ended and it was a beautiful sunny and calm winter day. Looking out our kitchen window I could see that there was a few feet of snow on the road and I knew that there would be no school today. I was anxious to eat my breakfast and get outside to go sliding with my toboggan on the fresh new snow.

I trudged through the deep snow up the long hill behind our farmhouse. I planned to climb all the way up to the head a twenty minute walk at least. Then I was going to slide back down to our house, maybe a two minute toboggan ride at the most. But it was going to be worth it. Suddenly I heard a loud noise or I should say roar coming from the other side of L'Anse-a-Brilliant by the church. Coming out of the woods on the line road which was a secondary unpaved road between L'Anse-a-Brilliant and Belle Anse was this big navy blue machine driving over the snow. I didn't know what it was and had never seen anything like it. It turned from the line road unto the highway and passed our farm going towards Seal Cove. I noticed this weird machine had large skis on the front of it and tracks on the bottom of it like an army tank. It has several round windows on the side like portholes you see on a ship. It was travelling at a good clip of speed and throwing out a big cloud of snow behind it. I was amazed how fast it was moving because the snow on the road was at least two feet deep .

I got on my toboggan and slid down to our house where my mother had come outside to call me in. She yelled "Bryan, Come into the house quick. You have to get ready for school."

"Mom", I replied. "There's no school today. It's cancelled because of the storm."

"No, it's not cancelled. That was the Bombardier. Mr. Girard, your school bus driver is driving it. He's come to take all you kids to school today. Your principal does not want you kids to miss any school days and had the drivers get out the old Bombardiers. Yes, Bryan you are going to school today. Get your book bag ready. The Bombardier will be here any minute for you."

I got ready for school in a hurry and when I got down to the road to wait for the Bombardier it wasn't long before I saw it coming down the hill. It stopped and a door opened. I looked in and I saw Mr. Girard.

"Good morning Bryan," Mr. Girard said. "I'd bet you thought you wouldn't be attending school today. I bet you were planning to go sliding on your toboggan today."

"I was sliding down from the head when I heard and saw you coming down the line road" I said. "My mom told me to get ready for school fast. I've never seen anything like this vehicle before."

"It's a Bombardier Bryan and it's made right here in Quebec. I'm going to give you the thrill of a lifetime today. We haven't had the snowmobile out for a few years and maybe by this afternoon the roads will be plowed and I'll be driving you home in the school bus. This may be your only chance to ride in the Bombardier. I stepped inside the snowmobile and said hello to all the six Syvret kids who were from Seal Cove. Instead of rows of seats like on the school bus there were bench seats along both sides and across the back of the snowmobile. If I remember correctly there was room for maybe fifteen or sixteen children. I sat near the back near my friend David Syvret and then we were on our way. We stopped and picked up more students along the way but some missed school that day because they weren't ready and didn't know that the Bombardier was coming for them.

The ride was fairly smooth on the highway but when we turned onto the line road the ride got rougher. There were no seatbelts and when we hit a snow drift or a rough spot we kids in the back of the snowmobile bounced around and were thrown up into the air. There were also some fumes from the motor noticeable inside the Bombardier. By the time we got to the school some of my fellow schoolmates said that they were sick to their stomachs and felt like throwing up. Fortunately it didn't happen in the Bombardier and I enjoyed the once in a lifetime ride to school in a snowmobile riding over the snow instead of the normal driving in a school bus.

At the end of that school day Mr. Girard's prediction proved to be correct as the roads had been plowed and we made the return drive home in the school bus. I was sort of sad in a way because I was looking forward to the return ride home in the Bombardier.

That was my one and only ride in the Bombardier but about ten years later they marketed a small snow machine that held one or two people but it was exposed to the elements. It was called a Ski Doo and became very popular. I have driven them several times over the years but for pure excitement they do not compare to that old Bombardier that I rode in so many years ago.

86. Don't Break Plates On My Head

Throughout my life my most favorite drink or beverage has been a cold glass of water. I don't mean city tap water that is full of chlorine, fluorides and other things they treat it with. I can't drink that water, not even a mouthful. The water that I grew up drinking on the farm was well water or spring water right from the ground and cold even in the summer. This water is pure and delicious the way nature intended it to be.

Our summers in Gaspe could be described as just right, not too hot, and not too cool. One summer however when I was about nine years old it was hot all summer long and some people were worried about their wells going dry. There had been no rain to replenish the underground wells.

One hot summer day I felt like having a drink of cold well water so I turned on the tap but the water wasn't cold so I ran it for a while. My mother got angry with me and told me to shut the tap off because I was wasting water. I told her that it wasn't cold yet.

Our tap water came from my grandfather's well under the other end of the house. It was pumped by an electric pump into a small water tank in his cellar and then to his kitchen and bathroom and also out to our end of the rather large house. My mom was right as I would have to waste a lot of water before it drew new cold water up from the well and over to our kitchen tap.

I went outside on the gallery where our old manual pump was located directly above our well. I pumped the old pump and held a glass under it until it was full. But the water was not cold enough for me so I threw out the water and kept pumping until the water got colder.

My mother came outside and started to give me heck for wasting too much water. She said that "I was going to pump the well dry."

I replied "I have to pump until the water gets cold. The water I pumped is not wasted because it seeps back into the well below through the ground."

My mother didn't buy it and ordered me to stop pumping immediately. I have always had a bit of a temper when provoked and my mother was pushing the wrong buttons. I figured since it was a hot day and she was a little hot under the collar she needed to cool down a mite. So I threw the

197

glass of water I had in my hand into her face. Did I mention that my mother had a bit of a temper as well? Because she had been drying her dishes when all this took place she had a plate in her hand and she promptly smashed it over my head in retaliation.

The fact that I am still here alive and almost well fifty years later means that no real harm was done although my mom was missing one of her favorite plates. Also by now you the reader may have figured out where I got my bit of a temper from.

87. My Mom (Frances De Vouge)

My mother Frances De Vouge was born in 1923 in the village of Dunfield on Trinity Bay in Newfoundland. At that time Newfoundland was not part of Canada. When she was just sixteen her father Will Wiseman decided to send her to Montreal, Quebec to live with her aunt and uncle who had already immigrated to Canada. Mom wanted to be a nurse and she was sent to nursing school. Later while working in a Montreal hospital helping sick people she contracted rheumatic fever herself and almost died. She spent six months in a convalescent home and when she recovered she did not return to nursing.

Mom decided to go to business college and on graduating started her career in the banking industry at The Dominion Bank of Canada in Montreal. She worked her way up and by the time she met and married my father in 1947 she was an assistant manager at the bank.

When I was ten months old and my father decided to move his family to Gaspe I don't know how it set with my mother. I don't think that she was too happy about it. She had lived in the beautiful modern city of Montreal where she had a good career going and she was moving to a farm in L'Anse-a-Brilliant which didn't have electricity, running water or an indoor bathroom. But eventually we got all those modern conveniences and she adjusted quite well.

My mother was now a stay at home mom and in 1953 my sister Donna was born. Over the years her business skills came in handy. When I heard a song on the radio that I liked I would attempt to write the words down while I listened to the song. I wasn't fast enough to do the job but my mother was. You see mom could take shorthand, a skill she learned in business college. When I asked her to write the words to a song we heard she used her shorthand and completed the task in no time at all. Her writings however looked like hen scratchings to me before she translated them back into English.

When anyone needed a professional letter written to a business or government agency they would come to our house and tell my mother what they wanted to say and my mom would type it out on her old "Royal" manual typewriter. I think she had the only one in L'Anse-a-Brilliant.

When we moved to Murdochville in 1961 my mother was sometimes called in to work part time for the manager and the executives of the local mining company when their secretaries went on holiday.

Later when my mom, dad and sister moved to St Catharines in 1966 mom worked for several years in a fruit canning factory and then in a nursing home. She sold Avon products as a sideline and won awards as the top saleslady in St Catharines many times.

When Avon started their new monthly campaign she would deliver the small catalogues to her customers and ask them to phone in their orders on a certain day. When I got home from school that day the phone would be ringing off the hook and I would be taking orders for two solid hours until she got home from work and took over. I joked to her that I deserved some compensation for my hard work on the phone so she would give me some Avon aftershave and cologne once in a while.

In summary, Mom was successful in everything she did including being a mom. After my father passed away in 1996 Mom lived another eleven years and she passed away in Liverpool, Nova Scotia in 2007. She is laid to rest alongside my father in Laurel Hill Cemetery near Port Mouton, Nova Scotia.

88. Dad, You're Going Bald

My father Herzil De Vouge was born in 1917 and was thirty-one years older than me. When I was a small child I remember him as having a full head of jet-black hair. I have several pictures of him circa 1949 proudly holding me up so my mother could take pictures of us with her old Kodak camera. Of course those old pictures are all black and white which really emphasized the blackness of my dad's hair. Dad always had a good haircut and his hair was always combed neatly with a nice wave in the front. He was in fact well groomed.

Ten years later my father was starting to go bald. Dad was in his early forties and while his hair was still jet-black, unfortunately he was losing it. That's when the plan went into action. In the late fifties many of today's male hair restoration products did not exist but there were a few available and my dad tried some of them in the hope of stopping his hair loss and maybe even growing some new replacement hair back in. These products, however failed to live up to expectations and my father continued to lose his hair.

I remember one day back in 1958 or 1959 when dad came home from work for the weekend and showed my mom a new product he had purchased that was guaranteed to grow hair on a bald head. It was imported from France and I believe it was called "Molly de Boeuf". This cure for baldness came in a small glass jar and was sort of brownish in colour. My mother massaged some of this stuff into my dad's scalp every day and we waited and waited for hair to grow. Mom and dad kept checking his head for any new growth of hair but were dismayed to find that there wasn't any appearing.

I knew that my dad was disappointed but I didn't know what the big deal was. I told him "Dad, your father is bald. Your three brothers are going bald. You can't stop baldness."

I don't think my dad wanted to hear this information but I believed it to be true. My uncle Glen who was younger than my dad was already very bald. My uncle Cyril, my dad's older brother was going bald and uncle Denzil, another younger brother still had a good head of hair but was starting to lose a bit.

My father eventually gave up on the hair restoration products and cures for baldness. He did what many men of that era did. It was called a comb-over and consisted simply of growing one's hair long on one side of one's head and combing it over the bald area. Dad's comb-over looked pretty good from a distance and he didn't really look bald. Close you could tell it was a comb-over but dad's still jet black hair still looked good.

Because Gaspe is a coastal region it is windier than most other parts of Canada. My dad's comb-over would blow back when it was windy and he wasn't wearing a cap or hat. His hair would then be short on one side and long on the other and dad would comb it back over with his fingers. the wind would promptly blow it back over once again.

I would say "Dad, you look like a pirate with your hair hanging down like that."

Dad would chuckle and comb it back over once again.

One day in 1977 when I was twenty-nine years old a co-worker came into the lunchroom at work, snuck up behind me and then tickled a spot at the top back part of my head.

I said "Glen, why are you tickling my head?"

Glen replied "I see a little bald spot coming in. Bryan, you are going bald. You have male pattern baldness."

I went home and did something I don't remember ever having done before. I picked up a hand mirror , went into the bathroom, stood in front of the bathroom mirror and checked out the back of my head. Yes, in the ocean of black hair I did see a small spot of my white scalp. I was going bald. So What!

Since that day in 1977 my forehead which was less than three inches above my eyebrows has stretched all the way over the top of my head and half way down the back. At the age of sixty-one I still have hair on the sides of my head and a little at the back. And my hair is still black, not gray. The ten or twelve hairs that still grow on the top of my head are like unwelcome guests. I have the hairstylist get rid of them fast. I flaunt my baldness. Long live the chrome dome.

89. License Plates From All Over The USA

Growing up in the 1950's in the Gaspe Peninsula one of my favorite summertime hobbies was observing and listing out of province license plates found on cars, trucks buses and trailers. When I saw a license plate from a state or province I would write it down on a list when I got home. I would report this to my teacher when I got back to school in September and would usually try to make it into one of my school projects for the year.

Despite being a bit isolated and being off the beaten tract the Gaspe Peninsula received many tourists every year. Although we were very far away from any big cities and consisted mainly of small towns, villages and farmland the Gaspe is tremendously beautiful and scenic. Around every turn there's another picture postcard view waiting to be captured by your camera and enjoyed by you. People who visit the Gaspe are sure to fall in love with it and are sure to return in the future.

There are ten provinces and three territories in Canada and we are one very large country but in the fifties it appeared that we were not a nation of travellers. Canadians did not go on vacation very much and if they did it was mainly to visit relatives who had moved to another province or to one of the big cities like Montreal in our own province. It was a very rare occasion that I would spot a British Columbia, Alberta, Saskatchewan, Manitoba, Newfoundland or Prince Edward Island plate. I don't ever remember seeing a Yukon or Northwest Territories license plate. Usually the Canadian license plates I saw were from Ontario, New Brunswick and Nova Scotia.

It was a different story however with our southern neighbours down in the United States of America. They obviously loved to travel and many of them came to the Gaspe Peninsula to visit in the summer. Not a day went by that I did not see a license plate from the USA.

It totally amazed me that in any one summer I would see between twenty-five and thirty different license plates from all over the USA. It made me wonder what all these Americans were doing here because we did not get that many Canadian tourists. Americans obviously loved to travel and loved coming to the Gaspe. They would flock to the tourist Mecca of maritime Quebec, the small town of Perce where the world famous Percy Rock is located. Percy was thirty miles away from our farm and when my family went there for an afternoon we would see many American tourists and I would get busy writing down all the different state license plates that I saw.

Our license plates in Quebec were simply white with blue letters and numbers on them. The American plates were so much more colourful and some had designs on them as well as the required numbers and letters. For example New York state plates have a graphic of the Statue of Liberty on it. Also there were so many different colours such as blue, white, yellow and even black. If you saw a green license plate from afar and you thought that it was probably Vermont your suspicions would indeed prove correct. If you ever visit Vermont you will understand why the powers at be there chose to make their license plate a green one.

It truly amazed me when I came across a car from states such as Florida and California. What were these people doing here? They had come from such beautiful places why didn't they just stay home and enjoy their own state? One day I was shocked to see a license plate from Alaska, a state that was so far away from the Gaspe that I couldn't imagine anyone driving this far on vacation. I figured Alaska must be at least seven or eight thousand miles away. And at the conclusion of their visit here they had to drive all the way back home again.

It's now been over fifty years since the day I saw that Alaska License plate. Since then I have adopted the American love of travel and I have visited nine provinces and twenty-five states all by driving in my car or truck. Of course my favorite destination is Florida in December, January and February. Since I retired ten years ago I have spent the majority of each winter here in Panama City Beach. I now look for Canadian license plates and so far this winter of 2009 I've seen one each from Nova Scotia, Saskatchewan and Quebec. I have also seen many, many plates from Ontario, hundreds of them in fact. Ontarians appear to love Florida in the wintertime.

90. Blue Haired And Other Weird Teachers

I attended Belle Anse Consolidated School from January of 1955 until January of 1962 except for the one year period when my family had moved to Murdochville in fifty-six and fifty-seven. Some years the school board had difficulty in hiring enough teachers to cover all the classes. You see the Gaspe Peninsula is a basically rural and isolated part of the province of Quebec and our teachers didn't earn as much money as other more populated areas and cities such as Montreal. Even young teachers that had just graduated university and were looking for jobs hesitated to come to the Gaspe to teach school. The end result was that the school board would take anyone that they could get, sometimes scraping the bottom of the barrel. They pulled former teachers out of retirement, hired immigrants from Europe and hired the local Anglican minister to teach.

One year we needed a new principal and the school board hired this old lady with blue hair. I don't remember her name or know how old she was but she looked older than my grandmother who was over sixty. In those days I don't recall any of the older ladies dying their hair in Gaspe. When the ladies got older and their hair went gray they left it gray. So why was our principal's hair bluish? When I asked my mother she said "It's a blue rinse that some ladies with gray hair use to highlight their hair."

Blue was my favorite colour but blue hair seemed weird to me and I didn't understand why a lady would want to have blue hair. Other than that this blue haired lady was an ok principle if not a little strict.

That same year the school board brought Mrs. Whitcomb out of retirement. If we thought the blue haired principle was old then Mrs. Whitcomb was positively ancient. It was quite a harrowing experience being a student in Mrs. Whitcomb's class because every day we students thought that this would be the day that Mrs. Whitcomb would drop dead on us. You see almost every day she fainted and collapsed unto the floor. This usually happened when she was standing at the blackboard for a prolonged period of time and this was too much for her. She seemed to be alright if she just sat at her desk and didn't get up.

The first time that Mrs. Whitcomb fainted our class panicked and the girls started crying and yelling "Mrs. Whitcomb, Mrs. Whitcomb, Mrs. Whitcomb." I ran out of the classroom and burst into the blue-haired principal's office without first knocking on the door. In a very excited manner I told the principle that something had happened to Mrs. Whitcomb and that I thought that she had died. Quickly the principal followed me back into the classroom and on seeing Mrs. Whitcomb laying on the floor turned to me and said "Bryan, go to the school residence and get help."

The janitor's wife who lived at the school with her husband also served as the school nurse and I went and got her. She and the principal applied a wet cloth to Mrs. Whitconb's forehead and she came back to life. We were so relieved to see that our teacher was ok and the class settled down once again.

In the weeks that followed this unfortunate occurrence was repeated several times and each time that it did I or one of my classmates summoned the blue -haired principal and she would revive Mrs. Whitcomb. It was evident that this could not continue and Mrs. Whitcomb was retired once again only partially into the school year. Now we needed another teacher.

One year my teacher was a young lady in her early twenties, a local girl who had graduated from Belle Anse School herself and who still lived with her parents less than a mile from our school. She was a teacher of different moods as one day she would appear to be angry or a word I must hesitate to use but must, bitchy, and then other days she would appear to be very cheerful, so happy in fact that she would let us students get away with a little mischief. We were puzzled why she changed her moods from day to day.

One day one of my classmates came to school and predicted that our young teacher would be in a good mood today. And she was, in fact she was positively glowing with joy.

"Good Morning class." she said. "Isn't it a beautiful day?"

We knew that we were in for a good day today. What we did not know was how our classmate knew in advance and had predicted it. An explanation was in order.

Our classmate in his brilliance had figured it out. He lived close to our teacher's house and knew the days that her boyfriend came over and took her out. These dates meant that her class would have a good day the next day. Also when her boyfriend didn't come around for a few days she became moody and that meant that my classmates and I had to watch our "P's and Q's." My classmate's prediction was bang on because his older brother had seen our teacher with her boyfriend at the local Lover's Lane the previous evening. For the remainder of the school year we could only hope that our teacher's boyfriend could keep her happy with many visits to Lover's Lane.

One of the weirdest and most controversial teachers I ever had was this young German teacher who had come to Canada to teach at Belle Anse School. He was a young man in his mid to late twenties and he proved to be a real dud. He was abusive to many of his students and as the complaints from parents about his conduct multiplied he was told to quit or he would be fired. I'm not sure of the exact circumstances of his leaving but the end result was that we were very happy to see him go.

It was apparent that he didn't like his male students but he really liked the female ones, especially the older teenage girls. There was this certain fifteen or sixteen year old girl in one of the senior classes. She was really beautiful and he openly flirted with her. Although I was only eleven or twelve when this happened we all knew that this was inappropriate. This young lady was in no way receptive to his advances and I think that she was quite embarrassed with the situation. The principal and other teachers realized what was going on and put a stop to it.

In my case I remember having my butt kicked and having my arm twisted behind my back by him.

We were preparing for a Christmas concert at Belle Anse School and like previous years I was going to sing a Christmas carol. Usually I sang in a choir but this year I was going to sing solo and the song was "Silent Night". Because Canada is both English and French I was asked to sing in both official languages. I readily agreed and started practicing, especially the French part of the song. I was surprised when my teacher gave me a sheet of paper written in German and told me that he wanted me to also sing "Silent Night "in German. I told him that I didn't know how to talk or sing in German and the teacher in charge of the concert had asked me to sing in English and French. He got angry with me and ordered me to learn the words to the song in German. He asked me to read the German words from the sheet he had given me and I tried to read them but having never heard the German language spoken before I totally mispronounced the words. This got my teacher more angry at me, so angry in fact that he took my arm and twisted it behind my back putting me in a great deal of pain. He accused me of mispronouncing the words on purpose and told me to have the words memorized for the next day.

My father was off to Murdochville for the week at his job so I told my mother what had happened.

Mom said, "No son of mine is going to sing "Silent Night" in German and she got quite angry. I don't exactly know what mom said in her note to the principal but the end result was my teacher never mentioning anything about me singing in German again. Of course there was still quite a bit of anti-German sentiment here a little over a decade since the end of the second world war.

Our school was located at Belle Anse on a hill overlooking a bay of the Atlantic Ocean. We had a good view of the famous Perce Rock and Bonaventure Island across the bay. That spring a school or I should say pod of whales came into the bay and we had a really good view of several of them right from our school. We had seen this before but our young teacher from Germany had not seen anything like this and he was really fascinated with the whales. He took the whole class down to the field below the road to get a better view. There was a steep bank, almost a cliff really down near the water and he warned us for our own safety to stay at least fifty feet from the edge. He said he didn't want any of us falling over the edge. He asked us to take a few minutes to observe what we saw before us; the whales in the bay, Perce Rock, Bonaventure Island and the high mountains on the other side of the bay. Then he asked us to write an essay describing what we saw before us.

A few of us boys edged a little closer to the edge of the bank even though our teacher had warned us not to. When he noticed this he became furious and because I was the closest he picked me up by the ankles and lifted me up in the air. Since I was upside down my head was dangling close to the ground. I was afraid that he was going to drop me but he held on to my ankles tight and he kicked my butt a few times with his foot all the time yelling at me and accusing me of disobeying him. I was too afraid to cry and wondered what was going to happen to me but when he put me back down I noticed that a few of the girls were crying and all of my other classmates had shocked looks on their faces. What should have been a wonderful experience with the whales in the bay turned out to be a nightmare for my classmates and especially for me.

Our so called teacher left our school shortly thereafter never to be heard from again. He may have gone back to Germany where that type of conduct may have been more tolerated but it was certainly not acceptable here in Canada. He was most definitely the weirdest and worse teacher I have ever had.

91. Verna Tells Off The Minister

In the preceding chapter I wrote about weird teachers and I didn't include the Reverend Thomson. I felt that he deserved a chapter all his own.

In 1958 I was ten years old and in grade five. Our local Anglican minister who had served our community for many years was the Reverend Apps and he retired and moved away. Our new Anglican minister was the Reverend Thomson and he and his family came to us from Wales in the British Isles. He served Anglican congregations in Mal Baie, Barachois and L'Anse-a-Brilliant and maybe one other that I'm not aware of. That meant preaching in three or four different churches miles apart which made his Sunday's very busy indeed.

At Belle Anse Consolidated school that year we were short a teacher and the Reverent Thomson was enlisted to fill the void. He did not become my home room teacher but roamed from classroom to classroom teaching different grades. I kind of liked him mainly because I became enamored with his ten-year old daughter Madeline who was in my grade five class. It appeared that she liked me as well and we were quite the item in our class for a while.

Back in the fifties the teacher would give us a cod-liver oil capsule just after the lunch bell rang. The idea was that the cod-liver oil was very good for us and would keep us in excellent health. However many of us had other ideas on what to do with these capsules. We would bite a small hole in the end and squeeze the capsule squirting the cod-liver oil on each other. This would stink up our clothes all day with a terrible stench. We would also bite into the capsule breaking it and then gargle with the cod-liver oil. This would give us terrible and I mean really terrible bad breath which we then exhaled onto our classmates discussing them.

When the Reverend Thomson came to our school to teach he ended this nonsense. When the lunch bell rang at noon he would shout out very loudly "Don't forget your capsules" and he would proceed to the door where we exited the classroom and pop a cod-liver oil capsule into our open mouths. He would ask us to swallow the capsule, open our mouths and stick out tongue so he could see that we had done as he had instructed. This reminds me of the television show "Survivor" where in the food competition the contestants have to open their mouths wide and shove out their tongues to prove that they had swallowed the ghastly maggot that they are forced to eat. Only with us it was cod-liver oil capsules.

At recess when we played baseball outside we would all practice the Reverend Thomson's favorite words "Don't forget your capsules" in our best Welsh accents.

The real reason that I'm writing about the reverend Thomson is to tell you what we didn't like about him as a teacher. When he asked a student a question he figured that the student should provide him with the correct answer. If the student answered wrongly the Reverend Thomson would often shout out 'You fool, you fool" in a loud manner. "You should know the correct answer to that question."

I was never called a fool but several of my classmates were and they didn't like it at all. It was very embarrassing for them to be called a fool by their teacher and they didn't think that it was right. Many of the schoolchildren informed their parents what was happening at school and it became a topic of discussion between some parents.

Verna Leggo was a second cousin of mine and was about four years older than me and in the upper grades at our school. We heard rumours on the school bus that Verna had a solution to the problem at school but we did not know what it was. Verna's grandmother and my father's aunt Ella had given her advice on what to do if Reverend Thomson ever called her a fool.

One day in Verna's class one of the students gave an incorrect answer to a question that Reverend Thomson had asked. He raised his voice to the student and said "You fool, you fool."

Verna had been waiting for this to happen and when it did she stood up from her desk and said to Reverend Thomson "Whoever sayeth to his brother thy fool shall be in danger of hellfire" which is a quotation from the bible.

It was said that on hearing this Reverend Thomson's mouth dropped open in astonishment. He had no response, however he never ever called a student a fool again.

92. I'm The Champ (Reading)

It's Wednesday January 14, 2009 and I'm sitting at the dining room table here in Florida watching the San Antonia Spurs versus the Los Angeles Lakers on TV. I like writing while watching a game be it baseball in the summer and fall or basketball in the winter. By the way' the Spurs are winning 98 to 89 and there's eight minutes and fifty-nine seconds left in the game. When the game is over I will put down my pen and paper, shut off the television and resume reading "The Shape Shifter by Tony Hillerman. I will finish reading the book tonight and it will be the fifth book that I have read in the past fourteen days.

Since I retired in 1999 I have read over eight hundred books, mostly fiction but also documentaries and biographies. I was reading over one hundred books per year but in the last few years I have cut back. In 2007 I read seventy-five books and in 2008 I really cut back only reading sixty-four, which is the lowest total of any of the past ten years. I buy all these books at bookstores or from the book club. I also receive books as gifts from my three sons. I do not borrow books from the library. When I want to read a book I buy it, read it and then store it. I have bookcases in every room in my house except the kitchen and the bathrooms. I have every book that I have ever read since I was a child. I have thousands and thousands of books, too many really. And still I buy more books.

It all started when I was a small child on the farm. Even though I couldn't read I would look at any book or magazine I could get my hands on. I would look at the pictures and wonder what the words said. My mother and father must have got tired of reading to me but I don't remember them ever refusing to read to me when I asked. Also my grandmother would read to me from the bible as she was very religious and the good book was her book of choice.

When I was about five years old my father got some old grade one and grade two schoolbooks and he taught me to read almost a year before I started school. In the years that followed I read and read anything and everything.

Around fifty years ago in 1959 when I was in grade six Belle Anse Consolidated School wanted to promote reading and we had a reading

211

competition. Whoever read the most books from the school library during this part of the school year would be declared the reading champion. We would take out books from the school library, read then on our own time and then on Friday give an oral book report to the teacher. I usually gave about three reports per week and at the end of the reading competition I had read eighty-three books and was declared the reading champion. No other student in the school was even close. I was very proud of my accomplishment like an athlete winning the championship in his chosen sport.

At Christmas and on my birthday I would receive books from my three aunts, my mother and grandmother. One year I received the same book from three of my aunts. Therefore two were exchanged for books I didn't have and all was well.

My favorite books were Whitman books with titles such as "The Lone Ranger" and others such as "Red Rider" and "Roy Rogers. I also loved "The Hardy Boys" series. After that I would make a list of books I wanted and give it to my mother and she would inform my aunts so that there was no duplication from then on. Nanny almost always bought me a religious book for children and I enjoyed reading it as well.

Friends and relatives alike use to tell me that I read so many books that I was likely to go blind. However fifty years later with the aid of eye glasses I am still reading and loving it.

A reader I was, a reader I am and a reader I always will be.

93. Holiday To Newfoundland, P.E.I. and Nova Scotia (1959)

In the spring of 1959 my mom and dad announced that we were once again going on vacation for two weeks in July. We would be visiting my mother's relatives in Newfoundland, my father's relatives in Nova Scotia and some friends in Prince Edward Island. Our road trip was to last two whole weeks.

The first day of our trip we drove as far as Moncton, New Brunswick and we stayed at the Green Acres Motel which was very close to Magnetic Hill, the number one tourist attraction in Moncton. We visited Magnetic Hill and dad drove to the spot indicated, shut off the car's motor, put the transmission in neutral and we coasted up the small hill supposedly as the result of magnetic force. It was very weird indeed but I think that it was some sort of optical illusion and we were actually coasting down the hill.

The second day we drove into Nova Scotia and over the bridge across the Strait of Canso to Cape Breton Island. We proceeded to North Sydney where we boarded the big ferry "The Cabot Strait" which would take us across the Cabot Strait overnight to Port aux Basques, Newfoundland. We stayed that night on board in a family cabin for four with two bunk beds . It was the first time I ever slept on a top bunk and on a ship no-less.

On the road again the next morning we drove to Corner Brook which was very scenic and I judged it to be a big town or maybe a small city. Remember I came from a country farm so even a small town seemed big to me. We visited one of my mother's nieces who lived there with her husband. I think her name was Carol.

Newfoundland had joined Canada in 1949 and now ten years later they were building Highway 1 which was the new Trans Canada Highway. There were long areas of construction and paving so the going was very slow and frustrating to drivers who had to stop and wait and wait for long periods of time before being allowed to proceed once again only to be stopped at another paving site five miles down the road.

The Trans Canada Highway does not go in a straight line from Port aux Basques in the west to St John's in the east but goes in a semi-circle first northwest to the north of the province and then southeast to the capital city of St. Johns. We were almost halfway across the island and we were stopped by a man with a portable stop sign. He informed us that there was a detour. We looked around but we didn't see any road to detour onto. The sign man told us that we had to drive across this farmer's field until we came to a gravel road and turn right and drive about five miles until we came to another man with a sign who would inform us of another detour. When we reached the second sign man he sent us on another long detour.

"I think we're going in the wrong direction " I said. "We should be going east towards St. John's and I'm sure we're going west."

"Yes" my dad replied. "But that's where the man directed us on this detour."

We eventually made it back to Highway 1 but low and behold we were stopped by the same construction worker with the stop sign as we were the first time. Once again he informed us that we had to go on a detour.

"Don't you recognize us?" dad asked. "You sent us on a detour an hour ago and now we're right back here where we started. We went in a complete circle."

Before the man could reply my mother lit into him but good. "What the hell are you people doing in this province? she asked. "You sent us on a wild goose chase through a farmer's field on a cow path in the wrong direction. I tell you Joey Smallwood is going to hear about this. In fact I'm so mad if I had Joey Smallwood by the neck I would choke him right now." My mother was so angry she was steaming and I thought I would see steam rising from her forehead.

"I'm sorry maam" said the construction sign man. The other sign man up the road made a big mistake and sent several people in the wrong direction."

I knew that Joey Smallwood the man that my mother had referred to was the premier of Newfoundland and was responsible for bringing his province into Confederation with Canada. I was surely glad that he was not there that day for I was sure that my mother might have strangled him.

We drove on and this time the second sign man sent us in the right direction. We were happily on our way after having wasted around ninety minutes due to the false detour.

About an hour later I noticed that my mom was asleep in the front seat and my sister was asleep in the back seat. I was engrossed in my Superman comic book when our car left the road and proceeded into the ditch. Apparently my father, the driver had fallen asleep at the wheel. As I yelled at him he awoke, regained control of the car and drove it up the bank, out of the ditch and back onto the road. We stopped and checked for damage to the car but it was undamaged. Several people had witnessed what happened and told us that it was a miracle that we were still alive and well. From that moment on I resolved to keep a close eye on my father while he was driving.

It was now almost five o'clock in the afternoon and we had not eaten anything since we had breakfast at my cousin's place in Corner Brook. It appeared that in the province of Newfoundland all restaurants, snack bars, etc. were closed on Sunday's. Finally we saw this roadside chip stand and a man was there opening the door to enter it. We stopped and my father asked the man if he was open for business.

"It's Sunday" he said. "We're closed. Everything is closed on Sunday's."

My mother got out of our car and said "We've been driving all day and haven't had anything to eat since breakfast. We're tourists from Gaspe, Quebec and we didn't realize that there would be nothing open on Sunday's. Where's a tourist supposed to eat today?"

The man replied "We don't get many tourists here."

"You're going to get more now that the Trans Canadian Highway is being completed " my mom said. "I think you'll have to start opening on Sundays. Could you open up for a half hour? We're starving."

The man said "Sure" and he opened the chip stand for us. We all has hamburgers, fries and pop and ate our meal at a picnic table. Boy, the hamburger and fries tasted some good and the Orange Crush tasted better than normal. I conclude that food tastes better when you're starving. My parents thanked the man for feeding us on this Sunday and we were on our way.

We actually made it to the village of Dunfield on Trinity Bay that day. It was where my mother was born and lived until she moved to Montreal when she was sixteen years old. Although my grandfather had passed away in 1952 and my grandmother had remarried and moved away my mother still had many cousins, friends and other relatives there. I had some memories of Dunfield because I had spent the summer of 1951 there with my mother when my grandfather Will Wiseman was still alive. We did not stay in my mom's old house. It was now owned by my mom's cousin Gilbert. Instead we stayed at one of my mom's oldest and dearest friend's house right across the street.

There were a few unusual things that I saw happen in Dunfield. I saw this herd of horses in an upper meadow outside the village. They seemed to be running wild and grazing on the grass up there. In the evening they came down from the meadow and paraded through the main street of the village and then exited Dunfield to an area where they could get a good drink of fresh water. It appeared that the horses that some called Newfoundland Ponies stayed in that area overnight and in the morning they paraded through the village streets once again and returned to the upper meadow to graze all day. When I asked who owned the horses I was told that several people owned them and that they were turned loose in the summer to look after themselves. In the fall the owner would round up his horse and put it to work hauling sleigh's of firewood out of the woods. This was different than back in Gaspe because we kept horses on our land and when they were thirsty they came to the barn where we provided them pails of water to drink. They also slept in the barn all year long.

I also noticed that the people here kept goats and not sheep like we kept in L'Anse-a-Brilliant. They drank goat's milk instead of cow's milk like I did back home.

My father and I were invited to go cod fishing with Gilbert and his co-workers. Gilbert wanted to show us his fish trap and how they went about catching their fish for sale. The trap was actually a big net out in the bay and we went out in two boats. We were in the bigger boat with most of the fishermen. A few men in the smaller boat closed the door to the large net trapping the fish inside. Then as the fishermen pulled the net into the larger boat the fish gradually surfaced until they ran out of room and the fishermen gaffed them into the boat. I'd never seen so many live codfish in one place in my life. it looked like there were at least a thousand codfish there. It took a very long time indeed to get all those fish into the two boats to transport them back to land. It was a different way of inshore fishing than we did back in Gaspe where we jigged cod. It was obvious to me that there were a lot of codfish in Trinity Bay.

It turned out that my father's 1958 Mercedes-Benz was quite an attraction to the people who lived in Dunfield, especially the children. Most people had not seen a car imported from Germany before and when I explained to some of the kids that it had a diesel motor which burned oil instead of gas they looked at me in amazement. When I explained that the motor had no sparkplugs they looked at each other and didn't say anything. I don't think they believed me.

The next day we drove to Bay Roberts which is located on Conception Bay, one bay over from Trinity Bay. We were going there to visit my mother's stepmother Amy who had remarried after my grandfather Will Wiseman had passed away. My grandmother's new husband was Mr. Jacob Mercer and he was a salmon fisherman. It was the first time that we met him since he had married my widowed grandmother. I now had a new step-grandfather.

The next day we had breakfast around seven o'clock in the morning. Then we had what I thought was our dinner at eleven o'clock. At two o'clock we did have our dinner although I didn't eat much because I wasn't hungry. The table was set once again at four o'clock in the afternoon and tea and cookies were served, sort of a snack. Supper was served between six and seven and later that night before bedtime we had a scoff (a snack).

I asked my mother "Mom, why are we eating six times in a day?"

"It's an old Newfoundland custom" was her reply. "The younger people don't do it anymore but the old people still do sometimes, especially when they have company."

"Six meals in a day" I said. "Breakfast, an elevener, dinner, a fourer,

supper and a scoff. Gee, That's a lot of dishes to wash. But you won't go hungry around here."

After a few days in Bay Roberts we drove to St. John's, the capital city of Newfoundland and visited my mother's older sister Gladys and her family. I met several of my cousins including a teenager named Francis who was named after my mother. I also went to a ballpark with one of my male cousins and played baseball with him and his friends.

When it was time to take the long drive across Newfoundland back to Port aux Basques to catch the ferry back to the mainland I wasn't looking forward to it. This time however, it was smooth sailing or I should say driving. Nobody sent us on wild goose chase detours this time and there were hardly any delays due to construction. We even got to stop and watch a moose who was eating lily pads close to the highway. That night we stayed at a small place along Highway 1 called South Branch. My dad rented a cabin and I noticed that it was located only about fifty feet or so from a train track. We were all tired and went to bed fairly early. I woke up about four in the morning and I was wide awake. I tried but I could not get back to sleep. It appeared that my mom, dad and sister were all still sleeping soundly. Then I heard a train coming and it blew its whistle because there was a railway crossing next to the motel and cabins. I thought it was stupid for the train engineer to blow the whistle so early in the morning because he would wake everybody up. But I guess that they had their rules that they had to abide by. I thought that my mother had awakened because I could hear her mumbling.

"There's a train coming" I said.

"Oh my God" my mom said. "My children will be killed."

I then realized that my mother was talking in her sleep so I replied "No, don't worry. Your children are safe."

"Oh, Thank God ." my mom replied. :My children are safe.

A couple of hours later when everyone else got up I asked my mother if she remembered talking to me at four in the morning. She had no memory of it at all so I informed her of our conservation when she was talking in her sleep.

There appeared that there wasn't any restaurant and we were all very hungry. When mom and dad went to pay for the cabin mom asked where the nearest restaurant was located. The lady replied that there wasn't any restaurant nearby but then she invited us into her home and told us that she would make us our breakfast. She said "There's no menu but I'll make you anything you want for your breakfast."

My mom and dad had bacon, eggs, toast and coffee while Donna and I had cereal and milk.

After dad paid the lady for the cabin and breakfast we were on our way to Port aux Basques to board the ferry back to Nova Scotia. This time we boarded the "William Carson", a very modern and gigantic ferry ship. It was so big that there were train tracks on the ship and I saw a train actually drive right onto the ferry. This time we were crossing the Cabot Strait in the daytime so Donna and I set to exploring the ship which had several decks. We found an elevator and pressed the button to take us to the bottom level. Exiting the elevator we walked along a corridor and went through the first door we saw. We found ourselves in a big noisy room with what looked like a gigantic engine which I then realized was the engine that ran the ship. I also noticed a sign on the wall which said "Authorized Personnel Only" or something to that effect. I was about to mention to my five year old sister that we better get out of there when I heard this loud voice behind me.

"What are you doing down here?" asked the man. "This area is off limits to passengers. Do your parents know that you're down here?"

"No" I replied. "We were on the elevator and must have pushed the wrong button."

"Then get right back on the elevator and go find your parents." he said. "And push the right button this time."

Donna and I found mom and dad and we all went to the ship's restaurant for lunch. It appears that mom and dad had not been too worried about our absence. They knew that when we got hungry we would seek them out.

I think the crossing from Newfoundland to North Sydney, Nova Scotia took about eight hours and then we drove off Cape Breton Island to mainland Nova Scotia and proceeded to Truro where my aunt Dot, uncle Glen and cousins Tommy, Freddy and Gary lived. We stayed there on Bible Hill Road for a few days and I remember the big fields of the Nova Scotia Agricultural College across the street. I also remember there was a midway or carnival located nearby that we attended and I went on a few rides.

A few days later we drove to Pictou where we took a car ferry to Wood Islands on the south shore of Prince Edward Island. The ferry was much smaller than the ones we took to and from Newfoundland and we crossed the Northumberland Strait in less than two hours. We drove through the capital city of Charlottetown and northwest to P.E.I.'s second city of Summerside. We stayed at my parent's friend's farm about five miles out of Summerside and I helped my dad pitch our old tent. It was the first time on this holiday that we were going to be sleeping in the tent and I was looking forward to it. We spent the day with my parent's friend's family and then spent a pleasant night in the tent. The second day it started to rain real hard and it was decided that we would sleep in the house that night. I still wanted to sleep in the tent but the powers at be decided otherwise. The problem was that I would have to sleep with my sister which I did not like to do. The solution was that we slept head to toe, toe to head which was acceptable to me and the bed was more comfortable than the leaky tent in the pouring rain.

Prince Edward Island is a mostly flat low lying island very different than the rough, rugged and mountainous Newfoundland. I think the country place where we were staying was called Cherry Hill and I was wondering why because when I looked around the land appeared kind of flat without any thing that I considered a hill in sight. All I could see beside other farmhouses were potato fields as far as the eye could see. It seemed that every square inch of farm land was devoted to growing potatoes. I surmised that potato farming was the number one industry here. The soil or clay appeared to be red in colour in contrast to the brown ground we had back in Gaspe.

The next day we departed P.E.I. at Borden and took another small car ferry to Cape Tormentine, New Brunswick. At this point the Northumberland Strait is at it's narrowest and the ferry ride only took an hour or so.

We completed the crossing and drove north through New Brunswick back to our home province of Quebec and to our farm in the Gaspe Peninsula. We had certainly crammed a lot of activity into a two week vacation. We had reconnected with many of our friends and relatives that we had not seen for several years. We had visited all four of Canada's maritime provinces which included three islands. It was quite the adventure but now it was nice to be back home.

94. Smuggling Margarine into Quebec

On our vacation trip to Ontario in 1958 I became aware of margarine which was something that was not available back home in the province of Quebec. Margarine looked like butter and tasted like butter. On a piece of bread I could not tell the difference between the two.

When I got back to Gaspe I read an article in the paper that the Quebec Government had passed a law banning the importing of margarine into the province of Quebec. I asked my dad why margarine was illegal in Quebec.

Dad said "Oh, they're crazy. They think that if they allow margarine to be sold here in Quebec that it will ruin the dairy industry here."

I read follow up articles in the paper that Quebec had the largest dairy industry of any province in Canada. Because margarine was less than half the price of butter the powers at be in the Quebec government felt that they had to erect protective barriers. I was only a ten year old kid and I didn't understand how Quebec could sell it's dairy products such as milk, yogurt and it's famous cheese to the other provinces like Ontario and then ban Ontario margarine from Quebec. It just wasn't fair.

In the following summer of 1959 we went on a vacation road trip once again, this time to the maritime provinces. We were reacquainted with the taste of margarine and my father informed us that he was going to buy some margarine to take back home with us.

My mom said "But Herzil, what about the law against margarine in Quebec?"

"What are they going to do?" my dad said. "Are they going to put me in jail for illegal food?"

At the end of our two week vacation and before returning home to Quebec we went shopping at a grocery store and dad bought two cases of Blue Bonnet margarine. Each case contained twenty-four bricks of margarine. Dad placed both cases on the floor of the back seat of the car, one case under my feet and one case under Donna's feet. He covered them with a blanket so they wouldn't be visible and we were on our way.

When we crossed the bridge from Campbellton, New Brunswick to Pointe-a-la Croix, Quebec we were stopped on the Quebec side of the bridge by two men in uniform. They weren't police but were some sort of Customs men. When one of them approached our car my dad rolled down his window.

"Good Day sir" the officer said. "Do you have any margarine in your trunk today?"

"No" was my dad's reply.

"Could you open your trunk for me please?" said the man and he glanced into the car at my mother, sister and me.

My father opened the trunk and the officer looked in. He saw our luggage, tent, sleeping bags and some groceries that we had bought. He rummaged through the groceries but didn't find any margarine. The officer thanked my father and said "Welcome home."

We were on our way. Nobody was going to jail today for importing margarine into Quebec.

Back home on the farm we opened up a margarine case and I discovered the rectangular bricks were not shaped like a brick of butter as they were long and narrow and they were white. There was a round capsule of food colouring in the middle that you had to bust with your thumb nail and knead into the white margarine until it became the yellow colour of butter. We used about one brick of margarine per week so our forty-eight bricks would last us almost a whole year. It became my job to bust the food colouring capsule and kneed the margarine once every week. I liked margarine because in the winter when it was colder in the house it was always soft and easily spread as compared to butter which was hard in the winter and almost impossible to spread evenly.

My mother told me not to tell my friends at school that I had margarine in the sandwiches that she made me for my lunch.

"You never know" she said. "Someone might inform on us having margarine."

In 1960 we went to Ontario on vacation and once again we brought back two cases of Blue Bonnet margarine. By now they had ended the practice of checking your car's trunk for margarine at the Quebec border. Margarine, however was still illegal in Quebec.

Some years after I left the province of Quebec in 1967 it became legal to sell margarine in Quebec with some conditions. Margarine had to retain its white colour to distinguish it from the beautiful yellow colour of butter. It was thought that most people would reject the idea of buttering their bread with a white spread.

Just a few short years ago in 2006 or 2007 it finally became legal to add food colouring to margarine to make it yellow like butter. It only took about fifty years to do so.

These days I prefer butter on my bread but still use margarine when I cook. As to the number of job's I've had and things that I have done I guess I can add illicit margarine smuggler to the list.

95. Sister Donna

My sister Donna is five years younger than me and she is my only sibling. When I think back to the days when we were children I remember that we got along quite well. In other words we didn't fight like cats and dogs like some brothers and sisters do and we didn't kill each other.

I do remember her tagging along with me when I went to visit or play with my friends. When you are twelve years old and want to hang out with your buddies who want their seven year old sister there as well? Sometimes I had to wait until she was otherwise occupied and sneak out of our house without her knowing.

One thing that aggravated me was that she got everything she wanted for free just by asking our parents. I, on the other hand had to pay fifty percent and sometimes the total cost of things that I wanted. For example when I was eleven I asked my dad to buy me my first bicycle. He informed me that if I worked during the summer and saved the money he would buy me a new bike but I had to put up half the money. After earning the money doing various jobs I presented my father with twenty dollars. He put in twenty dollars and he bought me my first new bike. At the same time dad bought Donna a new bike for free. She didn't have to put up one red cent.

A few years later in Murdochville someone stole the back wheel off my bike which had been parked behind our house. Because my bicycle was imported from England I had to order a new back wheel from England which took quite a long time to arrive.

I asked Donna "Can I borrow your bike?"

"No" was her answer. "But you can rent it for twenty-five cents for every half hour that you use it."

When I complained to my mother all she said was "that girl is going to become a banker."

I had to pay my ten year old sister rent every time I used her bike and you can bet that she was watching the clock.

One winter I had a nasty spill on the ski hill and I broke one of my skis: better the ski than my leg I guess. I don't remember Donna skiing but she did have skis and she rented them to me as well.

When my transistor radio broke she rented me her transistor radio which my parents had bought for her after she complained that I had one and she didn't. Of course I had paid for mine myself.

When my record player broke and could not be fixed she got one somehow and rented it to me. However she had no records of her own and I had a good collection. When she asked to borrow some of my records I said "Ok, but you'll have to pay me rent."

"No way" was her reply and she stormed away.

Every time I left the house or went out at night Donna would sneak into my bedroom, find my records and play them for free.

You guessed it. Yes, Donna did become a banker, a corporate lender in fact lending millions of dollars to company CEO's coming to her to borrow money.

96. The Hanging Tree

When you see or hear the expression "The Hanging Tree" you might think back to the old west when the good guys caught the cattle rustler or horse thief. Justice was usually quick and the good guys found the nearest suitable tree with a stout branch strong enough to hold a man's weight without bending. The outlaw was placed on a horse, a noose was placed around his neck and someone then slapped the horse on the butt. The end result was an outlaw hanged by the neck until he was dead. The tree became known as a hanging tree.

In the fall of 1959 or 1960 (I'm not sure which) when I was eleven or twelve the three Leggo brothers Lance, Denver, Zane and I went exploring up the L'Anse-a-Brilliant River one day after school. We had no particular destination in mind but wanted to go further than we had gone before. One of the Leggo boys pointed out something that none of us had seen before.

It was a birch tree growing out of the rather steep riverbank and it wasn't growing up towards the sky like the evergreen trees there. For some unknown reason it was growing out from the bank at a forty-five degree angle towards the river. It was very weird indeed.

Lance decided to climb this tree and the rest of us watched as at first he started climbing up and then as the tree bent with his weight he was climbing sideways directly above us. As he climbed further up or I should say along the tree it kept bending down and Lance became closer to the ground. Suddenly Lance unwrapped his legs from around the tree trunk and he dangled down from the tree just hanging there with his feet a few feet above our heads. The tree was now shaped like an archer's bow and we knew that it had some spring in it. Denver and I jumped up and each of us grabbed one of Lance's legs and pulled him down a bit. This was an incredible stupid thing to do because when we let go of Lance's legs the tree sprang upwards with Lance holding on for dear life. Because Lance was such a good and strong athlete he managed to hang on without any mishap but I'm sure if that was me on that tree I wouldn't have been able to hang on and would have fallen from the tree and broken my neck.

Once the tree was motionless Lance simply let go and dropped to the ground without hurting himself. The second time Lance climbed the tree I decided to join him and we both ended up hanging from the tree but this time we were closer to the ground because the tree bent more with the added weight of two of us on it. When we decided it was time for us to drop to the ground someone said "one, two, three, go" and we both dropped at the same time. This was great fun and we named the tree "The Hanging Tree". We also vowed to return once again for more fun.

The next day on the bus ride home from school we decided that as soon as the school bus let us off in L'Anse-a-Brilliant we were heading for the hanging tree. For the second day in a row we climbed and dropped, climbed and dropped and now we were becoming pros at it. We were hooting and hollering and having a great old time. Once again nobody got hurt and we went home happy and with all our bones intact.

On the third day on the bus ride home from school we debated whether we should visit the hanging tree for the third day in a row. Of course we were now addicted to playing on the hanging tree and the answer was yes, we were going. In fact we couldn't wait to get there we were so excited.

When we reached the hanging tree we were shocked, saddened and deeply disappointed at what we discovered. The hanging tree was not hanging anymore but lying on the ground. Someone had chopped it down.

For a moment we just stood there in silence with dejected looks on our faces. Then I got angry and wondered why someone would chop down our hanging tree and spoil our fun. We wondered who had done this despicable thing. Obviously it was not my father because he was working eighty miles away in Murdochville and only came home on weekends. I knew it was not my grandfather and it wasn't Basil Leggo, my friend's father because he was busy working at his store all day. Then who could it be? It was a great mystery.

I had my own personal theory of who had done the dastardly deed and why. There was a young man named Derean McCoy who lived nearby who was in his thirties and still lived with his parents. He was a curious fellow and I think that when he heard goings on in the woods a few hundred yards from his house he went to investigate what was taking place there. When he sneaked up through the woods and observed us hanging from the hanging tree he did not reveal himself but waited until we had our share of fun and left. He must have then gone back home, obtained an axe and then returned into the woods to chop down our hanging tree. Why did he do it? He obviously thought that what we were doing there was very dangerous and that eventually one of us children would fall off the hanging tree and seriously injure if not kill ourselves. He did not want to see this happen so he got an axe and chopped down the tree. End of our fun. End of the danger.

Now that is only my theory and after more than fifty years we still do not know who chopped down the hanging tree. Now that I'm a senior citizen I realize what a big favor the mystery man did us that day so many years ago. Thank you whoever you are as we are all still alive and well. But the mystery remains. Who really did cut down the hanging tree?

97. Return To Ontario (1960)

As the summer of 1960 approached my father announced to us that once again we were going on a July vacation trip to Ontario with a stop in Montreal along the way. I was overjoyed because we had visited Montreal, Toronto and the Welland area of Ontario in 1958. I loved it there and was so looking forward to watching television once again. We still did not have television reception in L'Anse-a-Brilliant and I was getting real tired of waiting for it to come our way.

When we reached Montreal we were to visit my uncle Cyril and his family in Park X and my aunt Leona who lived in the Rosemount area. We were also going to visit and stay with an old friend of my father's named Ernie who worked for the Montreal Canadiens. At the time I was born in Montreal in 1948 dad was friends with a few of the Canadiens players that he had met through Ernie and when we left Montreal and moved to L'Anse-a-Brilliant in 1949 dad had sold our cottage at Lac Echo in the Laurentian Mountains to one of the Montreal Canadiens players; I'm not sure which one. Ernie was not the coach or general manager of the Montreal team but was an executive of some sort with them.

When we arrived at Ernie's house we were invited down to his basement where his recreation room was located. His rec room was a shrine to the Montreal Canadiens with several team pictures on the walls and other memorabilia spread around. But the thing I loved the most was something that I could not believe. He had his very own pop cooler right there in his rec room. When Ernie was opening a beer for my dad he noticed me admiring the pop machine.

"Bryan" he said. "Get a pop for your sister and yourself."

I asked my father for twenty cents to insert into the pop machine for two soft drinks.

Ernie laughed and said "No Bryan, you don't need any money for that machine. Open the lid and grab two pop. The gate you pull them through is always unlocked."

I did what he said and removed two Orange Crush, one for me and one for my sister Donna.

"Thanks" I said. "I wish we had a pop machine like this in our house."

Ernie chuckled and said "Ask your dad to get you one."

"Fat chance" I thought.

As we continued on our vacation and entered Ontario my sister Donna and I noticed something new and exciting that was not there the last time we had visited Ontario two years before. There were Tastee Freeze ice cream franchises everywhere and it so happened that our father loved the new swirly soft ice cream. As our father drove along Donna and I would spot a Tastee Freeze sign and yell out in unison "Tastee Freeze, Tastee Freeze."

Although our yelling scared the wits out of dad while he was driving he would quickly pull over and buy us all an ice cream. We ended up making many pit stops during the trip.

As we had done two years previously we visited Mr. Dawson Baird and his relatives in the Welland area. One day we went out in the countryside and visited Les Selby who had a few sons around my age. On their property out behind their house they had an old fashioned swimming hole dug out of the ground with a bulldozer and filled with water. It wasn't an official swimming pool but on a hot July day in southern Ontario it sure did the trick even if the water was sort of muddy. While I was in the water I noticed some things that scared the bejesus out of me. There were several large bugs with very long wings flying around and it became very evident to the boys that I was afraid of them. Back home in Gaspe I had been stung by bumble bees, wasps and hornets and I didn't want to be stung by these nasty things. The boys told me not to be afraid.

"These are dragon flies" one of the guys said. "They won't bite or sting you. They are protecting us by eating up the mosquitoes that are after us."

"Thank God" I said. "I wish we had some of them in Gaspe."

Our vacation trip of 1960 was a very enjoyable one and before you knew it we were heading back to the Gaspe. But as our father was driving down the road concentrating on his driving he would suddenly be startled by Donna and myself yelling out in unison "Tastee Freeze, Tastee Freeze."

98. Throwing Snowballs

On of my favorite winter activities when we were kids in the Gaspe was throwing snowballs. We certainly got enough snow for it. The best time for making snowballs was late fall-early winter and in the spring when it was getting warmer out. In the colder months of the winter it was very difficult to make a good snowball because the snow lacked moisture and it was simply too dry. The best snowballs were made in the spring when the snow was starting to melt and had a large moisture content. This sticky snow was ideal and we took advantage of it by making hundreds of snowballs and throwing them at each other.

I remember one fine spring day when Lance and Denver Leggo, Reed De Vouge and I made two snow forts about thirty-five feet apart. We divided into two teams the De Vouge's against the Leggo's. Each team made about fifty snowballs and piled them behind our forts for easy access. When we were all ready someone said go and the battle was on. The ensuing snowball fight was very strategic. I would exit my fort and if a target presented itself I would throw a snowball as fast as I could. When Lance or Denver threw a snowball at me I would quickly duck back behind our fort. If either of the teams scored a rare direct hit then that team let out a gleeful cheer. On this day the worse thing did happen. One of the Leggo's got me good, right in the face. I fell down emitting a rather loud "aahaaa" and everyone stopped throwing snowballs and went silent thinking that I was hurt. When I quickly got up and I was laughing the three other guys also burst out in fits of laughter.

"Lance or Denver, Whoever threw that snowball got me good" I said. "You win. You win. But next time I'll get you, I promise."

The snowball fight was over and a good time was had by all. Tomorrow would be another day.

When I was at home alone I would practice throwing snowballs. I would set up and throw at the old outhouse from about forty feet away. Of course it was a sizeable and stationary target so I hit it every single time. Then I would throw at the clothesline pole which was like a telephone pole. I found that when I threw a fastball I was not as accurate as when I threw a curve ball. Since I was a pitcher when I played baseball at school I was also good at throwing snowballs.

One fine spring day when I was around eleven or twelve years of age Lance, Denver and I got into a bit of mischief. Well, ok, it was mostly my fault. You see we were at the corner of the highway and the old road (now called L'Anse-a-Brilliant Ave.) and I decided that we should throw snowballs at passing cars. Of course we would not throw a snowball at a car we recognized that belonged to a local person but any other vehicle was fair game.

The cars that passed were going about fifty to sixty miles per hour and we usually missed when we threw a snowball at them. The ones we did hit usually slowed down and stopped to try and see who had thrown the snowball. But we ran into the adjacent wooded area and they didn't see us. They went on their way. I saw this particular car coming and I threw a snowball at it. What I did not see was that the driver had his window wide open, perhaps because he was smoking and flicking his ashes out the window. My snowball went right into the open window. I don't know if it hit him or his passenger but I do know that I was in trouble because he jammed on his breaks and started backing his car up really fast to try and catch us. We of course ran into the woods once again but the man started chasing us all the while yelling and swearing at us. We ran farther into the woods but the man who was furious was still chasing us. Although he could not see us he could see our footprints in the snow and he was following them. I was really afraid that he would catch up to us and God only knew what he was going to do to us when he caught us. Fortunately for us he did not catch us as he was sinking up past his knees in the snow. When It became apparent that the man was no longer chasing us and was returning to his car we snuck to a spot where we could see him get into his car and drive away.

That was the last time I threw a snowball at a car. When you are a child you don't always think of the harm you can do when you're doing something that you consider fun. This could have caused an accident resulting in loss of life. I was very ashamed and sorry for what I had done. Thank God that no harm was done.

I did continue to throw snowballs and I got to be really good at it. I consider throwing snowballs to be a legitimate sport because it takes skill and determination to be a good thrower. Since it's a winter sport I think it should be included in the forthcoming Winter Olympic Games. I think the world audience would really enjoy a top notch snowball throwing competition. Teams from around the world could compete. If the Jamaicans can have an Olympic bobsled team then surely they could have an Olympic snowball throwing team as well.

These days I spend the majority of my winters not looking at winter snow but at the white sand beaches of Panama City Beach in Florida. However when I do get back to Sudbury in March there is always an ample supply of melting snow for me to make snowballs with. Although I'm in my sixties now I still like to make a few snowballs and throw them at the hydro pole on my neighbour's lawn. Just to see if I still have it. If anyone observes me doing this they probably must think that I'm off my rocker. Well, I'm not. Why should I give up throwing snowballs just because I'm a little older now? I'm still accurate but my velocity is down a bit. It must be because of that darn rotator cuff injury I had in my shoulder a few years ago.

I've stopped throwing snowballs for the time being however. It's May 10th. and all the snow melted away three weeks ago.

99. How I Got My First Bike

I have mentioned previously that Reid De Vouge taught me to ride his bike when I was eleven. I was now twelve years of age and I wanted a bicycle of my own. When the Eatons and Sears spring and summer catalogues came in the mail I went right to the bicycle sections. The bike that I decided I wanted was in the Eaton's Catalogue and it was an Eagle Glider single speed beauty. It was red and white and it was imported from England. I selected an adult size frame with twenty-six inch wheels. I had grown up quite a bit in the past year but if it was too big for me I knew that I would grow into it.

I showed my mother the bicycle I wanted and she asked me how much it cost.

I said, "forty dollars."

"Ask your dad," she said. "He's the one with the money."

I didn't think that dad was going to be a problem as two years before he had bought a brand new Mercedes-Benz, an expensive car that cost twice as much as a Ford or Chevy. Surely if he could afford to buy a Mercedes he could afford to buy me a forty dollar bicycle.

When my father got home for the weekend from Murdochville where he worked Monday to Friday I showed him the bicycle I had selected in the Eaton's catalogue. I told him that it cost forty dollars and asked him to buy it for me.

Dad said, "You bring me twenty dollars and I'll put in twenty dollars and we'll order you the bike."

"I don't have twenty dollars," I said.

"Well go earn it . You got all spring and summer and when you have twenty dollars to give me you'll get the bike," was my father's response.

I was very disappointed. I did not make any wages doing chores on my grandfather's farm. Sometimes I did small jobs for other people like pluck chickens or plant potatoes but my pay was in cents, not in dollars. How was I going to make twenty dollars? I had no idea.

I knew that my mom felt sorry for me but knew she wasn't going to argue with my father over it. But she had an idea.

She used to order her Christmas cards and some other items from the Regal Company and three or four times a year she would receive small catalogues from them. They had also wanted her to represent them by going around door to door selling Christmas cards in our community. She had declined because she didn't have the time or a driver's license.

At the age of twelve I became a Regal salesman and my mother had to sign the forms because I was a minor. I was sent a large box of Christmas cards which were to be shown to customers. The box had handles on it like a suitcase so that I could carry it from farm to farm. The boxes of cards were samples only and were not for sale. There were about a dozen different types and styles of Christmas cards and they came in different price ranges. I would make a hefty commission on each box of cards ordered and I was eager to get started. In the fifties everyone sent and received lots of Christmas cards every year. The exchanging of Christmas cards was in its height of popularity in that era.

One hot summer day I set off with my sample Christmas cards to take orders and the first person that I called on was Mrs. Rita De Vouge who lived two farms over and she was my friend Reid's mother. I knew that she would order some cards from me as I remember her showing me cards she had received from away and how she had loved the cards.

"Bryan, what have you got in the box?" Rita asked as I entered her house.

"Christmas cards," I answered, "And lots of them. I'm selling Christmas cards for Regal. I want to earn enough to buy a new bike."

Rita grinned at me and said "Bryan, you're selling Christmas cards in the middle of July. Christmas is five months away."

"It's a perfect time to take orders for Christmas cards," I replied.

"Let's have a look," she said and I opened my box and placed all of the sample boxes on her kitchen table. She looked through the various boxes and commented that they were very nice Christmas cards and that she would buy a few boxes. She went into another room and returned with some money. She chose two of the boxes she wanted, gave me the money and took the Christmas cards.

I said, "These cards are samples only and are not for sale. I have to take your order, send in the money and bring the cards you have chosen to you when I receive them in September or October."

Rita looked at me sort of puzzled and said, "I'm not going to pay you in advance. Remember what happened last summer: those university students going around selling magazine subscriptions. They showed us sample magazines and took orders. We had to pay them in advance and then we were gypped. We never received one magazine and we lost our money. Bryan, your own grandmother ordered magazines and she was taken just like me. I can't pay you in advance."

"But the guys who were selling the magazines were strangers and they were from Ontario or someplace," I said.

Rita replied, "You could send in the money and not receive any Christmas cards at all. I'll keep my money right here and when you bring me the cards in the fall then you'll get your money"

"Ok." I said. "I'll ask my mother if we can do that."

When I got back home my mother could see that I was a little disappointed. She asked me what was wrong and I explained that Rita ordered two boxes of the Christmas cards but would only pay for them on delivery. Mom said that she understood why and told me that she would put up the advance money I needed. Mom explained that to make twenty dollars in commission I needed to sell fifty dollars worth of Christmas cards. I could keep twenty and had to send in thirty dollars.

Over the next few weeks I visited every farm and house in L'Anse-A-Brilliant and even a few in Seal Cove. When I explained what I was doing and why almost everyone ordered Christmas cards from me. The majority of people did not want to pay in advance so I said that was ok but much to my delight some of them did pay me up front. Of course my mother, my grandmother and some other close relatives ordered cards and also paid me in advance.

Mom ordered my bicycle and it was shipped from the Eaton's catalogue warehouse in Moncton, New Brunswick. I received it on the first day of September , just a few days before the new school year started. It was beautiful, red and white and all shiny and new. I loved it. I rode it for hours and hours every day.

When the Christmas cards arrived later in September I delivered them on my new bicycle and I showed it to the people who had ordered Christmas cards from me. I thanked them for their business and came away with the feeling that we were all very happy: me for having a new bike and them for helping me get it.

100. Smoking Is Not For Me

In the fifties in the Gaspe the majority of people smoked. It seemed that most people over the age of sixteen were puffing away on cigarettes. Some old men smoked pipes of all shapes and sizes. When you saw someone smoking a cigar you knew he was a tourist or relative from away that came to visit. Not many Gaspesiens smoked cigars.

My family however was an exception to the rule. My grandparents and great-grandparents did not smoke. My great-grandfather Elias chewed tobacco and I'm not sure if he smoked earlier in his lifetime. My parents were social smokers, a term you may have not heard before. They did not smoke on a daily basis but only when company came over. If dad knew the visitors were smokers he would offer them a cigarette and light one up for himself as well. You could tell that my mother was an amateur smoker because of the way she held her cigarette, puffed and blew the smoke out without inhaling it.

My father couldn't wait to offer his friends a cigarette as he wanted to show off his cigarette dispensing machine. It was a rather decorative square box with a bird with an open beak on top of it. When you pulled a lever down the bird bent over and a small door would open and then as a cigarette elevated the bird would grab the cigarette in it's beak. The machine emitted a musical tone and the bird returned to its original position with the cigarette in its beak. When seeing this the visitors would laugh and say "Gee, I've never seen anything like that before."

A pack of twenty cigarettes lasted my mom and dad four to six weeks. When they ran out mom would send me to the store for a pack of Belvedre cigarettes. They came in a beautiful blue pack which I considered much nicer than their competitors pack's.

In those days there wasn't much discussion on the harmful effects of smoking on people's health. However I remember people saying that children shouldn't smoke because it would stunt their growth.

I smoked my first cigarette when I was twelve years old. It was given to me by a local teenager and when he noticed that I was puffing and blowing out the smoke like my mom did he told me to inhale the smoke into my lungs, keep it there awhile and then slowly exhale. I did this and the end result was me staggering around like a drunk. My lungs hurt and I got dizzy and lightheaded. I coughed a lot and thought that I was going to be sick but the teenager said that I was going to be alright and that I would get used to it after awhile.

Smoking was considered very cool by the kids my age so I decided that I would continue smoking. Since a pack of cigarettes cost forty cents I decided to buy tobacco and papers and roll my own cigarettes. Tobacco only cost twenty-eight cents a pack and papers were five cents. I learned to roll my own cigarettes and started puffing away. When I got home I would hide the tobacco and papers somewhere outside and hope that mom would not smell smoke on my breath. I also chewed bubble gum and ate mints.

One weekend afternoon I was down at the harbour wharf and my aunt Dot saw me smoking before I saw her. She mentioned it to my mom and I got a blast from my mother.

I decided to quit smoking, not so much because of getting caught but because I hated it. I couldn't understand why I should pay money out to do something that made me ill. That was not cool with me so I gave my half finished tobacco pack away. My experience of smoking cigarettes lasted approximately one week.

101. Raiding 101

There comes a time in every young Gaspesien's life when he learns a new skill that one doesn't learn in school. The skill is raiding and that's the way it was in L'Anse-a-Brilliant in the fifties. When a child evolved into a teenager he retired from raiding and a new group of up and comers took over the tradition.

Raiding is simply invading someone's garden or orchard and helping yourself to the fruit and vegetables within. It seemed that everybody had a garden but only a few had apple orchards and since children like apples more than vegetables most of the raiding we did was for apples.

There were three apple orchards that I remember but only two of them were raided. The first was Cecil De Vouge's and it contained my all time favorite Macintosh apples. The second orchard was at the top of the hill and was owned by the Quinn's. It contained Granny Smith type apples which are green and a little sour. It also contained those very small crab apples which normally were not eaten but made into crab apple jelly. However I liked to eat then as they had a completely different taste than most apples. This orchard was a fairly big one with lots of apples to raid. The third orchard was our own orchard of only three trees which was never raided.

I had found out fairly early in life that I didn't like our own apples as they tasted terrible. One day I asked my father why no one raided our apples.

"They're not fit to eat. They're only good for making pies" was his reply.

Over the years we raided the other two orchards maybe twice per year. We didn't take too many apples; just enough to satisfy our hunger so to speak. We stored our booty in our clubhouse which was the cuddy of a dry docked fishing boat. When we were down at the beach swimming and got hungry we would go over to our stash and eat an apple or two.

One year our raiding of apples almost came to an end. You see, both owners bought dogs to guard their orchards. My fellow raiders discovered this out and we were worried that our raiding days were over. Nevertheless we decided to think on it and try and come up with a plan.

Early in the summer when the apples were still small I renewed my friendship with Reid De Vouge whose father Cecil owned apple orchard number one. I got to know his new dog which was not vicious at all. In fact when I petted it and played with it we became friends very quickly. I mentioned to my friends that the dog and I were friends and his dog house was in amongst the apple trees where he stayed all night.

One night we waited until dark and snuck up to Cecil's farm. I went ahead of the others and called to the dog. He did not bark at me but came out of his dog house wagging his tale. I went up to him and petted him as we were friends. My friends then came and the three of them picked apples off the trees. That was how we solved the dog problem on orchard number one.

Orchard number two however was more of a challenge. There weren't any kids our age to make friends with so we couldn't make friends with the dog. Also this dog was a barker, a real loud one. He would bark at anyone even walking along the highway one hundred yards away. It was impossible to even approach the orchard without the dog barking like crazy and old Mr. Quinn coming out of his house to see what was going on. What were we going to do? One day I asked my mother if I could have fifty cents so I could go to Quinn's and buy some Granny Smith apples and maybe some crab apples as well. She gave me the money and a pillow slip to put the apples in. I walked up the hill with Zane Leggo and we approached the Quinn's house. The dog was barking like crazy and Mr. Quinn came outside. He saw me carrying a pillow slip and asked "What do you guys want?"

"Do you have any apples for sale ?" I asked.

He looked at me and said "Ha you didn't come here to raid apples this time."

"No" I replied. "We don't raid. We come to buy apples."

"Well sure" he said and we all went into the house including the dog.

"My mom sent me to buy fifty cents worth of apples," I said." She would like mostly Granny Smith but wants some crab apples as well if you have them."

Mr. Quinn took the fifty cents and my pillow slip.

I asked "Should I pick them off the tree?"

"No" he replied. "We have some here in the house" and he went into another room to get them. Meanwhile the dog was still barking and Mrs. Quinn yelled at the dog.

"Quit your darn barking!" she yelled.

The dog promptly stopped barking and became very quiet and laid down on the floor.

Much to my surprise Mr. Quinn came back with my pillow slip completely filled with apples. What a deal for fifty cents.

"Wow" I said. "You filled it right up. It's so heavy we'll each have to take turns carrying it home."

Mr. Quinn said "Come back anytime if you want to buy apples."

"Thank you very much. I will," I replied.

After talking to the Quinn's for awhile Zane and I left carrying our heavy pillow slip of apples. When we walked around the bend on the highway my two other friends were waiting for us. They also had a pillow slip full of apples which they had raided while we were in the house with the Quinn's. Of course they had waited until the dog who was inside the house was ordered to shut up.

We took the apples in my pillow slip to my mother and we took the other apples to our club house in the dry-docked fishing boat. Despite the obstacles we had succeeded and got the job done.

Since we were nearing our teen years we retired from raiding apples. It was safer and easier to just buy them. After all we had to make way for the next generation of raiders coming up. Remember future raiders the main Raiding 101 rule is "Where there's a will there's a way."

102. *Hurricane Donna*

The title of this chapter "Hurricane Donna" may give you the impression that I'm writing about my younger sister Donna. Well she was a hurricane when she got on my nerves. However this story is about the real hurricane "Donna" that hit the USA and Canada in September of 1960. Here in Canada we are not used to having many damaging hurricanes but in the 1950's and 1960's we had a few of them. The hurricane they called "Donna" affected me the most and will always be in my memory.

Hurricane Donna was classed as an official hurricane on August the 29th. and it lasted seventeen days until September the 14th. making it a very long lasting and destructive hurricane. In fact it was the longest lasting and most destructive hurricane in the history of the Atlantic basin. It was classed as a Category 5 hurricane and it was the most destructive hurricane of the season. Winds reached speeds of 128 to 150 miles per hour in the USA and fifty people lost their lives due to Hurricane Donna.

When it reached the Gaspe Peninsula on September the 13th. it caused great havoc to my family and me.

The fury that hurricane Donna threw at us was mostly in the evening and nighttime. There was a torrential downpour of rain like I had never seen before and the winds howled so loud and were so strong that I thought our old farmhouse was going to be blown away. I could feel the house shake and move a little when a strong gust of wind hit us dead on.

In the morning when I got up and looked out the kitchen window I saw that the river had overflowed its banks and that our lower valley was flooded. Fortunately there were no cattle grazing there at the time. The L'Anse-a-Brilliant River which was usually a shallow and mild slow flowing river was now a very fast and raging river which uprooted trees from along it's banks sending them downriver to the harbour and out to sea. The trees on our property were bending in the wind but except for along the riverbank I didn't see any that were blown down.

My grandmother visited us at our end of the house and told my mom "Herzil and Glen's boat is missing from the harbour and it must have washed out to sea."

My grandfather was out checking for damage done by the hurricane and had already verified this. Quickly I got on my brand new bicycle which I had for less than two weeks and peddled like crazy to get down to the beach and harbour to see the effects of the hurricane. When I was riding down the hill on the old gravel road I noticed that the road was washed out less than a third of the way down the hill. I slammed on the brakes to try and stop in time but I was going too fast and drove into the small gorge that the hurricane had caused to erode in the road. When my bike hit I was thrown over the handlebars and I flew through the air doing a somersault before I landed on my back on the side of the road. I was lucky to have landed on a grassy area and not on the gravel road, The wind was knocked out of me but fortunately I had no other apparent injuries. However my brand new Eagle Glider bicycle did not fare so well. I was very distraught to see that my front wheel was bashed in really bad and the tire was also flat. I obviously could not leave my damaged bike so I had to part carry and part drag it the rest of the way down to the harbour.

The first thing I noticed at the harbour was that there were a few swamped and damaged boats and yes, the eighteen foot wooden boat that my father and uncle shared ownership of was missing. There were several fishermen there checking things out and I asked one of them "What do you think happened to my dad's boat?"

He replied "I think that one or those trees that washed down from the river got between your dad's boat and the wharf and the current was so strong pushing the tree it broke the chain and sent the boat out to sea. God only knows where that boat is now."

He was right of course as the Atlantic Ocean is a very big ocean. The boat could also have sunk. I didn't expect I'd ever see dad's boat again.

As if he was reading my mind he said "You never know, when the storm is over someone may find it drifting out there."

I hoped he was right.

"You should go check out the waves breaking over the wharf" he said. "Biggest waves I've ever seen. Don't go on the wharf because it's too dangerous. Check the waves from the beach."

I walked over to the beach with a friend who was also there and observed that the gigantic waves were breaking six to eight feet over the longest wharf. Normally the wharf was about eight feet above water level so this was something I had never seen before. I saw that the longer wharf which extended further out into the bay was damaged. It used to be straight and level and now it was twisted and sunken down in some parts.

The noise that the waves were making was deafening it was so loud. My friend and I had to shout at each other to be heard. Walking along the beach my friend and I found the biggest lobster that I had ever seen. It was dead of course, killed by the hurricane. We remarked that it was probably not fit to be eaten because lobsters have to be alive until you cook them.

Hurricane Donna had now been downgraded to a tropical storm but I thought that it would be probably several days before it calmed down and the fishermen could go out fishing once again.

I walked my bike home and I saw my uncle Glen there with my grandfather. He had come out from Murdochville to see how things were on the farm. I was sort of glad that my father wasn't there because I knew he would give me heck for damaging my bike even if it wasn't my fault.

Uncle Glen noticed my bashed in front wheel and I explained what had happened to my bicycle. I also told him that one of the fishermen had said that someone might find his boat.

"I hope so, Bryan" he said. "I hope so."

Uncle Glen checked my damaged wheel and said "I think I can fix that wheel, Bryan."

He took my bike up to the barn to work on it and I went to tell my mom all about the waves breaking higher than the wharf.

My uncle Glen fixed my bike wheel and patched the inner tube inside the bicycle tire and presented my bike back to me as good as new.

I was very grateful and said "Thank You very much."

The good news came the next day. My dad and uncle Glen's boat had been found at Grand Greve which is almost directly across Gaspe Bay from L'Anse-a-Brilliant and five miles away by water, about fifty miles by road. Since we did not have a telephone on our farm as of yet the person who had found the boat phoned Basil Leggo and asked him to contact us with the good news.

The next day my dad and uncle Glen drove to Grand Greve and brought their boat back by truck. There was some damage to it but nothing that they couldn't fix.

So Hurricane Donna came and went. It caused us some havoc but in the end everything worked out ok. Our old farmhouse was not blown away as I had feared. Although there was some damage to property no lives were lost in the Gaspe. I must say however that it was one hell of a storm.

103. Don't Kill The Rooster

In the mid-fifties the Bairds, the family who lived on the next farm to ours left and moved to the city of Welland in Ontario.

About five years later Hazel Baird moved back to the old farm in L'Anse-a-Brilliant. Her children had all grown up and left and she and her husband had gotten divorced. She had decided to retire in the Gaspe.

Hazel had nobody to help her on the farm so I and several other children helped her out by running errands and doing some chores for her. We also cut and chopped firewood for her wood cook stove.

As Hazel was now retired she didn't do much farming but she did keep some chickens and roosters. The laying hens provided her with all the eggs she needed.

Once in a while she felt like cooking up a chicken for her supper but she was unable to kill her chickens herself. She was very kind-hearted and loved animals. She would ask me to go up to her barn and kill a chicken or rooster for her. I was usually with one or more of the Leggo brothers, Lance, Denver or Zane. We would go up to the barn while Hazel retreated to her farmhouse to wait it out.

Sometimes Hazel's chickens would be in her barn and other times they would be browsing around outside gobbling up chicken feed that Hazel had spread on the ground for them. Most times chickens are elusive and can be hard to catch but once you nab one and hold it by the legs just above its feet it stops squawking and thrashing around and when you turn it upside down it relaxes and becomes quiet. You then place it's neck and head on a wooden chopping block. Surprisingly the chicken or rooster remains calm and motionless and then your friend chops its head off with an axe. You then have to let it go because blood is squirting out of where its head used to be like water from a water pistol. Now headless the chicken flies around squirting blood, hits the ground and tries to fly again. When it loses enough blood it stops thrashing around and dies. Some say that the reason the chicken does this after its head is chopped off is because of its nerves receiving a last message from its brain.

We would take the dead chicken down to Hazel's house where she had a pot of water boiling on the stove. Dunking the chicken into the boiling water scalds it thus making it easier to pluck the feathers off the body. Hazel would thank us and we would be on our way knowing that in a few weeks she would ask us to do it again. Farm boys grow up watching the adults butcher the bigger farm animals which was a bit much for us but killing a chicken for Hazel was ok by us.

One weekend in 1960 when I was twelve my cousin Freddy came out from Murdochville with his family for a visit. I took him over to meet Hazel on the next farm and she asked us to kill a chicken for her.

"Hazel, we'll kill that big rooster for you, the one that's way bigger than all the others," I said

"No, not that one" Hazel replied. "That might be the one that's laying the double-yoked egg."

"Hazel, roosters don't lay eggs" I said with a chuckle. "Hens lay eggs"

"I know but I don't want to take the chance" she said.

"Ok, then we'll choose another one for you."

Freddy and I went up to Hazel's barn and I grabbed a big rooster and I made sure that it wasn't the really big one that Hazel didn't want killed. I asked Freddy to hold the rooster for me but he didn't want to do that. He wanted to be the one that chopped its head off. Freddy was a year and a half younger than me and he was not a farm boy. He had never done anything like this before but I decided that I would hold the rooster on the chopping block and he would chop its head off.

I was holding the rooster the proper way and I placed its head and neck on the chopping block. I told Freddy to go ahead and he aimed the axe and swung it down but with not enough force. He only succeeded in cutting the rooster's head half-off. Then all hell broke loose. I let the rooster go and it starting thrashing around, flying, crashing, running and squawking loudly all the time squirting blood.

I yelled at Freddy "You should have swung the axe harder. Now we have to catch that rooster fast and put it out of its misery."

It took me a while to catch the rooster again and this time when Freddy swung the axe he chopped it's head clear off.

I told Freddy on the walk down to Hazel's farm-house " Don't tell her what happened. She doesn't like to see any animal suffer. If you ever do this again swing the axe a lot harder."

It may have been the one and only time that Freddy had done the deed and a little over a year later I moved to the town of Murdochville. Someone else killed the chickens for Hazel. I didn't mind doing it for her while I lived there but it wasn't one of the pleasant experiences of growing up on the farm.

104. Don't Fool Around
On The Beach

It was August in the summer of 1961 and I was just a month away from turning thirteen . It was the very brief time in my life when I had started smoking.

Down at L'Anse-a-Brilliant beach there's a piece of land called Smokers Point. It was probably formed during one of the ice ages ions ago. It is about fifty feet high and is circular in shape with cliffs on three sides and a very steep bank on the other side. When you're young you can climb to the top where it's flat and treed and you can smoke where nobody can see you. I think that's why it was called Smoker's Point years or maybe generations before I was born.

Zane Leggo and I were up on Smoker's Point with a clear view looking towards the wharf. I took out the makings and rolled us each a cigarette. It was after supper and at this time of the day the beach was deserted. People usually come to the beach in the late morning and early afternoon and sometimes in the evening after dark to make a bonfire. However at this time of the day the beach was usually deserted.

We heard a car pull up and the doors slam on the other side of Smokers Point but we couldn't see who it was. A minute later a young couple in their early twenties came into our view on our side of Smokers Point. We did not recognize them so they were not from anywhere around L'Anse-a-Brilliant. They walked on the beach towards the wharf, stopped by this big log that had washed up high on the beach during some storm and looked around. Seeing that they were all alone they started to kiss and hug. It was obvious that they were very much in love with each other. Zane and I watched as they embraced each other with a long passionate kiss. Zane started to giggle and I quickly put my hand over his mouth and shushed him. I whispered into his ear "Be quiet and let's watch and see what they do."

The young couple laid down on the sand on the other side of that big log. Unfortunately that darn log obstructed our view and we could no longer see the young lady as she was flat on her back. We could see the young man however because he was leaning over her and kissing her. I guess things started to heat up and passion got the better of him because suddenly he rose up, had a quick look around and undid his belt buckle. When he unzipped his pants Zane and I knew that something dramatic was about to happen. We looked at each other in disbelief and I whispered in his ear what I wanted him to do.

The young couple continued whatever they were doing oblivious to the fact that there were two young boys observing them from the top of Smokers Point. Zane and I waited about a minute and then stood up and yelled "Hey, what are you doing? There's no fooling around allowed on the beach."

Panic ensued. The young lovers were in shock at being discovered in their activity. The young lady started sobbing and covered her face with her hands. She quickly departed towards their car even before her boyfriend had the time to get his pants zipped up. He had a quick glance up to the top of Smoker's point fifty feet above but he did not see us. He ran after his girlfriend and they quickly got into their car and burnt rubber getting out of there. I could only imagine their embarrassment. I didn't think that young couple would ever come back to L'Anse-a-Brilliant beach again.

105. Reid Got Plastered Drunk

Reid De Vouge was a friend of mine and he lived with his parents Rita and Cecil. Reid's parent's farm was located two farms over from us on the old road. Reid was about three years older than me and was the male friend that lived closest to me. We played together often and also went trout fishing in the river together many times.

In those days I was very grateful to Reid as he taught me to ride his bike when I was eleven years old. I didn't have a bicycle of my own so Reid decided to teach me to ride his on the old road which didn't have much traffic. Reid's bike was an adult model and much too big for me. Since I could not sit on the seat and reach the peddles with my feet Reid showed me how to put one leg through the frame under the crossbar and stand on the peddles to ride the bike. And that's how I learned to ride his bicycle. Whenever I wanted to take his bike for a ride he would let me and today I still remember how happy that made me.

When I was twelve and Reid was fifteen he started hanging around with older guys and by this time I had friends such as the Leggo's who were more my age.

One afternoon I was walking home along the highway and decided to take a shortcut by climbing the wire fence and walking up the field to our house. As I was walking by the ditch and culvert where the old road intersected with the highway I heard a low moan coming from the ditch. I thought it might be an animal that had been hit by a car and had been knocked into the ditch. I walked over to the ditch very slowly and I heard the moaning again. I was scared because I thought a wounded animal might attack me.

It was not a hurt animal in the ditch. It was Reid De Vouge.

I said "Reid, what are you doing in the ditch?"

He moaned and said "I'm dying."

"Were you hit by a car?" I asked.

"No, I'm sick " he replied."

"I'll run over and get Rita and Cecil" I said.

"No" he replied. "I'm plastered drunk. Get a gun and shoot me. Put me out of my misery."

I told him "I can't do that. Reid, you have to get out of the ditch. Come up to my house.

He said "No, I don't want your mother to see me like this."

When I helped him up out of the ditch I discovered that he was so drunk he could hardly walk. We decided to put him in the outhouse that was located behind our house. Since we had a washroom in the house the outhouse was not used so it was a safe place for him to hide until he sobered up. Reid entered the outhouse and sat down. He closed his eyes and said "If I'm not out in a half hour come in for me."

I closed the door and left him there. After a half hour I returned, opened the door and found him slumped over against the side of the outhouse sleeping it off. I decided not to awaken him but to check on him in another thirty minutes.

He was still there sleeping in what looked like a very uncomfortable position when I checked on him. Once again I left him alone and did not awaken him.

After I ate supper with my family I decided to wait a full hour before checking on him again. This time when I opened the outhouse door he was gone. I figured that when he woke up he was sober enough to go home.

I found out later that Reid had been with some older guys who had encouraged him to drink to excess. This was purely for their entertainment, watching a younger guy get drunk. I'm sure because the same thing happened to me six years later.

106. Cindy Was A Pig, A Real Pig

My grandfather Leslie had been a fisherman/farmer and when he got older he retired from fishing. But an old farmer doesn't retire from farming. He just scales back a bit. In the late fifties the cows, sheep and chickens were all gone and my grandpa decided to raise pigs.

In the spring of 1961 after the snow had melted away I saw a car on the road slowing down to enter our driveway and drive up to our house. My grandpa and I went out to see who the visitor was.

"Good Day Leslie. How are you?" was what the man said as he emerged from his car.

"I'm fine. How are you?" my grandfather replied.

"I hear that you're raising pigs for sale this year. If it's not to late to order I'd like you to grow me a pig."

My grandfather replied, "Yes, I can order you one and I'll be butchering when it gets cold in the fall."

Grandpa ended up ordering about a dozen piglets, one for him, one for my family, some for relatives and some for sale to the people who had ordered them. When the small little piglets arrived they were put in one of two big pens, each one containing a fenced in area for them to run around in and a small house to sleep in. The vet came and checked them all out and proclaimed them to be in good health.

My father wanted our pig separate from the others for some reason so it got it's very own private pig pen with it's own pig house. The other eleven had the larger pig pen and had to share their pig house.

I helped my grandfather feed the pigs every day. We made what he called slop which was pig meal mixed with water and we added boiled potatoes which we mashed before adding them to the mixture. The pigs loved it and over the summer and into the fall they grew from little piglets into big pigs.

My sister Donna was seven years old and she named our pig Cindy. When we got home from school in the spring she would go directly to Cindy's pig pen and talk to her, pet her through the fence boards and spend time with her. She made a pet of Cindy and they became friends. My parents were alarmed at this because after all we would be eating Cindy during the late fall and the winter months. To my mom, dad and myself Cindy was going to be pork chops and pork roasts on our dinner plate.

But to my young sister Donna, Cindy was her pet pig. When school was out for the summer she spent hours and hours with Cindy. Pigs are very intelligent animals and like dogs they can be trained to do tricks. Over the summer months Donna taught Cindy to shake a paw and to roll over on request just like dogs do. We all thought that this was amazing but my dad kept saying that Donna was getting too attached to the pig and he was worried how she was going to react when Cindy was butchered in the fall. I remember that even though I was twelve years of age I dreaded that day and how my sister Donna would be hurt.

In September I turned thirteen and in October Donna turned eight and we were back in school. In late October grandpa and his cousin Rupert Leggo set to butchering the pigs for the people who had ordered them. Every afternoon when we got off the school bus Donna would run up the driveway and check if her pet pig Cindy was still alive. She would be overjoyed when she discovered that Cindy was still alive and well in her pen.

One day however when we got home from school Cindy was not in her house or pen. Donna looked all around but Cindy was nowhere to be found. Donna was heartbroken of course and since that day some forty-seven years ago she has never eaten pork again.

107. Irma Said "I Hit Him"

When I bought my first bike when I was 12 years old I loved it so much I almost took it to bed with me at night like a small child with his teddy bear. I would ride it anywhere and everywhere usually within the boundaries of L'Anse-a-Brilliant.

A year later when I was thirteen I would go on longer road trips sometimes riding my bike to school fourteen miles away or seven miles if I took the shortcut through the line road.

One day my friend Irma and I decided to ride up to Douglastown which is five miles away. Irma didn't have her own bike but borrowed her older brother Wayne's bike. We rode to Douglastown and we may have bought an ice cream cone there, something we could not buy at home in L'Anse-a-Brilliant.

After riding about three miles on our return ride home we were riding through this wooded area about a half mile before reaching the Seal Cove River on the outskirts of Seal Cove. Because our local highway is only a two lane blacktop when I heard a vehicle coming up behind me I would slow down and pull over onto the gravel or grassy shoulder until the vehicle passed and it was safe to go back on the road. Better safe than sorry was my thought.

Irma was riding her bike close behind me and I heard a car coming and decided to pull off the road onto the shoulder which was very rough and uneven and the front wheel of my bike slid off the roadway into a hole about eight inches deep. I fell back onto the pavement whacking my face right into the pavement severely hurting myself. If that wasn't enough Irma ran over my head with her bicycle driving my face into the pavement a second time. I smashed my teeth into the pavement hurting my front teeth and cutting my lip severely. When I staggered to my feet I was bleeding profusely from my mouth. My arms and legs were ok and it was mostly my face that was damaged. I didn't take any time to talk to Irma or to blame her for running over my head. It wasn't her fault because she had no time to react when I fell off my bike. I got back on my bike and rode the last mile and a half to my house as fast as possible. Hopefully my mother being a former nurse could patch me up.

When I entered our house my mom took one look at me and said "Good God, what happened to you? Your face is a bloody mess."

I looked in the mirror and I was definitely in agreement with my mom's assessment of my face. I looked like I'd been in a fight with ten heavyweight champion boxers in a row and had lost all ten fights badly. I had cuts and abrasions on my face and a large goose egg on my forehead and my lips were cut and swelled up four times their normal size.

My mother cleaned and patched me up as best as she could. When my grandmother saw me later she said "Bryan, you are quite the sight". I didn't quite know what that meant but I don't think that it was good.

The next morning my mother woke me up to get ready to go to school and when I looked in the mirror I looked worse than the day before. My face was now black and blue and one side of my upper lip was puffed up. Also one of my upper front teeth had turned black overnight. I looked grotesque. My mom explained that my tooth had turned black because it had been bruised and that I was lucky that I had not knocked it out completely. She said that when the tooth healed it would be white once again.

When I got on the school bus I heard oohhs and ahhhs and I was asked what had happened to me. I explained to everyone on the bus about my bicycle accident and when I finished explaining I had to do it all over again because more kids were getting on the bus. And when I arrived at school word quickly spread and then three busloads of children were clamoring to get a look at my grotesque face.

Once in the classroom my teacher noticed me and was very alarmed at my appearance. She immediately asked me what had happened to my face.

I replied "I had a bicycle accident and fell off my bike and hit my face on the pavement." I thought she was asking me because if I had said that my parents or someone else had beaten me up then she would have reported it to the authorities.

"Oh come on Bryan, someone beat you up really badly. Tell me who beat you up."

No," I replied. "I really did have a bicycle accident and fell off my bike."

My teacher looked at me with concern and said "Bryan, tell me who hit you?"

Suddenly we all heard a voice from the back rows of the classroom and it said "I hit him."

We all looked back and saw that it was Irma that had uttered these words.

"Is that true Bryan? What did you do to Irma to make her beat you up so badly?" questioned the teacher.

I replied "After I fell off my bike and hit my face on the pavement Irma ran over my head with her bike. It was an accident."

The class erupted in laughter but I didn't think that it was very funny. My teacher told the class to settle down and then she asked Irma if that was what happened.

Irma said "Yes, it all happened so fast I couldn't stop in time."

Our teacher was satisfied with that explanation and then was concerned by how I felt.

I told her that I didn't feel too good but that my mother had told me that I would be back to normal in no time at all. I'd hoped that she was right.

In time the bruises went away, my lip healed up and went back to it's normal size. My black tooth eventually turned white again and all was right with the world once again. Irma and I went on more bike rides and there were no more mishaps.

I especially liked when Irma couldn't borrow her brother's bike. On those occasions she sat in front of me on the crossbar of my bike while I peddled. I knew that now she couldn't run over my head with her bike. Also I liked it when the wind blew her long brown hair into my face while we were biking along. That was sort of romantic.

108. Dad Makes Me Hunt

Hunting season for all game and birds came in the fall in the Gaspe Peninsula. In the 1950's most people hunted to put meat on the table for the winter like their fathers and grandfathers had done before them. People hunted for partridge, duck, deer and moose. Most people did not hunt bear.

The most southernmost herd of caribou in Canada is located in the interior of the Gaspe but they were protected and it was illegal to hunt them.

My father hunted for partridge and moose. If he took holiday time off work to hunt he usually went elsewhere to a hunting camp with his hunting partners. If he was just hunting on the weekend it was in the woods on our own land or close by. My father was not interested in hunting ducks or deer. I figured that dad had seen the movie "Bambi" and thus didn't want to shoot a deer. Actually I think dad didn't like eating venison because when one of his friends offered him some he would always politely say "no thanks." However in the years when dad did not get his moose he would gratefully accept free moose meat from his friends.

What I didn't like about hunting season was when dad woke me up very early in the morning to go hunting with him. We would eat breakfast and walk into the woods to hunt even before the sun came up. Dad would be carrying his "303" rifle in case we saw a moose and I would be carrying the "22" rifle in case we saw a partridge. At eleven of twelve years of age I did not have a hunting license and my sole purpose of being there with on the hunt was to carry the second rifle. If he saw a Partridge he would signal me to hand him the "22" and he would give me the "303" to hold for him. He would then shoot the partridge and put it in a tote bag: we would exchange rifles once again and then be on our way.

I would attend school Monday to Friday and would be looking forward to sleeping in on Saturday and maybe later playing with my friends but it was not to be because the next weekend my father woke me up once again before daylight to go trudging through the woods hunting for partridge and moose. We never did see a moose to shoot those times I went hunting with my father but we managed to bag several partridge and I sure did enjoy eating the partridge soup and partridge stew that my mother cooked up.

A few years later when we were living in the town of Murdochville my father came to me and said "Come on, we are going for a ride in the woods."

"Why?" I asked. "Hunting season doesn't start until next week and you said I didn't have to go hunting with you this year."

My father looked at me and said "No Bryan, you don't have to hunt with me this year but we're going to the area where my hunting partners and I are hunting this year to check things out in advance."

We met up with some of my father's hunting buddies in two other four wheel drive vehicles and we were on our way. After driving on the road for a half hour we went off-road on an old bush trail which was very rough and bumpy. No car or half-ton truck could handle this so called road.

After it seemed like we had been driving forever we came to a river with a cleared area with an old cabin. This cabin was where my father and his hunting buddies were going to stay on their hunting trip. The only problem was that you had to cross the river to get to it and the bridge was washed out. This was the only place where you could cross the river and the river banks were at ten feet high making this a gorge. Therefore a new bridge had to be built and the men discussed what they had to do. They seemed very disappointed and said that it would take too long to build a new bridge. If they shot a moose a mile back of the cabin how were they going to get it back to the camp and across the river?

My father came up with a solution. They would cut down four big trees, chop the limbs off, then they would nail and lash two of the logs together and lay them across the gorge. Then they would do the same with the two other logs and he would drive his Jeep across the gorge to the cabin on the other side. The other guys reluctantly agreed to this but they said they were too scared of falling in the river with their vehicles to cross on the temporary bridge.

Dad told me to get in his Jeep and with men on both sides of the new bridge directing dad slowly drove across the bridge to the other side.

Everyone carried supplies for the hunting trip across the temporary bridge and stored them in the cabin. The cabin was checked out and found to be ok and then the door was locked with a padlock. Everything was ready for the moose hunting season which started in one week.

One of the other hunters commented that they had done all the work and some other hunters might come and take advantage of all our hard work by crossing our bridge themselves. There were many moose in this isolated area and the less hunters here the better. Again my dad came up with a solution.

He would haul the logs for the temporary bridge over behind the cabin with his Jeep and leave it there with the logs. When other hunters came on the hunting season opening day they would find that there wasn't any bridge to cross the river and they would go elsewhere to hunt.

On the day before the hunting season started my father and his friends left for the hunting cabin and on the way in they met other hunters coming out who stopped and told them that it was no use going in that area to hunt because the bridge was out. My dad and his friends thanked the hunters for the information and continued on to their hunting camp to get prepared for an early start to moose hunting season which opened the next morning. They ended up having the whole area to themselves and were successful in providing us moose meat for our winter.

109. Playing Shinny On The River

In the 1950's most Canadian boys couldn't wait to get a pair of skates, get on an outdoor rink or into an indoor arena and learn to skate and play hockey. The problem in L'Anse-a-Brilliant was that we didn't have an outdoor rink much less an indoor arena. But we did have the river to skate on if we had a cold winter and the river froze over. The ice conditions were less than ideal however and the ice was lumpy and cracked and thin at times because the river was still flowing under the ice on it's way out to the sea. Nevertheless we made do with what we had and at times we found an area of smooth ice to skate and play shinny on.

My friends and I would play until we were tired or the ice broke and one of us fell through. Fortunately for us the river was less than a foot deep where we skated and usually it only meant wet feet if the ice broke below us. That was not a big problem because we all brought extra socks with us and we would take off our skates and wet socks and put on dry socks and our winter boots and mosey on home.

There was this flat clear area where the river widened below the bridge where the river flowed under the highway. It was sort of a flood plain but it was totally dry most summers. One fall the river was high and flooded that area. When winter arrived this area froze over and it became an excellent place to skate and play shinny. The ice was actually smooth and not cracked perhaps because the water below was still water and was completely frozen.

One day my friends and I were playing shinny on this so called frozen pond of ours and one of my worst fears happened. No, I did not go through the ice. I wound up to take a snapshot and I broke my hockey stick. You see I was not the most talented of hockey players. I took the pieces of the broken hockey stick and I told the group that my dad would fix it. My dad could fix anything.

My dad gave me heck for breaking the hockey stick.

"I don't have enough other things to do" he said. "Now I'm going to have to fix that stick."

"I bought it three years ago at Henry's store." I said. "It only cost me seventy-five cents."

"Still I'm going to have to fix it" he said and the next time I went to play shinny it was repaired and as good as new.

One year in the late fifties someone built an outdoor rink in Seal Cove which was only about one mile away. I was disappointed to learn that I couldn't go skating on it. It was only for hockey players to practice and play on. I was very happy when I found out that one of our L'Anse-a-Brilliant boys had made it unto a hockey team and would be playing at the new rink. Wayne Leggo who we called Buzz was our best shinny player and now he was an official hockey player.

After Christmas in 1961 my family and I moved to the town of Murdochville which was eighty miles away. They had a brand new recreation center with an indoor rink. However I had hurt my right ankle pretty badly and had to give up skating for a few years. Oh Well!

110. Gaspe Water Is The Best

Over the past sixty years I have consumed many different types of beverages including beer, alcoholic drinks, fruit juices, hot chocolate, soft drinks, milk, tea. coffee and water. I love coffee and have two or three cups of java every day. When I was a child I loved soda pop and I would drink as much as I could get my hands on or as much as my mother would allow me to drink. In the 1950's the most popular soft drinks were Coke, Pepsi, 7 Up, Orange Crush, Teem, Kik Cola, Canada Dry ginger-ale, Kist orange and others such as the Sussex brand of pops that came to us from the Maritime provinces. I loved and drank them all.

I also drank a great deal of milk which came directly from my grandmother's milk cows. Nanny had the machine that pasteurized the milk and made it safe for us to drink.

Back on the farm the liquid that I drank the most was water pumped up manually from our well and it was fresh, clear, cold and pure as the good lord intended it to be. When I was thirsty I would go outside on our gallery and pump myself a cold glass of water and then a second one if I was still thirsty.

They say that the best drinking water in Canada is found in the province of Quebec , especially the water found in the Gaspe peninsula, the Laurentian Mountains and the glacial pools of the far northern part of Quebec. I believe it is so for I have never tasted water better than the Gaspe water I drank as a child.

There were more sources of water in L'Anse-a-Brilliant other than the wells. When my friends and I were swimming at the beach on hot summer days and we got thirsty someone would eventually say "Hey, I'm thirsty. Let's go over to the pipe and have a drink. About four or five of us would leave the beach and cross the bridge over the river to get to the other side of the harbour. Sometime before my time someone had shoved a long two inch steel pipe right into the side of the bank of the hill located behind Basil Leggo and Henry Snowman's stores. This pipe was propped up and all a child had to do was bend over and drink the cold spring water. Adults however had to kneel down to drink from the pipe as the pipe was located too low for them. On a hot summer day people at the beach and fishermen who had their boats docked in the harbour would go to the pipe for a drink. I would hear comments such as "Man, that water is cold" and "Wow, that water is some good." This source of good pure spring water was known as "the pipe".

Another source of good spring water was known as "the hose" which was located on Arnold Johnson's property next to the old road. When Arnold married and built a small house just below the highway he didn't have a well so he ran a very long plastic hose down from his brother--in-law Raymond Leggo's property where a good spring was located up in the field. The long hose passed through a culvert underneath the highway and Arnold had the hose propped up next to the ditch into which the water flowed. Everyone was welcome to come and drink from the hose and many people came for a drink of good spring water and also filled up canteens and containers to take home with them.

Another source of good and cold spring water was Tell Wee's well which was located on my grandfather's land about one mile back in the woods close to the base line where our land ended and Crown Land began. I did not know it was there but one day when I accompanied my dad when he was hunting for birds he said "Let's go to Tell Wee's well for a drink of spring water."

"Who is Tell Wee?" I asked.

"He was am old hermit who lived in a shack back here in the woods all by himself." he replied. "A little ways up the trail on your grandfather's land there's a spring and Tell Wee dug out a small pool and when we were kids my brothers and I called it Tell Wee's well.

When we arrived at Tell Wee's well I discovered that it was located in a small depression and I had to lay down on my belly and put my face down into the small pool to get a drink. Sure enough the water was cold and tasted great. I told my dad that the next time I came here I'd bring a small glass with me. I don't think that many people knew about Tell Wee's well as it was located a mile away from civilization so to speak and not too many people ventured back there.

When my father was home on the weekends we would often visit friends and relatives. We would go up to Seal Cove and visit Cecil Leggo and his family. Cecil and Gladys had a rather large family including Roger and Harry, two boys who were younger than me and who I enjoyed playing with. When their mother Gladys asked me if I would like something to drink I would always ask her for a glass of water because their source of water was a spring out behind the house.

"Wouldn't you like a pop instead Bryan?" she would ask.

"No, I really like your spring water " I replied.

Gladys looked at me and smiled. "Gee, you're easy to please" she said.

I would drink the glass of water she gave me and sometimes even had a refill. It was good water.

When I moved away from the Gaspe, first to Montreal and then to St Catharines and Sudbury, Ontario I could never really get used to tap water. I call it crap water because that's what it is when you compare it to the good spring and well water I drank as a child.

I got married in the early 1970's and my father-in-law showed me a spring near his camp on Naraka Lake. It was really good water and I would fill up several containers to bring back to Sudbury with me. This spring is located on Trout Lake Road and is about thirty miles south and east of Sudbury.

In the 1980's they started to sell spring water in the grocery stores and that was my salvation. I remember people asking me at my son's soccer games why I was buying bottled water when tap water was free.

"The taste, the Taste" was my reply. "There's no chlorine in it. I like to drink good water. I am a connoisseur of water."

I have visited L'Anse -a-Brilliant several times since I moved away forty-eight years ago. I have drank from the pipe and the hose but have not visited Tell Wee's well since 1961.

In the summer of 2008 I visited L'Anse-a-Brilliant once again, this time with my oldest son Zac. The pipe is not there anymore and the hose is nowhere to be found as well. I guess the people that live in Arnold Johnson's house must now have a well. I wasn't about to walk a mile back into the woods to try and find Tell Wee's well.

My son Zac and I visited Cecil Leggo who now is an eighty-four year old widower. I had not seen him in ten years but he recognized me and invited us into his house. During the visit he offered us a coffee, a beer or a pop. I declined all three offers and asked him for a glass of water, just like I used to ask his wife Gladys over fifty years ago.

"We don't get our water from the spring anymore, Bryan" stated Cecil. "The spring froze up one cold winter a few years ago so I decided to put in a well. But the water's still good."

And of course it was; so good in fact that I had a second glass.

Well all this writing has made me thirsty. I have a special bottle of "Eska" water from the glacial pools of Northern Quebec chilling in the fridge. Excuse me . I'm going to have a drink. Bye for now.

111. The Next Time Hit Him Harder

In 1961 when I was thirteen years old my mother, sister and I moved to Murdochville the mining town eighty miles from L'Anse-a-Brilliant to be with dad seven days a week instead of just two days a week.

We had lived in Murdochville for one year in 1956-57 but a violent strike at Gaspe Copper Mines Ltd. had convinced my father to move his family back to the farm. When the strike was over he went back to work in Murdochville and we stayed at the farm in L'Anse-a-Brilliant with my grandparents.

Our second move to Murdochville happened between Christmas and New Years when my sister and I were on Christmas break. We moved into a basement apartment for a few months until we could move into a new house that dad had bought at 720 2nd Street.

Early in January of 1962 I started the winter term in my new school. Right on the first day I was called "farm boy, farm boy" over and over again by some of the other kids. They were teasing me because I was wearing a homemade winter coat that was made for me by Mrs. Camelia Hotton, a friend of our family. She was a very talented clothes maker and also made winter coats. I was proud of my coat and it was nice and warm and it fit well. However it was a red patchwork pattern and the kids teased me saying "homemade coat, homemade coat". I endured the teasing but it was getting to me.

That day on the walk home from school I picked up our mail at the post office and was approached by my cousin Freddy who was with his friends Scottie and Dennis. Freddy was a year and a half younger than me and the other guys were also a year or so younger than me. As we walked down C Avenue and turned into 3 rd. Street they teased me about my coat calling me "farm boy". I was very disappointed with my cousin Freddy as I thought that he should support me and not be against me.

Then it got physical. The three of them ganged up on me, took my mail and book bag and threw them over the snow bank. I had to climb over the snow bank in waist deep snow and retrieve the mail and my book bag.

I knew I was tougher than them. I did hard work on the farm and was strong for my age. They were just town boys. And then they made a mistake and started pushing me around. I had enough of this and started fighting back. Scott and Dennis started running away and I punched my cousin Freddy a hard one in the head. He ended up in the snow bank flat on his back and I turned and walked home.

An hour or so later my mother received a phone call from Fred's mother, my aunt Dot. She told my mom that they had to take Fred to the hospital because he had a lump the size of an egg on his forehead. She said that Fred was at home now and would be all right.

My mother gave me a blast of crap and a stern lecture on fighting. She said, "Wait until your dad gets home. He'll deal with you."

When my dad got home from work my mom brought him up to date on what had happened and promptly left the room so that dad could deal with me.

My dad asked me, "What happened?"

I told dad the whole story about what had happened at school and how I was teased. When I told him about Fred and his friends I could see that dad was getting angry. He was getting his blood pressure up as he used to say. He turned to me and just as my mom had predicted he did raise his voice to me. In a very loud voice he said "THE NEXT TIME HIT HIM HARDER!"

112. You Have To Change His Diaper

When my family and I moved eighty miles away from the farm to the mining town of Murdochville just after Christmas of 1961 I was thirteen years old. Suddenly I was in the town where six of my eleven De Vouge cousins lived. Two of my father's three brothers all worked at Gaspe Copper Mines Ltd. where my dad worked as well. My cousins ranged in age from Tommy who was in his late teens down to Dana who was a newborn baby.

My uncle Denzil, aunt Ina their two daughters Daphen and Laurel and their newborn son Dana lived on D Avenue just a minutes walk from our house on 2nd Street.

In September of 1962 I turned fourteen and that fall my aunt Ina asked me if I would like to baby-sit one night every third week for less than three hours. She and my mom had joined the ladies bowling league and bowled on the same team together one night every week. My uncle Denzil had to work afternoon shift once every three weeks so he would not be able to look after his children. When she said that she would pay me seventy-five cents for less than three hours of babysitting I quickly agreed and I thought she was being generous because I was her nephew. That was good money in those days when many people paid less than that. The fact that I liked Daphen and Laurel and that they were very well behaved kids was a plus. There seemed to be only one problem.

"Aunt Ina," I said. "I don't know how to change a diaper. I've never changed one before."

"Don't worry Bryan" was my aunt's reply. You won't have to change Dana's diaper. I'll change him just before you get here and he'll be good until I get home."

And right she was. Everything went very well the first time I babysat. I did not have to change Dana's diaper. He actually went to sleep for most of the time I was there that night. His older sisters Daphen, the quiet one and Laurel, the more talkative one were very well behaved, a babysitter's dream so to speak. When Aunt Ina returned home and asked me if there had been any problems I told her no and that everything had gone great. She paid me the seventy-five cents and I was on my way.

I babysat this trio of young cousins several times in the next few months. Baby Dana was not a problem and I enjoyed playing cards and other games with his older sisters. I thought that babysitting was a very pleasant experience and I got paid well for it. I need to mention that when I sometimes had to baby-sit my sister Donna I did not get paid one red cent.

One night in the middle of the winter the babysitting was going ok when all hell broke loose. I was playing a game with the two girls when we heard what seemed like a small explosion coming from the direction of Dana's playpen.

Laurel the seven year old said, "Dana pooped his pants. You'll have to change his diaper."

"Oh my God, no" was my response. "your mother told me that I would not have to change his diaper. She said that he would be ok until she got home."

"It's not ok this time" Laurel replied. "Look it's running down his leg and in a minute he's going to start crying real loud. You'll have to change his diaper."

"Oh my God, What am I going to do?" I said. "I'll call my mother. No, I can't. She's bowling with your mom. I'll call my dad. No, I can't. He's babysitting my sister Donna. What am I going to do?"

Laurel stated once again "You'll have to change his diaper."

"I don't know how was all I could say. I looked to the nine year old Daphen for support but she had retreated way back into the corner of the kitchen where she was observing us and not getting involved in any way.

"How do I change his diaper ?" I asked.

"I'll tell you how" was my seven year old cousin's response. "I've watched my mother do it lots of times."

Laurel informed me that first I had to wet a washcloth, then take off his dirty diaper and clean him up. Then all I had to do was put a new diaper on him.

"Easier said than done." I whispered to myself.

In those days the disposable diaper with the plastic pull tabs had not been invented as of yet. My aunt Ina used the old-fashioned reusable cloth diaper which needed two safety pins to hold it up.

When I undid the pins on Dana's diaper what I discovered was nothing short of sickening. He must have had a really upset stomach because there was a large yellow mustard looking mess for me to clean up. It was all over him, even all over his legs. This was not the routine of changing an everyday regular diaper. This was a major operation, an unlikely experience to have when one is changing his first ever diaper. However I got through it ok with the help of my seven year old cousin Laurel. I could not have gotten the job done without her giving me the proper direction.

When my Aunt Ina returned from bowling Laurel told her that I had to change Dana's messy diaper. Aunt Ina inspected the job I had done in putting the new diaper on Dana and she turned to me with that beautiful smile of hers and said "Bryan, I'm proud of you. You did an excellent job."

"Thank You Aunt Ina." I replied. "Laurel taught me how to do it. She's a good teacher."

When she grew up my cousin Laurel went on to graduate from Queens University in Kingston, Ontario in Veterinary Medicine. She is a life long animal lover and has taught Veterinary Medicine at Nova Scotia Agricultural College for many years.

I grew up, got married and had three sons of my own. In the late seventies and early eighties I changed hundreds of my son's diapers, some of which were messy like my cousin Dana's. I am most thankful that my little seven year-old cousin Laurel had taught me well.

113. Gary, You Can't Swim

In the last chapter I wrote about my youngest cousin Dana in Murdochville. I had another young cousin living there as well. He was Gary and he was seven years old and seven years younger than me.

When my family moved to Murdochville just after Christmas of 1961 I was overjoyed that there was an indoor swimming pool in the recreation centre. However it was closed for the winter months and I eagerly awaited it's opening in the spring. I had been swimming back at L'Anse-a-Brilliant since I was about three years old and I was a good swimmer. When the pool opened for the summer I became a regular visitor.

One day my aunt Dot called me over to her house on 2nd. St, the same street that I lived on. She said "Gary wants to learn how to swim and since you're such a good swimmer Bryan I thought I'd ask you if you would do me a favor and take Gary to the rec centre with you and teach him to swim."

"Sure" I replied.

As Gary and I walked to the rec centre I couldn't help but wonder if Gary would be like his older brother Freddy who was around twelve years old but seemingly afraid of the water.

We arrived at the rec centre and after we changed into our swim trunks I informed Gary that it was a rule that we had to take a shower before we would be allowed in the pool.

As we entered the pool area I watched as Gary looked all around taking in the surroundings. He noticed the two diving boards and I explained to him that the low board was three feet above the water and the high board was ten feet above the water. He watched as several teenagers took turns running and jumping off the high board. All of a sudden Gary ran to the high board and starting climbing the ladder.

I yelled "Gary, get down from there. You can't jump off the high board. Gary, you can't swim."

But much to my astonishment Gary ran and jumped off the high board towards the side of the pool. My heart was in my throat as I ran around to the side of the pool where Gary resurfaced and simply grabbed the side of the pool. I helped Gary out of the water and he was real excited and wanted to do it again. The older teenagers there had seen Gary jump and they were obviously impressed that this little seven year old kid had gone off the high board.

"Gary" I said. "You have to learn how to swim before you start jumping off the high board. If your mom knew what you did she'd kill you or maybe me because I'm supposed to be teaching you how to swim. Now let's go to the shallow end and start your swimming lesson."

When we were both in the shallow end of the pool I demonstrated the several different swimming strokes that I knew and then informed him that it was best to start with the dog paddle, the easiest way to learn how to swim. I put my hand under his belly and supported him as he paddled with his hands and kicked with his legs. Then I took my hand away and let him swim for a moment until he started to sink. Quickly I would put my hand back under his belly and prop him up once again. He started to do better and I knew that he was going to be a good student. I also started to teach him how to thread water which is very important to someone learning how to swim.

While the lesson progressed Gary kept looking at the high board at the other end of the pool. I knew that he wanted to jump off it once again but I told him "No way Gary. Don't even think about it. Remember that first you have to learn how to swim before you ever jump off the high board again."

He agreed and when we got back to his house Aunt Dot asked me how he did.

"He's a good student " I replied. "He is obviously not afraid of the water and already he can swim a few strokes. It won't be long before he'll be swimming the length of the pool."

I neglected to mention the stunt that he had pulled by jumping off the high diving board.

114. Janet's Non Run Leotards

Hi, My name is Donna. You guessed it. I am Bryan's sister. Bryan asked me to write a chapter for his book, a chapter about my Mom and a chapter about my Dad .

This chapter is about my dear mother Frances who has now passed away.

When I was very young (a really long time ago) say about the age of seven or eight, at that time all the girls wore leotards to school every day. I was very good at all sports and I was on the running team.

I managed to get many runs and large holes in my leotards almost every day. My mom was always telling me that I was very hard on my leotards. She told me that she was spending so much money just replacing my leotards.

Janet and I were the top runners at that time and our teacher was very proud of our performance.

When I returned home from school one day, my mom told me that she was so happy because she had now solved the leotard problem. She told me that she had now purchased non run leotards for me. She purchased many pairs of different colors. She seemed very happy about this.

The next day at school wearing my non run leotards, I told my teacher that I could not run today. She said "Ok". I guess she thought that I was not feeling well and she did not ask me why I could not run.

For days and days I kept telling my teacher that I was not able to run. Finally she told me that I needed to bring in a note from my mother stating the reason why I was unable to run.

I spoke to Janet and she told me that she was wearing non run leotards. When I arrived home after school that day I told my mother that I had not been running at school for days and days and that I now needed a note for my teacher telling her the reason that I had not been running. Mom asked me why I had not been running at school. I told her it was because of the non run leotards. I told her that Janet had non run leotards and she could still run in them. My mother laughed so hard she almost fell off her chair. She then explained that non run meant a non run in the leotard and that I was able to still run while wearing them.

My mother wrote the note to my teacher who also had a good laugh about this.

I then returned to my running wearing my non run leotards.

This was my mother's favorite story about me.

P.S. I really did become much smarter later on.

115. My Dad Takes Me Moose Hunting

Hi. It's Donna again, Bryan's sister. I am going to tell you a story about my Dad.

My Dad was an exceptional hunter and almost always got a moose whenever he went hunting. He spent many hours practicing moose calls. He had records that he played over and over to learn how to call a moose. He had this large cone shaped object that looked like a funnel and he made loud grunting sounds into it. It was so funny watching Dad practicing his moose calling. He took this very seriously.

My brother Bryan went hunting with Dad on various occasions however when he turned fifteen, he did not want to go anymore. Dad then took Mom moose hunting with him, however this did not work out very well because my mom was praying to God that a moose would not come. I thought that this was so funny. Well guess what? It was now my turn to go moose hunting with Dad.

The most exciting thing about going moose hunting with Dad was the fact that I would get to ride in Dad's Jeep. I always loved riding in the Jeep every chance I got. You see Dad had this Jeep that in the winter he would have the cab on and in the summer it became a convertible as he took the cab off.

It was always so much fun for me riding in the Jeep. This is the main reason that I wanted to go moose hunting with Dad.

I was not afraid of guns and that is because Dad had taught Bryan and I about guns at a very young age. I learned how to carry a gun and how to shoot a twenty-two and a three-O-three rifle.

We set out early one morning, I guess I was about ten years old at that time. We went through the woods in the Jeep. We finally came to a stop and walked to where Dad was going to set up. There was a very high tower that Dad called a scaffold. We climbed to the top and we were above the tree tops. We had to look down in the forest.

After awhile I heard Dad say, "a buck is coming," and sure enough I could see a large moose coming toward us through the woods. He was coming very fast. Dad got his rifle ready and as soon as the moose got within shooting distance Dad shot him dead.

I felt very sorry for the moose because I love all animals, however the moose was a food source for us at that time. I remember Dad preparing the moose steak for us to eat. He would cook it and Mom would assist him. It was so good tasting because Dad knew how to cook it properly.

This was the first and last time that I went hunting with my Dad as he moved us to St Catharines, Ontario.

Donna

116. - My Brother Bryan

Hi. It's me again Donna, Bryan's sister. I am going to tell you a story about my only sibling Bryan.

As you probably know already, my brother Bryan is five years older than I. I bet he didn't tell you that he used to bribe me constantly to do things for him.

I hold my brother entirely responsible for my sweet tooth. You see I am a really sweet lady and when I was young I was always a sweet girl. What I really mean is that all through my life I have eaten a tremendous amount of sweets each and every day. I eat lots and lots of cake, ice cream and chocolate bars.

When Bryan and I were both young Mom would have milk and bakery products delivered right to our front door. Mom would order Vachon Products from the milk and bakery truck. Vachon's were many different kinds of cakes such as Joe Louis and Ah Caramel. Mom and Dad always shared everything four ways. Bryan would always save his cakes and bribe me with them to clean his room. I would clean his room and then he would give me his cakes.

As the years passed I would rent my bicycle and my skies to my brother for money, and then I would buy Vachon cakes and chocolate bars with the money.

When money got tight I would also blackmail my brother for money. For example whenever I found out something on him, I would tell him if you don't give me money I will tell Mom and Dad on you. Yes, I was a real brat. Bryan would pay me and I would not tell on him.

When I was seven years old, I caught my brother smoking cigarettes with his friends. I told him that if he did not let me smoke a cigarette that I would tell Mom and Dad on him and his friends. Bryan agreed and gave me a cigarette to smoke. I smoked the whole thing and later I got very sick. I am so thankful for this experience as I never took up smoking.

On another occasion when I was about ten years old my brother and his friends wanted me to go into a grocery store and purchase beer for them.

In Quebec beer is sold in grocery stores to those who are adults. When the grocery store clerk saw the beer, she said "Who are you getting this beer for?"

I told her my father is outside in the truck and that he sent me in to purchase the beer because he does not like shopping and standing in line. She believed me and I purchased the beer for my brother and his friends. My brother and his friends paid me a lot of money for that one.

My Mother and Father never found out about this.

I was a girl that always had money to buy many Vachon cakes and chocolate bars, thanks to my brother.

Therefore, it is wonderful to have a big brother.

Afterword

Dear Reader

Wow, I can't believe that this book is finally finished. It took me over fourteen months to write, edit, proof read and key into a file on the computer to e-mail to the publisher.

I have found that writing a book is an insurmountable task but one that must be surmounted. I said I was going to do it and I did it.

It amazes me that when you sit down and try to remember things from your childhood to write about how the memories start slowly filtering back when you need them. I guess that our childhood memories are important to us and somehow our brain finds a way to retain them.

At first I found that writing can be difficult especially when the only writing I've been doing for the past forty-three years has been signing checks when I pay the bills. But as you go along it becomes easier and sometimes even enjoyable. It certainly is time consuming. If you're looking for a cure for boredom this could be it. Perhaps I'll start on a second book.

Anyway I just looked out the window. The sun is shining. It's a beautiful day. Bye for now.

Yours Truly

Bryan De Vouge

PS. I'd like to thank my sister Donna De Vouge for contributing three of her own memories of her childhood. I'd also like to thank my son Jesse De Vouge for showing me how some things work on the computer.